# The Evolution of John Dewey's Conception of Philosophy and His Notion of Truth

## MELVIN TUGGLE

University Press of America, Inc.
Lanham · New York · Oxford

**Copyright © 1997 by**
**University Press of America,® Inc.**
4720 Boston Way
Lanham, Maryland 20706

12 Hid's Copse Rd.
Cummor Hill, Oxford OX2 9JJ

**Library of Congress Cataloging-in-Publication Data**

Tuggle, Melvin
The evolution of John Dewey's conception of philosophy and his
notion of truth / Melvin Tuggle.
p. cm.
Includes bibliographical references and index.
l. Dewey, John, 1859-1952. 2. Philosophy. 3. Methodology. 4.
Truth. I. Title.
B945.D4T84    1997    191—dc21    97-37404 CIP

ISBN 0-7618-0916-3 (cloth: alk. ppr.)
ISBN 0-7618-0917-1 (pbk: alk. ppr.)

⊖™ The paper used in this publication meets the minimum
requirements of American National Standard for information
Sciences—Permanence of Paper for Printed Library Materials,
ANSI Z39.48—1984

# Contents

# Foreword

I am happy to write this foreword to *The Evolution of John Dewey's Conception of Philosophy and His Notion of Truth* for at least two reasons: first, because of the importance of Dewey's philosophy and its relevance for contemporary human predicaments, and second, because Dr. Melvin Tuggle, whether or not one agrees with him on every point, after extensive study of Dewey and his critics, has some fresh and helpful thoughts on the evolution of Dewey's outlook and a conviction that Dewey's position is both important and relevant for our time.

Dewey is one of our greatest and most productive philosophers. He lived for more than 92 years and had an active career of teaching and writing of more than 70 years and published versions of his writings were coming out up to and beyond the year of his death, 1952. For example, the Southern Illinois University Press has just completed publishing in 37 volume his collected writings. As might be expected, moreover, Dewey's views underwent significant changes during his writing career as he worked over and rethought his ideas on such important topics as world view or metaphysical perspective, philosophical method, truth, the role of philosophy, and essential components of one's religion. But some of the dominant motifs of his mature outlook appeared quite early. For the most part, however, after his early shift from intuitionalism to Hegelian idealism, he worked his way slowly and almost imperceptibly from one position to another, retaining much of the earlier along with the new.

Dewey's vast array of publications understandably has called forth a battery of able but diverse interpreters, but there is still room for another interpreter with his own distinctive outlook like Dr. Melvin Tuggle, who agrees with them in large part but also differs from them in significant ways. As will be obvious from his notes and bibliography, Dr. Tuggle has done a prodigious amount of work both on the immense body of Dewey's writings and the major secondary sources as well. In addition to his insights on the cluster of Deweyan concepts he treats in his book, he has a keen eye for organic relationships between

Dewey's central ideas. Also, a further strength of Dr. Tuggle's book is the fact that he is alert to the relevance of his study to moral and social problems faced by contemporary American democracy. For example, his narrative sheds light on such tangential issues as black and other minority representation in the field of philosophy and various other educational and cultural issues and the suggestions Dewey might have for handling them.

One interesting case in point with reference to possible changes in Dewey's outlook is his conception of God. As Dr. Tuggle indicates, the God of Dewey's 1887 *Psychology* is the traditional Biblical deity, and Dr. Tuggle apparently believes that Dewey's conception of God is a consistent and persistent guiding thread running throughout his entire philosophic career; but most Dewey scholars hold that Dewey had moved away from his early Congregationalism with its supernatural leanings by the time he went to the University of Chicago in 1884, and they contrast his naturalistic *A Common Faith* of 1934 with his early supernaturalism. In the latter book, of course, Dewey expresses his reservations on both aggressive atheism and supernaturalism as being too exclusively preoccupied with man in isolation from nature.

Dewey's method of reflective or critical inquiry for resolving indeterminate or problematic situations, I think, may well have a better claim to providing a continuing and persistent guide to his thought. Versions of this method may be found as early as his *Psychology*, and *How We Think* offers his classic statement of the steps in a complete act of reflective inquiry. A more sophisticated version of the method may be found in 1938 *Logic: The Theory of Inquiry*. Indeed, it might argued that this method offers the most important new way of tackling relevance since Aristotle's classic formulation in terms of a metaphysics of natural classes. It seems to me, moreover, that Dewey's thesis that through proper use of intelligence, reflective inquiry, we humans can better come to terms with the problems facing us, still stands as a challenge to renewed endeavor and the best thought of which we are capable.

Dewey produced a world view which for imaginative sweep and relevance to human predicaments warrants consideration alongside the views of Plato, Aristotle, Democritus, Hegel, Leibniz, and the other great figures of Western philosophy he cited so often in attempting to clarify his own outlook. *Experience and Nature* was his major statement of a world view, and late in life when considering a new edition of this work, he declared that if he had to do it over he would call it "Culture and Nature." Whatever the title, however, he considered experience and nature or culture and nature, not as polar opposites but rather as partners in transactions. In our world, he maintained, change rather than permanence is primary. We live in a world in which the incomplete and the precarious are as genuine as the relatively complete, stable, and well established. To meet the challenges of such a world we must seek intelligent ways of redirecting ongoing affairs, stabilizing patterns we find good and seeking ways of averting or reconstructing, if possible, patterns we find bad.

Both Dewey and Dr. Tuggle stress the idea that human growth, or problem solving, is both the moral end and goal of education. For fixed notions of the good Dewey substituted the idea of growth or problem solving and held that the central concept in ethics is not "good" but "better." A good person is one who is improving, whatever that person's place on some absolute scale. The test of social and political institutions is whether they make for continued education and growth. Moreover, education is not simply for the young but rather is something for all of us. For Dewey, Jefferson, and Dr. Tuggle education is of crucial importance for democracy, and Dewey went so far as to say that democracy is belief in "the ability of human experience to generate the aims and methods by which further experience will grow in ordered richness." Perhaps I should add that Dr. Tuggle is not merely an apostle of growth; he is an exemplar of it.

Dr. Tuggle and Dewey also emphasize the importance of communication for enabling people of diverse cultures and backgrounds to work together. For example, Chapter 5 of Dewey's *Experience and Nature* begins with the sentence "Of all affairs, communication is the most wonderful." And, of course, communication is not merely a matter of conveying statements in language. Art may have a greater claim to universality.

In this foreword I have touched on only a few of the interesting topics and questions treated by Dr. Tuggle, but hopefully, I have said enough to make clear that this book is well worth looking into.

Lewis E. Hahn
Department of Philosophy
Southern Illinois University at Carbondale
Carbondale, Illinois 62901-4505

# Preface

The content of this book emanates from my research for a doctoral dissertation under the direction of Professor David S. Clarke, Jr., Department of Philosophy, Southern Illinois University at Carbondale. The main thesis of this book is that John Dewey's conception of philosophy began and culminated with his concern about the problem of truth. It is asserted here that Dewey's mature conception of philosophy and his notion of truth may be quite profitable for solving some of our more recent contemporary philosophical problems. In hope of clarifying his mature thoughts about philosophy and truth, this book surveys the stages of Dewey's development during his long life-time of ninety-three years.

Using a general approach, I trace the historical progression of his thinking and try to show the relevance of his conceptions of philosophy and truth to our contemporary problems. In doing so, I attempt to elucidate the terminological difficulties that he encountered with language while trying to communicate his own concept of philosophy and his notion of truth. Moreover, I examine criteria that may be used to judge Dewey's work in the field of philosophy in the Western tradition. Under the headings of Early, Middle, and Later years, I provide a triadic survey of his life-work, focusing on his academic and religious views. My reflections try to provide pertinent information concerning the biological, semiotic, and psycholinguistic basis of his perspective, as it eventually evolved into a form of pragmatic naturalism.

I conclude the book by emphasizing Dewey's belief that the business of philosophy should deal with cultural problems. Focusing on the implications of his matured position, I try to show that his perspective may be useful for solving some of our critical social problems in a practical manner. Moreover, a careful examination of his logic, as I try to make clear, indicates that open-minded and honest communication must be a keystone to understanding his mature concept of philosophy and his notion of truth.

*Preface*

Since a preface provides an opportunity for authors to acknowledge those who helped make their particular works possible, I will pause here to express my gratitude. I'm indebted to several Professors of Philosophy at Southern Illinois University; namely, Elizabeth R. Eames, John Howie, M. Browning Carrott (History), and to Lewis E. Hahn I owe a special debt for his editorial Foreword. Moreover, I'm indebted to Gene G. James, Professor of Philosophy at the University of Memphis and Reuben H. Green, LeMoyne-Owen College, Memphis, TN. Although I am clearly acknowledging my debt to all of them for their advice, criticism and teachings, it should be understood that they are not accountable for my use (or misuse) of their instructions.

It also seems fitting here to acknowledge the family members who indirectly helped make this book possible. First I am grateful for the guidance of my grandmother, Addie (MomPete) McKinney Woodson. Though she died in 1990 while I was attempting to complete the Ph.D. requirements, it should be noted that my memories of her loving kindness helped me keep my eyes on the prize and receive the reward. Similarly, I am indebted to Menola Tuggle. As my biological mother, she persistently exhibited the love and confidence that I needed to help me obtain my goal. On the other hand, I'm grateful to my dad, George Tuggle; he trained me to always tell the truth; and I'm indebted to his mother, Cora L. Tuggle, who repeatedly emphasized the importance of a good education. Last, but not least, I wish to acknowledge the encouragement that I received from my brother, Calvin Tuggle. He died in 1996 after battling with leukemia for twenty years; but before completing his earthly pilgrimage, he read the entire manuscript and shared his constructive criticism.

As a final note, I'm thankful to Dorothy Albritton and L. Pilar Wyman for their excellent professional services. Moreover, I am thankful to all of the individuals who are affiliated with The University Press of America; thanks to each of you for helping make the publication of this book a reality.

# Chapter 1

ଞ୍ଚଓଃ

## *Introduction*

The evolution of John Dewey's conception of philosophy began and culminated with his concern about the problem of truth. The narration in the following chapters is an attempt to sustain this thesis. We shall take a rather general approach to discussing his thoughts about philosophy and truth. By doing so, the narrative endeavors to shed some light on the historical progression that led to Dewey's mature conception of philosophy, and the reason why he came to see truth as an endless process of inquiry.

For instance, after studying philosophic inquiry for nearly forty years, in 1917 Dewey concluded that in America there was an urgent need to recover philosophy. We find him saying, "I believe philosophy in America will be lost . . . unless it can somehow bring to consciousness America's own needs and its own implicit principle of successful action."[1] Apparently, though, as this study tries to make clear, Dewey's conceptions of philosophy and truth have been misconstrued by some of his critics. For example, in 1930, more than a decade later we find him still defending the same position, as he says, "I think it shows a deplorable deadness of imagination to suppose that philosophy will indefinitely revolve within the scope of the problems and systems that two thousand years of European history have bequeathed to us."[2] As he viewed the role of philosophy in America, Dewey argued that "a chief task of those who call themselves philosophers is to help get rid of the useless lumber that blocks our highways of thought, and strive to make straight and open the paths that lead to the future."[3]    But unfortunately, it seems that he was unable to get enough American philosophers to see his view.

The reader should understand, however, as this study tries to show, that Dewey's conception of philosophy was far from being that of a narrow-minded nationalist.    Rather, during the time of his philosophizing, he simply recognized that in America, "The growth of the nation has coincided in time with the change known as the industrial revolution."[4]  "Not only have the two been contemporaneous," Dewey observed, "but the United States has contributed more to effecting the transformation than has any other people, and it has experienced the consequences more fully.    It is *the* industrialized nation, *par excellence*, of the world."[5]    At the time he was writing, then, Dewey was well aware that "In the past forty years the transformation has gone on at an accelerated pace, so that from an agrarian nation we have become a manufacturing and distributing people with the centre of gravity transferred from open country to congested city."[6]  In his efforts to help philosophy keep pace with the acceleration, however, as this study shows, John Dewey was misconstrued by some of his critics and commentators as a materialist seeking pecuniary profits.

In Chapter 2, as an attempt to clarify Dewey's mature concept of philosophy and his notion of truth, we examine one of his most important doctrines, Instrumentalism.    The study shows that he formulated it after being attracted to pragmatism by William James and Charles S. Peirce.    In the context of this background, the study additionally shows how Dewey's efforts to define instrumentalism were challenged by Bertrand Russell, whose vexing criticism of pragmatism had intensified a difficult problem of communicating ideas through language.    As we shall see, though, Dewey kept insisting that philosophers need to get the subject matter of philosophy straight, if we ever expect to reach any worthwhile agreements about what truth really is.    Thus, the narration in Chapter 2 concludes by indicating that Dewey's theory of human communication must hold the key to understanding his logic.

By employing this narrative form of expression to disclose Dewey's views, the present writer attempts to get away from the customary argumentative paradigm that is practiced by traditional positions and schools of philosophy.    That is to say, in 1932 Dewey explicitly stated that

> What professional philosophy most needs at the present time is new and fresh imagination. Only new imagination is capable of getting away from traditional positions and schools—realism, idealism, pragmatism, empiricism and the rest of them. Nothing much will happen in philosophy as long as a main object among philosophers is defense of some formulated historic position.[7]

It is in keeping with this vein of thought that the narrative tries to clarify Dewey's ideas about philosophy and truth. Chapter 3, for instance, renders an overview to provide a general survey of his conceptions of philosophy and truth. The chapter tries to furnish sufficient background information to illustrate the direction in which Dewey developed his own philosophy of truth. In doing so, we consider the value of his mature philosophy in light of evaluations by some mainstream contemporary philosophers, such as Melchert, McDermott, Lavine, and Sleeper. Following Sleeper's interpretation, as an attempt to assess the value of Dewey's views, a triadic survey of his life-career works is furnished. This enables us, it is hoped, to scrutinize the stages of his development during his early, middle, and later years.

In Chapter 4 we pay close attention to Dewey's early educational endeavors, and his initial religious activities as well . Consequently, what we find is that Dewey seems to have firmly fixed his beliefs about religion during his youth. As we proceed, though, we observe that his religious concerns seem to diminish after gradually drifting away from the Absolutism of Morris's Hegelianism. In any case, perhaps it is needless to say that Dewey kept philosophy as his life-career pursuit, and education apparently became his number one passion.

In Chapter 5 we consider some of the shifts that occurred in his thinking about philosophy and truth as he came to be more and more impressed by the potentials of the pragmatic movement. Building on the insights of Peirce and James, we note how Dewey formulates his intrumentalism or experimentalism to determine the meaning of truth apart from dogmatic religious teachings. As our study shows, in his effort to become more scientific in his approach, he employed a genetic method of reference when defining the word "truth," and other words as well. We observe in addition, however, that this new procedure apparently led Bernstein to draw the conclusion that Dewey was a half-hearted metaphysician. Our narrative, of course, endeavors to show why Dewey, following the ideas of American philosophers such as Emerson, Peirce, James, and Mead, should not be classified as a half-hearted metaphysician.

Subsequently, in Chapter 6 we give due consideration to an apparently neglected influence upon Dewey's conceptions of philosophy and truth, namely, Thomas Jefferson. As we shall see, there is a resurgence of Dewey's concern about religion, or let us say religious attitudes, which he manifests in his defense of Jefferson's democratic ideals. Also in the sixth chapter, we note how Dewey tried to direct philosophic debates away from problems posed by the Cartesian dualisms and the Greek notion of two orders of existence. Hence we shall observe that he employs his philosophic literature to get educators and philosophers to direct their attention towards the study of patterns in human culture. For this is where he believed that philosophy may have a great work to do.

As our study endeavors to show, Dewey desired to get the general public involved in philosophy. Indeed, our narrative reflects upon his desire to get more heterogeneous students to climb the "continuous ladder" of higher education, and help us bring to light more measures of truth. It is this unbiased scientific frame of mind, as the narration tries to show, that truly reveals the wisdom of his common sense view of philosophy and truth.

In concluding, Chapter 7 provides a summary of several implications that seem to follow from Dewey's mature conceptions of philosophy and truth. It is hoped that after carefully observing the way he uses the term "God" in philosophic literature throughout his career, as displayed in Chapters 2-6, we shall be in a better position to determine the bearings that his use of the term had upon his ideas about philosophy and truth. Also, as our narrative tries to show, it is possible that a key to understanding his logic and his theory of human communication may turn on correctly comprehending his conception of God as a proper subject matter of philosophic discourse. For instance, the final chapter gives consideration to his assessment of several writings by Alfred North Whitehead that seems to shed some light on Dewey's view of communication. What we find is that Dewey apparently thought that he had good reason for his optimism.

In other words, it seems that he believed in "the God" of Abraham, Isaac, Jacob, Jefferson, and Emerson (to name just a few believers). Consider, for example, his article "A God or The God" (1933), where he reviews *Is There a God? A Conversation* (1932), by Nelson Wieman, Douglas Clyde Macintosh, and Max Carl Otto. In this writing Dewey says,

I have found much of the discussion in these Conversations elusive and hard to follow. I have found it difficult to put my finger, intellectually speaking, on the subject of discussion. . . . In consequence the most considerable part of my reflections has been devoted to trying to find an explanation of the trouble I have experienced in establishing a continous identification of the subject under consideration . . . .

[T]he difficulty seems to centre about the use of the indefinite article in the title: Is there a God? I should not have experienced a similar difficulty if the question were put with a definite article: Is there the God? For I should have known at once that the question was elliptical in form, and that some indicated context would serve to define and specify the nature of the object referred to. It might be the God of Abraham, Isaac and Jacob; of the Aristotelian metaphysics; of the Homeric Olympus; . . . of Islam . . . of Kant's Critique of Practical Reason, to mention a few of the possibilities. In every case there would still be difficulty in arriving at a satisfactory answer.[8]

As the narrative tries to show, Dewey apparently believed that if philosophers could come together and reason about the term "God" as a proper subject of philosophy, then most likely we shall be able to resolve some of the problems of society on a large scale. It is hoped that Dewey's perspective becomes quite clear by the time we reach the concluding chapter, where we consider his review of Macintosh's *Social Religion* (1940). In any case, it is hoped that the discussion of Macintosh's and Whitehead's work enables the reader to see that honest and open-minded discourse is definitely our best way of obtaining truth.

Let us therefore prepare to turn to the narrative, as I endeavor to shed some light on the maze of confusion that has gathered around the evolution of Dewey's thoughts about philosophy and truth. The personal pronoun "I" has been intentionally employed here to acknowledge all responsibilities for my interpretations and suggestions as they appear in the ensuing chapters. As for the significance of noting my employment of the personal pronoun "I," this procedure is in keeping with Dewey's assertion that, "Only when a person tries to get control of the *conditions* that determine the occurrence of a suggestion, and only when he accepts responsibility for using the suggestion to see what follows from it, is it significant to introduce the 'I' as the agent and source of thought."[9]

The ensuing chapters of this book, in other words, have a twofold purpose. That is, I disclose the research findings of my doctoral dissertation and I try to show how this study may help to improve the status of American philosophy within the near future. So, not only is this book designed to benefit future researchers, but it is hoped that those who are familiar with Dewey's work already will be able to grasp the explicit as well as implicit suggestions that are adumbrated here.

Perhaps this point can be made clearer if we consider Dewey's observations as to the efficient functioning of a dissertation committee. For instance, in his reflections upon the problem of methods in philosophy and the sciences, Dewey says,

> Now it seems to me that a good deal of what are called social problems in a technical social sense are self-set problems. A Ph. D. student— I don't say a member of a faculty, but a Ph. D.—thinks his own show would make a nice problem for a hundred people, while it hasn't anything to do with any problem that demands action and organized action for its solution. . . . In other words, I don't think that fact-finding is out—it merely is a type of intellectual missile—I think it is a necessary consequence of any procedure that fails to relate the social problems of action, problems that can only be settled by action, and that fails, therefore, to form the ideas and hypotheses, to collect the kinds of facts that are relevant to problems of action.[10]

Dewey seems to be saying that if a dissertation project is not too narrowly restricted, it should be possible for the Ph. D. student and the committee to actively effect a change in some pressing social problems. As Dewey explains it, "A philosophy based upon actual experience is so framed, in other words, as to react, through the plan of action which it projects, back into an experience which is directly realized and not merely conceived."[11]

We are informed by Dewey that "philosophy is vision, imagination, reflection— and these functions, apart from action, modify nothing and hence resolve nothing."[12] Therefore, according to Dewey, philosophy shouldn't be conceived of as only a "device for dealing with the problems of philosophers"; instead, it should be "a method, cultivated by philosophers, for dealing with the problems of men."[13] Indeed, he reminds us that "what serious-minded men not engaged in the professional business of philosophy most want to know is what modifications and abandonments of intellectual inheritance are required

by the newer industrial, political, and scientific movements."[14]
Moreover, we are reminded that, "Unless professional philosophy can
mobilize itself sufficiently to assist in this clarification and redirection
of men's thoughts, it is likely to get more and more sidetracked from
the main currents of contemporary life."[15]

In keeping with Dewey's reminder, I try to provide some new and
fresh ideas that are relevant to the main currents of contemporary life.
This study, in other words, tries to explicate Dewey's conceptions of
philosophy and truth in light of the following statement.

> I shall begin by stating briefly the standpoint from which I see
> philosophy—[i. e.] the business of philosophy. . . . I think that from
> my point of view, the poorest idea about philosophy is that it is a
> about "being," as the Greeks called it, or about "reality,". . . . As
> I may suggest later . . . it's becoming recently clear that philosophy
> hasn't made any great success in dealing with "reality."

> My standpoint is that philosophy deals with cultural problems, using
> culture in the broad sense which the anthropologists have made clear
> to us—dealing with the patterns of human relationships. It includes
> such subjects as language, religion, industry, politics, fine arts, in
> so far as there is a common pattern running through them. . . . The
> principal task of philosophy is to get below the turmoil that is
> particularly conspicuous in times of rapid cultural change, to get
> behind what appears on the surface, to get to the soil in which a
> given culture has its roots. The business of philosophy is the relation
> that man has to the world in which he lives. . . .

> The hope for philosophy is that those who engage in philosophy
> professionally will recognize that we are at the end of one historical
> epoch and at the beginning of another. The teacher and student
> should attempt to tell what sort of change is taking place. . . . We
> are undergoing the same kind of change . . . that happened when the
> medieval period lost its hold on the people's beliefs and activities.[16]

The relevance of Dewey's statement for our own times can be seen, I
think, if we consider it in light of the following observation. Just
midway between the time of Dewey's death in 1952, and our present
predicament in 1996, some social scientists reported that

> The problems of black and white America are enormous. The destiny
> of a major world power hinges upon its capacity to handle this situation
> and to resolve the issues it raises.[17]

Given the information that recent social scientists and anthropologists have made clear to us, what has philosophy or philosophers done to "handle" the latter situation and to resolve the issues it raises? In response to this question, let us note that only six years ago it was reported that

> The June issue of the [APA] Proceedings (Volume 62, Number 5) gives survey data concerning the numbers of blacks and other minorities in philosophy. Unsurprisingly, the proportion of blacks in the discipline is considerably below their proportion of the population. . . .
>
> The significance of these findings for our profession (as for the rest of society) is that black representation in a field can be expected, absent any discrimination, to decrease as the intellectual demands of the field increase. . . . Making the most optimistic assumptions, given that blacks constitute 12% of the population, only 2% (not 12%) of the profession will be black. That is close enough to current figures for all philosophers to regard themselves free from any discriminatory guilt.[18]

Clearly in line with this statistical report, David Hoekema provides us with some further insight regarding the disparate percentages of blacks and whites in philosophy. He tells us that four years ago he attended the "largest annual congregation of philosophers in the United States," and to the best of his knowledge, in the world, "viz., the Eastern Division meeting in Atlanta."[19] Reminiscing the occasion, Hoekema says, "I wondered what an anthropologist, attempting to understand an unfamiliar culture, would find noteworthy about this gathering of philosophers. I imagined the contents of the field notes she might take back to her study: Demographics: est. 80 percent male, 95 percent white . . . ."[20]

With respect to the latter statements concerning the statistics of whites, blacks, and other minorities in philosophy, the reader should understand that the subsequent chapters make no explicit attempt to address such issues. However, the narrative does endeavor to shed some light on the way Dewey would probably want us to handle them. For instance, consider America's educational problem of schooling near the turn of the century. Dewey expresses his common sense view of the problem as follows.

The intermingling in the school of youth of different races, different religions, and unlike customs creates for all a new and a broader environment. Common subject matter accustoms all to a unity of outlook upon a broader horizon than is visible to the members of any group while it is isolated. The assimilative force of the American public school is eloquent testimony of the efficacy of the common and balanced appeal.[21]

Though Dewey expressed this view more than half a century ago, it appears that some educators and philosophers are yet baffled by the wisdom of Dewey's thinking. Hence, it is hoped that our procedure in this study can help clarify his philosophical stance for truth, justice, and the American way.

Within rather recent times (1984), for instance, Spencer J. Maxcy has pointed up J. Christopher Eisele's questionable attempt to "read too narrow a conception of group life association into Dewey's work."[22] However, as Maxcy additionally recognizes and points up, "Dewey's abstruse writing style often makes it difficult to locate the proper referent for his theoretical statements. Eisele is not alone in misreading Dewey."[23] Thus, in contrast to Eisele's approach to interpreting him, Maxcy says,

It seems to me that Dewey's interest-group cultural pluralism represents the practical and the theoretical wedge between pluralistic culture as a descriptive notion and cultural pluralism as a normative ideal. Dewey, far more than Kallen and other pluralists of his day, recognized that once immigrant, racial, or religious groups were viewed as static and fixed, the possibility of future growth and development in sociocultural terms was cut off.[24]

Judging from Maxcy's interpretation, it appears that he has correctly grasped Dewey's position. Moreover, as for the philosophic context of the cultural pluralism debate, Maxcy seems to think that, "At the heart of it, Dewey's conception of cultural pluralism is a philosophic articulation incorporating his views of culture, social organization, democracy, and schooling. More than this, it is the precise meanings of these notions in the context of cultural pluralism as a norm that needs addressing in the research."[25] Now in light of Maxcy's argument about the direction in which researchers of Dewey's works should direct their efforts, this study tries to help provide some insight. For example, as we examine the evolution of Dewey's conceptions of philosophy and truth during his early, middle and later years, we shall investigate the trail marked by his writings; and as a result we note some of the reasons that were probably responsible for what Maxcy refers to as Dewey's "abstruse writing style." For indeed, we shall note some of the great thinkers—Emerson, G. Stanley Hall, Hegel, Morris, Peirce, James, Mead, Plato, and Jefferson—who influenced Dewey's complex writings. Thus, by considering their influences, this study may help clarify some of the questions regarding Dewey's notion of ethnic and cultural pluralism.

Why is it that Dewey's critics and commentators have encountered such difficulty with his writings? From the present writer's perspective, the main themes that create the puzzle in Dewey's work gathers around his attempt to make clear the subject matter of philosophy and not his educational theories about the problem of ethnic and cultural pluralism. We are informed by Morton White, for instance, that "Dewey has said that his earliest writings were clear, that his youthful prose was direct and clear. . . . It was only later, he thinks, when he began to try to create new ideas, to say things he thought had not been said before, that he began to be troubled about his prose style, about his capacity to communicate his thoughts to others."[26] Now as the present writer sees the problem, Dewey's effort to "create new ideas" and "say things he thought had not been said before," does indeed pose some questions regarding his conceptions of philosophy and truth; but with respect to his theory of education, it seems that Dewey makes his position quite clear in *The School and Society* (1902), where he says,

> What the best and wisest parent wants for his own child, that must the community want for all its children. Any other ideal for our schools is narrow and unlovely; acted upon, it destroys our democracy. . . . Only by being true to the full growth of all the individuals who make it up, can society by any chance be true to itself.[27]

As we can see, his notion of a true society and true democracy includes "all individuals." Dewey's employment of the quantification term "all" indicates how the "proper referent" for his theoretical statement should apply to the ethnic and cultural pluralism debate. More than three decades later, in his article "Education and Social Change" (1937), Dewey seems to leave little need for questioning what the proper referent of his statement is; for he says, "Our public school system was founded in the name of equality of opportunity for all, independent of birth, economic status, race, creed, or color."[28]

Above a decade earlier, in *Reconstruction in Philosophy* (1920), Dewey expressed his common sense view of the issue quite explicitly; for he reminds us that, "Government, business, art, religion, all social institutions have a meaning, a purpose. That purpose is to set free and to develop the capacities of human individuals without respect to race, sex, class or economic status."[29] Dewey even goes so far as to specifiy the historical context of Western philosophy and asserts that, "In his day, Aristotle could easily employ the logic of general concepts superior to individuals to show that the institution of slavery was in the interests both of the state and of the slave class. Even if the intention is not to justify the existing order the effect is to divert attention from special situations."[30] But clearly moving away from the old Aristotelian employment of logic, Dewey's common sense view regards *all* individuals as humans, if they possess human qualities.

Dewey, no doubt, was convinced that "Without strong and competent individuals, the bonds and ties that form society have nothing to lay hold on. Apart from associations with one another, individuals are isolated from one another and fade and wither; or are opposed to one another and their conflicts injure individual development."[31] Because of this perilous aspect of human existence, moreover, Dewey additionally reminds us that "Law, state, church, family, friendship, industrial association, these and other institutions and arrangements are necessary in order that individuals may grow and find their specific capacities and functions."[32] How much clearer could Dewey make his position than this?

> The best guarantee of collective efficiency and power is liberation and use of the diversity of individual capacities in initiative, planning, foresight, vigor and endurance. Personality cannot be educated by confining its operations to technical and specialized things . . . . Full education comes only when there is a responsible share on the part of each person, in proportion to capacity, in shaping the aims and policies of the social groups to which he belongs. This fact fixes the significance of democracy. It cannot [or ought not] be conceived as a sectarian or racial thing . . . .[33]

Now doesn't it seem hardly possible that Dewey could be more explicit in stating his common sense view of educational theory, as it comes to a head under the umbrella of philosophy? At any rate, as we prepare to investigate the evolution of his conception of philosophy and his notion of truth, notice that in concluding *Reconstruction in Philosophy,* Dewey ends it with the eloquence of Emerson's American scholar, as he reminds us that

> Poetry, art, religion are precious. . . . They cannot be willed into existence or coerced into being. The wind of the spirit bloweth where it listeth and the kingdom of God in such things does not come with observation. . . . [But] When philosophy shall have co-operated with the course of events and made clear and coherent the meaning of the daily detail, science and emotion will interpenetrate, practice and imaginaton will embrace. Poetry and religious feeling will be unforced flowers of life. To further this articulation and revelation of the meanings of the current course of events is the task and problem of philosophy in days of transition.[34]

With the preceding observations in mind, as we turn to the narrative, let's see how he dealt with the task of philosophy in days of transition. Let us consider the historical progression of his philosophic concerns about religion, art, education, and politics.

As we turn to the narrative, however, the reader is urged to remember that in 1946 Dewey still was trying to improve the status of his beloved discipline; for he held that

> Philosophy still has a work to do. It may gain a role for itself by turning to consideration of why it is that man is now so alienated from man. It may turn to the projection of large or generous hypotheses which, if used as plans of action, will give intelligent direction to men in search for ways to make the world more one of worth and significance, more homelike, in fact.[35]

And finally, in a 1952 publication, Dewey leaves us with the following message.

> The way ahead is hard and difficult for philosophy as for every other phase of human endeavor. . . . Philosophy can hardly take the lead in introducing that new epoch in human history which is now the alternative to ever increasing catastrophe. But it can, if it has enduring courage and patience, engage cooperatively in the prolonged struggle to discover and utilize the positive ways and means by which the cause of human freedom and justice may be advanced in spite of the uncertainties, confusions, and active conflicts that now imperil civilization itself.[36]

With regard to Dewey's message, before we turn to the next chapter and consider his new way of thinking about philosophy and truth, it is suggested that the reader also bear in mind the following problem, which certainly seems to be brewing (so to speak) in America's "melting pot of cultures," and it has international ramifications. For example, about two years after Dewey's death, George G. M. James, a professor teaching at a small college in Arkansas published *Stolen Legacy* (1954), and in it he claims that "Greeks were not the authors of Greek philosophy, but the people of North Africa, commonly called the Egyptians."[37] In contrast to James's assertion, however, as the next chapter shows, Dewey addressed the question of philosophy's origin in western civilization and he concluded that "European philosophy in Greece supplies the natural beginning."[38] Now it should be understood, of course, that the pertinent point for the purpose of this study is not a matter of whether Dewey or James is correct about the beginning of philosophy. What is much more important for our purpose is the manner of treatment that James's book has received.

As recently as 1987, for instance, it was noted by Martin Bernal that James, "relying on ancient sources, showed the extent to which the Greeks admitted they had borrowed their learning from the Egyptians during the Iron age. . . . James claimed that the Egyptians had been Blacks, and the work ended with a moving appeal calling for a change in black consciousness."[39] Also, and even more importantly, Bernal tells us,

> I had to try twice to have a copy of *Stolen Legacy* accepted by the university library at Cornell before it was finally placed in a smaller branch library. It is not recognized as a *proper* book. Nor has it been read outside the black community. Within intellectual circles in this community, however, it is highly prized and very influential.[40]

Then too, indicating some significant international connections, Bernal notes that

> *Stolen Legacy* is generally linked in people's minds to the school of thought pioneered by the late Senegalese nuclear physicist Cheikh Anta Diop. Diop wrote prolifically on what he saw as the integral relationship between black Africa and Egypt, and in the course of this generally assumed the Ancient Model of Greek history and James' theories in *Stolen Legacy* to be true.[41]

In 1988, approximately one year later, Asa G. Hilliard, a professor at Georgia State University published some findings that seem to sustain Bernal's claims about his attempt to get *Stolen Legacy* "accepted" by the library at Cornell. Hilliard tells us,

> One day in 1954, shortly after *Stolen Legacy* had been published, Professor James said goodbye to his close friend, John Howard, indicating that he would return soon. . . . Shortly after he left the campus at Pine Bluff, the news came by phone to Professor Howard that George G. M. James had died. . . . In 1976, as *Stolen Legacy* was being reprinted for the first time in twenty years, no copy of the book was in the general library at the University at Pine Bluff. However, in the private collection of President Smith there was a single copy. . . . Few were those who really knew about and understood the magnitude of the scholarly contribution of Professor James.[42]

Now in view of Hilliard's observations regarding James and his work, and also in view of Bernal's observations, what alarms the present writer is the way in which it *appears* that James's work has been deliberately kept away from the general public by the ruling class, or status quo. If this is actually the case, as it appears to be, then more than likely such a procedure is taking us in the wrong direction. For as this study tries to show, based upon Dewey's mature concept of philosophy and truth, such a procedure destroys instead of builds the foundations of a democratic society.

John Dewey has reminded us that, as he puts it, "If one wants to know what the condition of liberty is at a given time, one has to examine what persons *can* do and what they *cannot* do."[43] In light of Dewey's reminder, then, let us ask ourselves: Was it not merely a coincidence that James's unexpected death occurred "shortly after" *Stolen Legacy* had been published? Were there any attempts to suppress the ideas or work of James in America?

If there is an affirmative answer to either of the latter questions, then undoubtedly the enormous problems between black and white Americans, according to Dewey's view, are not being handled properly. That is to say, similar to Mahatma Ghandi's efforts some years before Martin Luther King endeavored to raise our consiousness regarding the need for non-violence, Dewey likewise was trying to do so. For he adamantly and persistently maintained that "acceptance in advance of the inevitability of violence tends to produce the use of violence in cases where peaceful methods might otherwise prevail."[44] Well aware of the diverse views in America's melting pot of cultures, Dewey plainly tells us,

> Of course, there *are* conflicting interests; otherwise there would be no social problems. The problem under discussion is precisely *how* conflicting claims are to be settled in the interest of the widest possible contribution to the interests of all—or at least of the great majority. The method of democracy—inasfar as it is that of organized intelligence—is to bring these conflicts out into the open where their special claims can be seen and appraised, where they can be discussed and judged in light of more inclusive interests than are represented by either of them separately. . . . [For indeed] what generates violent strife is failure to bring the conflict into the light of intelligence where the conflicting interests can be adjudicated in behalf of the interest of the great majority.[45]

Now in view of Dewey's suggestion, let us suppose that there were deliberate attempts to suppress the work of James. Couldn't such actions still be costing us today? Couldn't it be impeding the progress of stamping out ignorance throughout America and the world?

In response to the latter questions, and in keeping with Dewey's suggestion, it is hoped that the subsequent chapters can help show that we need more open and honest dialogues with the heterogeneous individuals in our society. For as Dewey plainly puts it, "The argument, drawn from history, that great social changes have been effected only by violent means, needs considerable qualification, in view of the vast scope of changes that are taking place without the use of violence."[46] Moreover, regarding the economic principles involved, seemingly Dewey did not believe that philosophers should have to "ask the helms on Wall Street" about our economy's condition and its effects; he tells us,

> It is said that the dominant economic class has all the agencies of power in its hands, directly the army, militia and police; indirectly the courts, schools, press and radio. I shall not stop to analyze this statement. But if one admits it to be valid, the conclusion to be drawn is surely the folly of resorting to a use of force against force that is so well intrenched. The positive conclusion that emerges is that conditions that would promise success in the case of use of force are such as to make possible great change without any recourse to such a method.[47]

However, in rather recent times (1985), Dewey, along with Bertrand Russell, has been accused of being overly optimistic about improving the human condition. For example, we find Samuel Meyer saying, "To the generation that has grown to maturity since World War II the most pertinent criticism both philosophers [Dewey and Russell] would face today lies in their nineteenth century liberal optimism and their lack of the sense of tragic vision."[48]  Is Meyer right?  Was Dewey indeed too optimistic?  Apparently no one can answer for certain whether Dewey was overly optimistic. In other words, it seems that any time we make assertions about future predictions, as Dewey did during his era, one can only justify one's position satisfactorily with a degree of probablity, as I see it.  Therefore, in this book I do not attempt to demonstrate that he was not overly optimistic about the plight of human beings, but I do try to elucidate the reason for his optimism.

In any case, however, if we are going to gain the confidence of heterogeneous researchers such as Professor Asa Hilliard, or the students of George G. M. James, for instance, then evidently we need to be fair in our dealings with them. What we should be aware of, as Dewey reminds us, is the dictum that "We must act not only with justice, but with the appearance of justice." He points up this reminder in "The Case of Odell Waller: Supreme Court to Be Asked Again to Hear Negro's Petition" (1942); in this work we find Dewey saying,

To the editor of the *New York Times:*

Once more our colored citizens, already deeply aroused over discrimination against them in the armed forces and defense industries, have been presented with a grievance. The United States Supreme Court, on May 4, declined without opinion to review the case of Odell Waller, colored sharecropper, convicted of first degree murder in the shooting of his white farmer landlord during a quarrel induced by Waller's attempt to get his share of their wheat crop. Colored people regard this unexplained refusal as just one more evidence that when white people speak of fighting to preserve freedom, they mean freedom for their own race.[49]

Surely, then, Dewey stressed the need to give heterogeneous people a "Fair Deal." And it appears that his unbiased attitude regarding fairness and justice may be attributed in part to the open-minded scholars who he associated with, or befriended. One excellent example may be found in his "Tribute to James Hayden Tufts" (1942), where he tells us,

For a considerable number of years I enjoyed the privilege of intimate association with James Hayden Tufts, first at the University of Michigan at Ann Arbor, and then for ten years here in Chicago. . . . the association was more than professional. It went deeper than being a faculty colleague, fellow-teacher, an active collaborator in philosophical research and publication, significant as these contacts were in my own life. I think of our friend as a scholar, a teacher, a writer, and of him as one who gave freely of his time, energy, and thought to civic issues. . . . One always knew where Mr. Tufts stood in any situation which arose and where he would stand whenever any moral issue came up. . . .

Another trait that made companionship with him attractive and rewarding was that the habit of judiciousness which New England has bred in its best children was strong in him. . . . I am glad to have been one of the large number whose faith in our common human kind and in the possibilities of human life has been rendered more robust and enduring because of his life and work. . . . When I renew acquaintance with the pages of his earlier work, I find no words occurring oftener than "fair" and "unfair." The world and our own America were never more in need of the Fairness which was the chief note of Mr. Tufts' life than in the tragic years we are now passing through.[50]

Now in light of Dewey's tribute to Tufts, think about how blacks, for example, just like whites, were supposed to benefit from the New Deal under President F. D. R.'s administration. And let us ask ourselves: Did blacks receive a fair share of the benefits? Is the treatment of James's *Stolen Legacy* an indication of social progress in the area of race relations? Philosophically speaking, what would Dewey say? The ensuing chapters try to shed some light on these questions, though the issues are not specifically addressed.

At this point, however, let us also ask ourselves: Just how much difference was there, if any, between the way Odell Waller and George G. M. James were discriminated against ? In light of this query, let's consider some consequences that such discriminatory actions may have on philosophy's future and our quest for truth. Dewey appears to provide an adequate context for our purpose when discussing "Logical Method and Law." For example, after citing the syllogistic premises "Socrates is a man" and "Socrates is mortal," he says,

In a certain sense it is foolish to criticize the model supplied by the syllogism. The statements made about men and Socrates are obviously true, and the connection between them is undoubted. The trouble is that while the syllogism sets forth the *results* of thinking, it has nothing to do with the *operation* of thinking. Take the case of Socrates being tried before the Athenian citizens, and the thinking which had to be done to reach a decision. Certainly the issue was not whether Socrates was mortal; the point was whether this mortality would or should occur at a specified date and in a specified way. Now that is just what does not and cannot follow from a general principle or a major premise. . . . to quote Justice Holmes, "General propositions do not decide concrete cases." No concrete proposition, that is to say, one with material dated in time and placed in space, follows from any general statements or from any connection between them.[51]

An important point that Dewey tries to make clear, no doubt, is that our logical reasoning should be reflected in "concrete cases" of everyday life, and not merely in text book rules. So what is wrong with some of our logic and our laws here in America? Dewey says the problem is due to our "lack of imagination in generating leading ideas. Because we are afraid of speculative ideas, we do, and do over and over again, an immense amount of dead, specialized work in the region of 'facts.' We forget that such facts are only data."[52] Therefore Dewey's plea for philosophy is, as he puts it, "a plea for the casting off of that intellectual timidity which hampers the wings of imagination, a plea for speculative audacity, for faith in ideas, sloughing off a cowardly reliance upon those partial ideas to which we are wont to give the name facts."[53]

Approximately five years later Dewey published "What Are Universals?" (1936), where he points out the possibility of some errant views yet lurking in some logicians. He says,

In this paper, I propose to discuss the nature of universals as that nature is determined by their identification with the content of *if-then* propositions. I shall begin by recurring to the equivocal meaning of *inclusion*. In one sense, it means being part of a collection or a member of a kind. Thus when it is said that "Negroes are human beings" and that "Sambo is a Negro," a kind of existence is first included in a superior kind [human], having other members, and then an individual thing [Sambo] is affirmed to be a member of the first kind. . . . Here *inclusion* designates falling within the scope of a definition:   determined as one of the modes of the relation of characters that are fixed by the definition.   . . .   "Human being" would still have a meaning if no Negroes were known. Inclusion here is a matter of necessary relations of meaning, not of conjunction of observable facts.   . . .   [Moreover] it would be an awkward linguistic expression that would say "Human beings comprehend

Negroes," while it would be a natural expression to say that the idea of humanity necessarily comprehends treating Negroes as human.[54]

With respect to Dewey's view of universals, as indicated by the statement above, it seems that he was concerned about those philosophers who continue to think in terms of Locke's way of understanding humans, which had been formulated in terms of Aristotle's logic.

For instance, Locke disclosed his view of the universal term "man" when he wrote and published *An Essay Concerning Human Understanding* (1690). Explaining how white Englishmen formed their ideas about Negroes during his era, we find Locke saying,

> First, a Child having framed the *Idea* of a *Man*, it is probable that his *Idea* is just like that Picture, which the Painter makes of the visible Appearances joined together; and such a Complication of *Ideas* together in his Understanding, makes up the single complex *Idea* which he calls *Man*, whereof White or Flesh-colour in *England* being one, the Child can demonstrate to you, that a *Negro is not a Man*, because White-colour was one of the constant simple *Ideas* of the complex *Idea* he calls *Man*: And therefore he can demonstrate by the Principle, *It is impossible for the same Thing to be, and not to be, that a Negro is not a Man* . . . .[55]

Then too, in addition to the influences of Locke's British way of thinking about Negroes, it seems that Dewey had reason to be concerned about Continental philosophy, seeing that it had been pervaded with Kant's influential views. Apparently before Hume was able to awaken Kant from his dogmatic slumber, he already had established his beliefs about Negroes. For instance, consider Elmer Duncan's and Miodrag Lukich's article entitled "Kant's Rigorism: A Problem and A Solution" (1965). As they point out, "Kant intended his ethic to apply only to moral agents. It did not apply to sub-human organisms." They tell us, "Kant argued that women and Negroes are not to be considered on a par with men in moral affairs"[56] And clearly exhibiting his view of blacks, we find Kant saying,

> Father Labat reports that a Negro carpenter, whom he reproaches for haughty treatment toward his wives, answered: 'You whites are indeed fools, for first you make great concessions to your wives, and afterward you complain that they drive you mad': And it might be that there were something in this which perhaps deserved to be considered, but in short, this fellow was quite black from head to foot, clear proof that what he said was stupid.[57]

Obviously, of course, Dewey was aware that both Kant's and Locke's ideas had pervaded the thinking of many Americans, and especially philosophers. John Locke, for example, "had more influence on Thomas Jefferson and people that drew up our Declaration of Independence and so, than any other individual," says Dewey, "and in a way the democratic principles as they evolved in this country and later in France were very closely connected with the later development of [Locke's] appeal to experience and the ultimate thing."[58]

As for Dewey's perspective, however, as this study tries to show, he had risen above the biases that keep homogeneous and heterogeneous individuals from freely communicating. Indeed, the following chapters attempt to provide some insight into the way Dewey's concept of philosophy and truth developed in light of this problem. As we have seen already, he held that the business of philosophy should be dealing with cultural problems. Also, we have seen how Dewey would probably respond to the cultural pluralism debate, as Maxcy has noted regarding Eisele's position. However, in light of what appears to be the case with James's *Stolen Legacy,* it is hoped that this study can help show how Dewey would doubtless suggest that we handle such matters. As I try to illustrate in the narrative, he evidently believed that philosophical problems, just like political problems, should be handled publicly, and not privately or secretively.[59]

Instead of concealing or suppressing James's *Stolen Legacy*, most likely Dewey would have seen the work as a means of bringing to light more measures of truth. Even though James's work may have been regarded by some as not being a "proper" book, to use Bernal's terminology, apparently Dewey would have at least regarded it as a *poor* form of art. In other words, with respect to Dewey's concept of art, he reminds us that,

> In the case of material things, possession by one excludes possession, use, and enjoyment by others. In the case of the intangibles of art the exact opposite is the case. The more the arts flourish, the more they belong to all persons alike, without respect to wealth, birth, race, or creed. The more they flourish the less they are privately owned, and the more they are possessed and enjoyed by all. This is what is meant when we say that art is universal—more universal than is that other intangible, science, since the arts speak a language which is closer to the emotions and imaginations of every man.[60]

As we can see, then, based upon Dewey's view of art, it is "the values of the arts which nourish the human spirit with the accomplishment of our past history which strengthens that legitimate pride, which enables one to say, 'I am an American citizen!'."[61] What is more important for our purpose, though, let us note that in concluding his discussion of "Art as Our Heritage" (1940), Dewey says, "I do not want to close without mentioning a fact which I could bring home to you only if television were at my command."[62] It is obvious, of course, that when he made the latter statement above a half century ago, "television" was not a household word or item like it is today. However, in view of the tremendous changes that have occurred since 1940, evidently we could—if we wished to do so—bring home to the American public the issues raised by James's *Stolen Legacy*; and in keeping with Dewey's notion of a true democratic society, this is what I would suggest that we do.

Adequately doing so, of course, shall require the proper employment of propaganda. For as Dewey has reminded us,

> Intelligence in politics when it is identified with discussion means reliance upon symbols. The invention of language is probably the greatest single invention achieved by humanity. . . . The nineteenth-century establishment of parliamentary institutions, written constitutions and suffrage as a means of political rule, is a tribute to the power of symbols. . . . "Propaganda" is the inevitable consequence of the combination of these influences and it extends to every area of life.[63]

As for the proper employment of the propaganda, perhaps it is rather unfortunate that we find Dewey saying, "The discussion of propaganda and propagandism alone, however, demand a volume, and could be written only by one much more experienced than the present writer."[64] Yet he does tell us, "Propaganda can accordingly only be mentioned, with the remark that the present situation is one unprecedented in history."[65] Hence, in view of Dewey's observations about the use of television and propaganda, it seems safe to say that we can improve the image of American philosophy at home and abroad as well; and we can do it all-at-one-time.

In the subsequent chapters, however, rather similar to Dewey, I do not try to give specific details about what we should do to improve the status of philosophy in America. Nevertheless, it should be understood here that whatever course of action we take, I think that it ought to be done on a voluntary basis. For as Dewey reminds us, "political activity can, first and foremost, engage in agressive maintenance of the civil liberties of free speech, free publication and intercommunication, and free assemblage."[66]  He believed, in other words, that "the government can do much to encourage and promote in a positive way the growth of a great variety of voluntary cooperative undertakings."[67]  Moreover, he says, "By equalizing conditions, I do not doubt that for some time to come political activity will move in the direction of support of underprivileged groups who have been oppressed and made insecure by the growth of concentrated industry and finance."[68]  Therefore, like Dewey, I believe that "The way is open for a movement which will provide the fullest opportunity for cooperative voluntary endeavor.  In this movement political activity will have a part, but a subordinate one."[69]  Very much like him, I'm convinced that "It will be confined to providing conditions, both negative and positive, that favor the voluntary activity of individuals."[70]

At any rate, with respect to the present disparity between whites, blacks, and other minorities in the field of philosophy, let us ask ourselves:  What kind of public image is being displayed or exhibited in America's philosophical arena?  Are the statistics that we noted earlier by Levin and Hoekema a good indication?  With these questions in mind, as we turn to the ensuing chapters, let's also remember that Dewey says, "When the parties involved in any transaction are unequal in status, the relationship is likely to be one-sided, and the interests of one party to suffer."[71]  In order to counteract such a problem, which seems to be similar to James's situation, Dewey says, "If the consequences appear serious, especially if they seem to be irretrievable, the public brings to bear a weight that will equalize conditions."[72]

In other words, I think that Dewey makes this position quite clear when he says, "Only through constant watchfulness and criticism of public officials by citizens can a state be maintained in integrity and usefulness."[73]  As the following pages try to show, the latter statement is indicative of the kind of open-mindedness that evolved from Dewey's concept of philosophy and truth.  So let us turn to the narrative and give due consideration to his new way of thinking about philosophy and truth.  Although there is no attempt made to provide a solution to our problems of communication, it is hoped that this study at least helps to clarify the evolutionary stages of Dewey's development and his perspective on our problems.  For as he reminds us, "the way and degree in which we use or fail to use freedom of inquiry and public communication may well be the criterion by which in the end the genuineness of our democracy will be decided in all issues."[74]

In keeping with Dewey's reminder, my hope is that this study will help create the kind of communicative environment that Dewey longed for. Just imagine what it could mean to the future of philosophy if a dissertation committee and a Ph. D. student could aid in resolving some of our philosophical problems concerning truth. In this respect, it is hoped that this research may appeal to my own contemporaries; but if not, at least it may generate some speculative ideas for future researchers. Either way, though, it seems clear that adequate organizational efforts will require some brave volunteers; for apparently social conditions are not much better now, if any at all, than they were when Dewey said,

> Only a few years ago the names of some of the leaders of thought in this country were on the black books of departments in Washington as dangerous characters, potentially seditious because they had indulged in criticism of our tendencies in industry and were not afraid to put their fingers on sore spots like suppression of free speech.[75]

Dewey goes on to point up the unfortunate consequences of this kind of danger, and he informs us that

> There are scores and scores who are induced to keep quiet, to gloss over social ills, and to accustom students to believe that all is for the best in this best of all possible countries. The result is that the great majority of the students in our schools go forth unprepared to meet the realities of the world in which they live. They have been filled with highly idealized pictures of the actual state of things, idealizations created in part by omission of any reference to ills and unsolved problems, partly by excessive glorification of whatever good things exist. Then the graduates find themselves in a very different kind of a world. . . . for the sensitive and thoughtful [person] it requires a painful readjustment to find the gap which exists between what they had been taught to believe and things as they are.[76]

In light of his assertion, and in concluding this introductory chapter, let's ask ourselves: What difference would it make if philosophers finally agree to use a correspondence theory of truth, a coherence theory of truth, or a pragmatic theory of truth in philosophic discourse, as long as the masses of ordinary people remain blind, or in blissful ignorance? With this question in mind, now let us carefully examine the evolution of John Dewey's conception of philosophy and his notion of truth, as he developed them over the years; let's see what else he thought and said about the future of philosophy and the problem of truth.

# Notes

1. Dewey, "A Need for a Recovery of Philosophy," in *Creative Intelligence: Essays in the Pragmatic Attitude* (New York: Octagon Books, 1917). p. 67.
2. Dewey, "From Absolutism to Experimentalism" (1930), reprinted in *Later Works,* Vol. 5, p. 159.
3. Dewey, "From Absolutism to Experimentalism" (1930), reprinted in *Later Works,* Vol. 5, p. 159.
4. Dewey, "The Social-Economic Situation and Education" (1933), in *Later Works*, Vol. 8, p. 49.
5. *Ibid.*
6. *Ibid.* Also indicating that Dewey was not a narrowly focused philosopher we find him pointing out that, "Men relied upon the growing interdependence of the peoples of the earth to bring about advance in the desired direction. Commerce, industry, growth of the means of communication between countries physically far apart, did in fact produce interdependence. . . . [But] we now live in what to all intents and purposes is One World. Distance, the isolating and divisive power of seas and vast spaces, has been overcome." See "Between Two Worlds" (1944), in *Later Works,* Vol. 17, p. 453.
7. Dewey, "Charles Sanders Peirce" (1932), in *Later Works,* Vol. 6, p. 277.
8. Dewey, "A God or The God" (1933), reprinted in *Later Works,* Vol. 9, p. 213.
9. Dewey, *How We Think* (1910), in *Later Works*, Vol. 8, pp. 145-46. In more recent times, the importance of noting the "special features of first person avowals" has been pointed up by D. S. Clarke Jr.; for he says, "As forms of language parasitic on ordinary descriptive language their use poses special problems." See *Principles of Semiotic* (New York: Routledge & Kegan Paul, Inc., 1987). p. 137.
10. Dewey, "Methods in Philosophy and the Sciences" (1937), in *Later Works,* Vol. 17, pp. 446-47.
11. Dewey, "The Underlying Philosophy of Education" (1933), in *Later Works,* Vol. 8, p. 84.
12. Dewey, "The Need for a Recovery of Philosophy" (1917), in *Creative Intelligence,* p. 65.
13. *Ibid.*
14. Dewey, "The Need for a Recovery of Philosophy" (1917), in *Creative Intelligence*, p. 5.
15. *Ibid.*
16. Dewey, "The Future of Philosophy" (1947), reprinted in *Later Works*, Vol. 17, p. 466-68.

17. Gerald R. Leslie, Richard F. Larson, Benjamin L. Gorman, *Order and Change* (New York: Oxford University Press, 1973). p. 456.
18. Michael Levin, "To the Editor" (1990), in *The American Philosophical Association, Proceedings*, Vol. 63, no. 5, p. 63.
19. David A. Hoekema, "Letter From the Editor" (1990), in *The American Philosophical Association, Proceedings*, Vol. 63, no. 5, p. 3.
20. *Ibid.*
21. Dewey, *Democracy and Education* (1916), p. 21.
22. Spencer J. Maxcy, "Ethnic Pluralism, Cultural Pluralism, and John Dewey's Program of Cultural Reform:  A Response to Eisele," in *Educational Theory*, Summer 1984, Vol. 34, No. 3, p. 302.
23. *Ibid.*, p. 301.
24. Spencer J. Maxcy, "Ethnic Pluralism, Cultural Pluralism, and John Dewey's Program of Cultural Reform:  A Response to Eisele" , in *Educational Theory*, Summer 1984, Vol. 34, No. 3, p. 301.
25. *Ibid.*,  p. 305.
26. Morton G. White, *The Origin of Dewey's Instrumentalism* (New York: Octagon Books, Inc. 1943). p. 134.
27. Dewey, *The School and Society* (Carbondale and Edwardsville: Southern Illinois University Press, 1902, 1976). p. 5.
28. Dewey, "Education and Social Change" (1937), in *Later Works,* Vol. 11, p. 416.
29. Dewey, *Reconstruction in Philosopy* (1920), p. 186.
30. Dewey, *Reconstruction in Philosopy* (1920), p. 191.
31. *Ibid.*, p. 188.  Perhaps it should be noted here that Dewey takes care to warn us that, "Because the individual does not participate in collective projects of social planning and control, he feels himself submerged and paralyzed by forces too large and blind, apparently, for any control. The final result is a spirit of fatalism combined with one of reckless speculation." See "The Social-Economic Situation and Education" (1933), in *Later Works*, Vol. 8, p. 64.  Most likely, so it seems, the best kind of collective efforts to organize individuals in our American society, would have to be accomplished by employing the classic Greek's method of public debate.  For as Dewey reminds us, "In Athens not merely political but legal  issues were settled in the public forum." See "Logic" (1933), in *Later Works*, Vol. 8, p. 3.
32. *Ibid.*, p. 188.
33. *Ibid.*, p. 209.
34. Dewey, *Reconstruction in Philosophy* (1920), pp. 212-13.  It is interesting to note that Dewey's concluding statement appears to contain a paraphrase of biblical scripture.  His message seems to echo Jesus's alleged assertion that, "The wind bloweth where it listeth, and thou hearest the sound thereof, but canst not tell whence it cometh, and whither it goeth: so is every one that is born of the Spirit" (*St. John* 3: 8, KJV).

35. Dewey, "Introduction" to *Problems of Men: The Problems of Men and the Present State of Philosophy* (1946), in *Later Works,* Vol. 15, p. 169.
36. Dewey, "Modern Philosophy" (1952), in *Later Works,* Vol. 16, p. 418.
37. George G. M. James, *Stolen Legacy* (New York: Philosophical Library, 1954).
38. Dewey, "Philosophy" (1934), reprinted in *Later Works*, Vol. 8, p. 19.
39. Martin Bernal, *Black Athena* 2 Vols. (New Jersey: Rutgers University Press, 1987). Vol. 1, p. 435.
40. Martin Bernal, *Black Athena* 2 Vols. (New Jersey: Rutgers University Press, 1987). Vol. 1, p. 435.
41. Martin Bernal, *Black Athena* 2 Vols. (New Jersey: Rutgers University Press, 1987). Vol. 1, p. 435. Concerning Bernal's reference to the work of Cheikh Anta Diop, consider the following observation made by John Henrik Clarke, Professor Emeritus, Department of Africana and Puerto Rican Studies, Hunter College, New York City. In the "Foreword" to Diop's *Civilization or Barbarism*, Clarke writes, "All African people, everywhere, are closer to a better understanding of their history and destiny because of the personality and work of Cheikh Anta Diop. . . . He was not only an innovative theoretician, but he was also a pragmatist. . . . he went beyond Pan-Africanism: he was a scholar-activist, dedicated to science in the interest of his people. He saw Africa and its people as the hope of humanity. *Civilization or Barbarism* is Cheikh Anta Diop's magnum opus and the last of his great contributions to the clarification of African world history. . . . Through this book he has left us an historical legacy that will inspire future historians and researchers who seek the truth about the role of Africa in world history. Before his untimely death he had stated that this would be his last scholarly work. . . . His work was a revelation to me, because I had not encountered, in print, an African scholar so forthright in challenging prevailing misconceptions about African history and putting forth a new creative view, with documentation. . . . When I attended the second meeting of the International Congress of Africanness in Dakar, Senegal, which met at the University of Dakar in 1967, I sought out Dr. Diop. I was surprised to learn that his office and laboratory were located on the campus of the university, less than three hundred yards from the assembly hall where the Congress was being held, yet he was not one of the participants at the conference. The sponsoring organization, the African Studies Association, was then dominated by white scholars, and to this day it has not recognized the scholarship of Cheikh Anta Diop and his contributions to a new concept of African history. Neither his name nor his work was mentioned at the conference. . . . I returned to the United States and spent the next seven years trying to convince American publishers that the books of Cheikh Anta Diop should be translated into English and published in the United States." See *Civilization or Barbarism* (Brooklyn, New York: Lawrence Hill Books, 1981, 1991). pp. xiv-xv.

42. Asa G. Hilliard, "Bibliographical Notes: George G. M. James," in the 1988 reprint of *Stolen Legacy*. With regard to the credentials of James, Hilliard also informs us that, "Professor George G. M. James was born in Georgetown, British Guiana, South America. He was the son of Reverend Linch B. and Margaret E. James. He earned the Bachelor of Arts, Bachelor of Theology and Master of Arts degrees from Durham University in England. . . . He was an external student and conducted research at London University. He did postgraduate work at Columbia University where he read for his Phd. Professor James earned a teaching certificate in the State of New York to teach mathematics, Latin and Greek. . . . [He] served as Professor of Logic and Greek at Livingston College, Salisbury, North Carolina, for two years; Professor of Languages and Philosophy at Johnson C. Smith, Charlotte, North Carolina, for ten years; Professor of Mathematics and Dean of Men at Georgia State College, Industrial College, Georgia, for two years; Professor of Social Sciences at Alabama A. & M., University of Arkansas, Pine Bluff, Arkansas, for five years." Also, says Hilliard, "Professor James was a member of the Asssociation of University Professors, the American Association for the Advancement of Science, the American Classical League, the National Education Association, and the American Teachers Association" *(Ibid.)*.

43. Dewey, "Liberty and Social Control (1935)," reprinted in *Later Works*, Vol. 11, p. 360.

44. Dewey, "Renascent Liberalism" (1935), in *Later Works*, Vol. 11, p. 55.

45. *Ibid.*, p. 56.

46. Dewey, "Renascent Liberalism" (1935), in *Later Works*, Vol. 11, p. 58.

47. Dewey, "Renascent Liberalism" (1935), in *Later Works*, Vol. 11, p. 59. Perhaps it should be mentioned here that in an additional footnote Dewey goes on to say, "It should be noted that Marx himself was not completely committed to the dogma of the inevitability of force as the means of effecting revolutionary changes in the system of 'social relations.' For at one time he contemplated that the change might occur in Great Britain and the United States, and possibly in Holland, by peaceful means" *(Ibid.)*.

48. Samuel Meyer, ed., *Dewey and Russell: An Exchange* (New York: Philosophical Library, 1985). p. 14.

49. Dewey, "The Case of Odell Waller: Supreme Court to Be Asked Again to Hear Negro's Petition" (1942), reprinted in *Later Works*, Vol. 15, p. 356. In concluding this particular article, it is interesting to note that Dewey again reflects upon the problem of economic principles—supply and demand— and he tells us, "It is clear from the record that both the slayer and the slain were victims of the economic forces which for some decades have exerted terrible pressure on both white and colored farmers. The white man was a debt-ridden renter; the colored man a destitute sharecropper" (p. 358).

50. Dewey, "Tribute to James Hayden Tufts" (1942), reprinted in *Later Works*, Vol. 15, pp. 321-23.

51. Dewey, "Logical Method and Law," in *Philosophy and Civilization* (New York: Capricorn Books, 1931). p. 133.
52. Dewey, *Philosophy and Civilization*, p. 11.
53. *Ibid.*, p. 12.
54. Dewey, "What Are Universals?" (1936), reprinted in *Later Works*, Vol. 11, pp. 105-06.
55. John Locke, *An Essay Concerning Human Understanding* (Oxford: Oxford University Press, 1690, 1975). Ed. Peter H. Nidditch. Book iv, Chapter vii, Section 16, p. 607. As for Locke's influence in the United States, for instance, Frederick Mayer reminds us that, "To the founders of American Independence, John Locke's *Two Treatises On Civil Government* were almost as authoritative as the Bible." See Mayer's *A History of Educational Thought*, p.230.
56. Elmer H. Duncan and Miodrag S. Lukich, "Kant's Rigorism: A Problem and A Solution." *Southern Journal of Philosophy*, Winter, 1965, p. 189. As for Kant's notion of a virtuous woman," it is interesting to note his assertion that, "Woman is intolerable of all commands. . . . They do something only because it pleases them and the art consists in making only that which please them which is good. I hardly believe that the fair sex is capable of principles, and I hope by that not to offend, for these are also extremely rare in the male" (*Ibid.*, footnote #9).
57. *Ibid.*
58. Dewey, "Problems of Contemporary Philosophy: The Problem of Experience" (1933), reprinted in *Later Works*, Vol. 17, p. 437. Also, rather indicative of Kant's influential position, Dewey tells us, "The Western world was reared under the influence of the doctrines and sacraments of the Church. Contrast between the old Adam which is 'natural' and a higher self which is 'spiritual' remained the assumption of philosophers who avowedly repudiated supernaturalism—as in the striking case of Kant." See Dewey's "Anti Naturalism in Extremis" (1943), reprinted in *Later Works*, Vol. 15, p. 47.
59. For a more elaborate discussion of this issue, the reader may consider Dewey's article "Practical Democracy" (1925), which is a review of Walter Lippmann's *The Phantom Public* (1925), in *Later Works*, Vol. 2, p. 213; also see Dewey's "Liberalism in a Vacuum: A Critique of Walter Lippmann's Social Philosophy" (1937). For present purposes, though, perhaps we should note Lippmann's close involvement with the origin and actions of the CPI (Committee on Public Information). Stephen Vaughn , in the "Preface" to *Holding Fast the Inner Lines: Democracy, Nationalism, and the Committee on Public Information* (1980), reports that, "The CPI proved spectacularly sucessful in mobilizing public opinion behind the country's participation in the World War of 1917-18, popularizing the notion that the struggle was a great crusade to save democracy. In retrospect there must be little doubt that its appeal promoted national unity, but there has been considerable skepticism as to whether

the CPI strengthened democracy, which, in the United States, has been associated with individual liberty and human equality under law" (p. xi.). With respect to Lippmann's involvement, Vaughn tells us, "The newspaperman Walter Lippmann corresponded with Wilson and apparently had some influence with the president. Lippmann's correspondence in the months before entry into the war revealed a concern with such matters as recruiting an army, censorship, and a rationale for abandoning neutrality and entering the war that would win support of the many dissident groups within the United States. . . . [Lippmann maintained that] problems with the press would not come from unpatriotic Americans but from 'those who persecute and harass and cause divisions.' It was important to control untruth but not to suppress truth, as had been done in Europe. A healthy public opinion was of paramount importance. The ideas Lippmann had in mind for mobilizing public opinion—a rationale for abandoning neutrality and entering the war—appeared in a letter and memorandum he submitted to Wilson on March 11, 1917" (p. 5). However, says Vaughn, "There is no evidence that Wilson replied to these suggestions of March 11, but Lippmann likely discussed his ideas with the president in mid-March. . . . There is evidence that the president's confidant, Colonel Edward M. House, asked Lippmann to help set up a 'public bureau,' and the response was an outline of such an agency on April 12, 1917, just one day before creation of the Committee on Public Information. Lippmann proposed a clearinghouse for information on government activities, a monitoring of the foreign press, a taking into account of the motion-picture industry" (p. 6). In connection with Lippmann's actions, Vaughn also says, "In retrospect, it would appear that [Arthur Bullard] should receive much of the credit for the administration's decision to establish the Committee on Public Information" (p. 7). Accordingly, says Vaughn, "When Bullard's article on diplomacy appeared in the *Atlantic* in April 1917, it argued that all the nations of Europe had been victims of secret diplomacy and that the United States conducted its foreign policy in a scarcely better fashion; American diplomacy, Bullard contended, was hardly more democratic than that of Russia. The culprits of this depressing situation were the professional diplomats who hated publicity and defended secrecy. Bullard proposed to make it impossible 'for a few men in secret and uncontrolled conclave to decide the fate of nations.' He would do so by going over the heads of any foreign office that stood in the way, appealing directly to the people" (p. 11). Thus, as Bullard saw things, "Nothing would 'be more gloriously American and more heartily welcomed by the Liberals of all the world than the devising and demonstrating of means by which diplomacy could be democratic'" (p. 11). As Vaughn puts it, "Bullard's ideas for propaganda organization were nothing if not detailed. He clearly had been thinking a great deal about the subject. A healthy public opinion required free discussion. . . . The best method of combating dangerous opinion was publicity, 'by constantly giving the man in the street something wholesome to think about'" (p. 13). So, it seems that Bullard's view, as opposed to Lippmann's, was much more in accord with Dewey's. Like Lippmann, however, we can see that Dewey also believed in directly confronting America's chief officer, if necessary. For on one occasion during the era of the Great Depression, we find him boldly writing a letter to President Hoover, and bluntly criticizing him, saying, "It is a misfortune when a person in high and responsible office is committed to ideas and policies which are absolutely contrary to the actual and inevitable course of events. It is not only a misfortune for his own political career, but a calamity for the nation, and even for humanity." See "President Dewey Calls on Hoover to Recognize Government Responsibility for Unemployment" (1931), reprinted in *Later Works*, Vol. 6, p. 372. To be sure, it is evident that Dewey believed in speaking out against wrong regardless of who commits it. He obviously believed in rendering criticism when due. We can see that he courageously exemplifies his straightforward stand for truth in his closing remarks to Hoover, where he says, "we are living under new conditions which demand new ideas and new measures on the part of those in public life," that is, "On behalf of our suffering fellow-citizens"(p. 373). So indeed, Dewey even wrote boldly to the highest ranking officer in America.

60. Dewey, "Art as Our Heritage" (1940), in *Later Works*, Vol. 14, pp. 256. As for the suppression of art, or ideas, Dewey also informs us that "One of the chief occupations of states has been the waging of war and the suppression of dissentient minorities." See *The Public and Its Problems,* in *Later Works,* Vol. 2, p. 280.

61. *Ibid.*, p. 257.

62. *Ibid.*

63. Dewey, *Liberalism and Social Action* (1935), in *Later Works*, Vol. 11, p. 51.

64. Dewey, *The Public and Its Problems* (1927), in *Later Works*, Vol. 2, p. 348.

65. *Ibid.*

66. Dewey, "I Believe" (1939), reprinted in *Later Works,* Vol. 14, p. 93.

67. *Ibid.*

68. Dewey, "I Believe" (1939), reprinted in *Later Works,* Vol. 14, p. 93. We are reminded by Dewey on another occasion that "Industrial entrepreneurs have reaped out of all proportion to what they sowed. By obtaining private ownership of the means of production and exchange they deflected a considerable share of the results of increased productivity to their pockets." See *Liberalism and Social Action (1935), in Later Works*, Vol. 11, p. 53. Maybe, then, in view of their enormous amout of earnings, what we should do is allow them the opportunity to put some money back into American communities. For instance, we could organize philosophers and ordinary citizens from every stratum of social life in

America (on a volunteer basis, of course) to create a public forum like they held in ancient Athens, when philosophy was still in its state of infancy. The event could also be used as an attempt to get the name of God straight as a proper subject matter of philosophy; and thereby the event could also contain some of the thrills and excitement that allegedly took place at Mount Sinai, where "the sight of the glory of the LORD was like a devouring fire on the top of the mount in the eyes of the children of Israel." See *Exodus* 24: 17. In other words, we could use propaganda to advertise the event, and we could allow some of the major business corporations in America to sponsor it, as they advertise their products or services. In this respect, we could put our many bureaucratic agencies to work for us; that is, we could organize the event as a telethon that enables each individual citizen to make a financial pledge or contribution to help eliminate our federal deficit.

69. Dewey, "I Believe" (1939), reprinted in *Later Works,* Vol. 14, p. 95.
70. *Ibid.*
71. Dewey, *The Public and Its Problems* (1927), reprinted in *Later Works*, Vol. 2, p. 274.
72. *Ibid.*
73. Dewey, *The Public and Its Problems* (1927), reprinted in *Later Works,* Vol. 2, p. 278.
74. Dewey, "Contribution to *Democracy in a World of Tensions*" (1951), reprinted in *Later Works*, Vol. 16, pp. 403-04. Perhaps it should be mentioned here that regarding the form of genuine democracy, it seems quite evident that Dewey would be opposed to those philosophers who think that "our rulers will have to administer a great quantity of falsehood and deceit for the benefit of the ruled" (*Republic* V: 459c). Quite contrary to the latter way of thinking, Dewey boldly and candidly says, "It is terrible enough that so many youths should have no opportunity to obtain employment under the conditions set by the present economic system. It is equally terrible that so many young people should be refused opportunity in what we call a public educational system, to find out about the causes of this tragic situation, and, in large measure, should be indoctrinated in ideas to which the realities about them give the lie. Confusion and bewilderment are sufficiently rife so that it is not necessary to add to them a deliberately cultivated blindness." See "Youth in a Confused World" (1935), reprinted in *Later Works,* Vol. 11, p. 354.
75. Dewey, "The Economic Situation: A Challenge to Education" (1932), reprinted in *Later Works,* Vol. 6, p. 124. With respect to the problem of "fear," it is interesting to note that at the age of ninety we find Dewey telling us, "Of the various kindly and generous, often over-generous, things that have been said about my activities on the occasion of my ninetieth birthday, there is one thing in particular I should be peculiarly happy to believe. It is . . . that I have helped to liberate my fellow-human beings from fear."

As he additionally points out, however, he had come to recognize that "democracy is an educative process," and "This educational process is based upon faith in human good sense and human good will as it manifests itself in the long run when communication is progressively liberated from bondage to prejudice and ignorance." See "John Dewey Responds" (1949), reprinted in *Later Works,* Vol. 17, p. 86.

76. *Ibid.*, p. 125.

# Chapter 2

ജ‍യ‍ര‍

# A New Way of Thinking
# About Philosophy and Truth:
# Dewey's Instrumentalism

John Dewey undoubtedly viewed "truth" as an English word, a word that had undeniably caused wrangling among many English speaking philosophers. Yet he apparently recognized that disputes about truth are not novel to people who speak English. Except for the alphabetical characters that constitute the word "truth" (e. g., "verite" in French and "wahrheit" in German), and except for the different vocal sounds employed to pronounce the term, evidently disputes about "truth" have existed since the dawn of philosophy. Dewey, no doubt, believed that disputes concerning the problem of truth have been passed down to us from the ancient Greeks. When he reflects upon Western philosophy in its initial stages, for instance, Dewey tells us that

. . . the origin of European philosophy in Greece is the natural beginning. For not only does the name "philosophy" come from Greek thought, but also the explicit consciousness of what is denoted by the term. Greek thinkers moreover distinguished the branches into which philosophy is still conventionally divided; they laid the foundations logic, cosmology, metaphysics, ethical and political philosophy, and to a lesser degree, aesthetic theory. Even if these foundations are not always built upon, it is impossible to understand departures and innovations apart from some reference to Greek thought. In Greek philosophy the problems of western philosophy are either formulated or adumbrated.[1]

As Dewey interprets the history of philosophy, then, disputes about the problem of truth must be seen in light of the early Greeks. The statement above seems to clearly express the context in which he believed the philosophical problem of "truth" should be taken. In their effort to resolve the problem, Dewey points out that they had postulated "two orders of existence." They had described one as "permanent and complete, the noumenal region, to which alone the characteristic of Being is properly applicable," and the other was said to be "transitory, phenomenal, sensible, a region of non-Being, or at least of mere Coming-to-be, a region in which Being is hopelessly mixed with non-Being, with the unreal."[2] For the ancient Greeks, only the former region was considered to be the domain of knowledge, of truth. They regarded the latter region as the territory of opinion, confusion, error. This division of the universe, however, did not set well with John Dewey. He thought that their attempt to provide a satisfactory way of dealing with the problem of truth had resulted in a dichotomous universe, a form of dualism. Thus, adamantly rejecting this view, he raised the question, "How could *knowledge*, truth ever come about upon such a basis?"[3]

Dewey held that like knowledge itself, "truth is an experienced relation of things, and it has no meaning outside such a relation."[4] This is why his philosophy emphasizes the "intending" character of knowing, and the "relational" character of truth. For Dewey, neither "truth" nor "falsity" are properties of any experience or thing in and of itself. So he questions the classical Greek notion of truth because it tends to suggest metaphysical absolutes outside experience.

In other words, after the classic Greeks divided existence into two realms, a higher one of perfect being (noumenal) and a lower one of deficient reality (phenomenal), how could theories about the noumenal region be confirmed? Dewey questioned whether they could be. In any event, evidently he was convinced that the notion of truth inherited from the classic tradition, which was passed on to medieval philosophers, and then to us, has caused many of our disputes about the problem of truth.

For the most part, as John Dewey interpreted the climate of mainstream philosophy during his epoch, the Greek conception of "two orders of existence" had still been retained in philosophic discourse. Rather unfortunately, perhaps, instead of the two orders characterizing the universe itself, one was regarded as the universe, while the other was regarded as the individual mind trying to know that universe. But Dewey, however, rejected this questionable notion of a dichotomous universe. On his view, this notion has been a major hindrance to developing a tenable definition of the word "truth." Therefore, throughout his mature philosophical career, Dewey kept trying to dispel it.

Indeed, Dewey's ardent endeavor to dispel the Greek notion of "two orders of existence" marks the beginning and the end of his attempt to provide a defensible pragmatic conception of truth.[5] As the following pages point out, John Dewey was proselytized to pragmatism by the preaching of Charles S. Peirce and William James. Then, after his conversion, Dewey spent the remaining years of his life trying to clarify his own notion of truth. Though it is difficult to say exactly when he was converted to pragmatism, apparently it occurred near the turn of the century. Dewey says himself that

> I have been engaged by means of published writings in developing the essentials of my present philosophical views for at least thirty-five years, beginning with my essays in the *Studies in Logical Theory* in 1903.[6]

He additionally says,

> I did not hit upon my position as a ready made and finished doctrine. It developed in and through a series of reactions to a number of philosophic problems and doctrines. During the early nineties, practically all important philosophizing in the English language was influenced by Neo-Kantian and Hegelian idealism. Pragmatism and all versions of realism are of later growth. . . . But I gladly admit that my philosophic views did not develop in a vacuum and that I took seriously philosophic doctrines that were current.[7]

In "The Development of American Pragmatism" (1925), Dewey clearly acknowledges the effects that Peirce and James had upon influencing his notion of truth. He tells us that the purpose of the article is to "define the principal theories of the philosophical movements known under the names of Pragmatism, Instrumentalism, or Experimentalism."[8]

Moreover, he tells us that "the origin of Pragmatism goes back to Charles Sanders Peirce."[9] However, he explains that "James narrowed the application of Peirce's pragmatic method, but at the same time he extended it."[10] Further distinguishing between the methods of these two proponents of pragmatism, Dewey tells us that "James extended the use of the pragmatic method to the problem of the nature of truth."[11] That is, as a specialist in psychology, and as a humanist, James propounded a new notion of what it means to say of a proposition that it is true. Peirce, on the other hand, as a specialist in logic, had advanced a pragmatic theory of the meaning of linguistic signs. Dewey, however, despite the different orientations of the two thinkers, followed the insights of both Peirce and James. As he explains his position, Dewey tells us that

> I myself, and those who have collaborated with me in the exposition of instrumentalism, began by being Neo-Kantians, in the same way that Peirce's point of departure was Kantianism and that of James was the empiricism of the British School.[12]

What is Pragmatism, Instrumentalism, and Experimentalism? Let us first consider a provisional definition for the former term, and then the latter two terms, respectively. James defines Pragmatism *not* as a "theory" of truth, but as a "means" of discovering truth.[13] According to him, Pragmatism provides a "conception of truth." James held that it is mostly a "method" for ascertaining the nature of truth. He describes it in the following way.

> The pragmatic method is primarily a method of settling metaphysical disputes that otherwise might be interminable. Is the world one or many?—fated of free?—material or spiritual?—here are notions either of which may or may not hold good of the world; and disputes over such notions are unending. The pragmatic method in such cases is to try to interpret each notion by tracing its respective practical consequences. What difference would it practically make to anyone if this notion rather than that notion were true?[14]

Evidently, then, in light of James' description, we may provisionally define Pragmatism as a method or means of inquiring into the nature of truth.

Instrumentalism is an outgrowth of Pragmatism. John Dewey's elaboration of Instrumentalism is a modified version of the theory of meaning that James got from Peirce, and extended its application to conceptions of truth. However, just as James was reluctant to define Pragmatism as a "theory" of truth, likewise we should be careful about defining Dewey's Instrumentalism as a theory of truth.[15] It would be more appropriate, perhaps, to follow James Gouinlock's suggestion and say that "instrumentalism when fully explicated is a theory concerning the nature of intelligent conduct."[16]

No doubt a strong defense for Gouinlock's suggestion can be sustained by the definitive meaning of "truth" that Dewey gives in *Experience and Nature*, where he says,

> Sometimes the use of the word "truth" is confined to designating a logical property of propositions; but if we extend its significance to designate characters of existential reference, this is the meaning of truth: processes of change so directed that they achieve an intended consummation.[17]

From Dewey's extensive definition of the meaning of truth we see that its function is to designate "characters of existential reference." On his view, then, truth may be defined as the "processes of change" that make designations (propositions) possible. So, on his definition of truth, it is an "organic process of inquiry" that discloses distinct referential qualities of its existence.

As for his method of discovering the nature of truth, Dewey does not make a sharp distinction between Instrumentalism and Experimentalism. On one hand, for instance, Dewey says, "Instrumentalism is an attempt to establish a precise logical theory of concepts, of judgments and inferences in their various forms, by considering primarily how thought functions in the experimental determinations of future consequences."[18] Moreover, as Dewey further defines his version of Instrumentalism, he informs us that it "assigns a positive function to thought, that of reconstituting the present stage of things instead of knowing it."[19] Thus, according to Dewey's definition, "Instrumentalism maintains that action should be intelligent and reflective, and that thought occupy a central position in life. That is the reason for our insistence on the teleological phase of thought and knowledge."[20] However, it is clear that Dewey draws no rigid distinction between Instrumentalism and Experimentalism, for he also says,

> Pragmatism and instrumental experimentalism bring into prominence the importance of the individual. It is he who is the carrier of creative thought, the author of action, and of its application. . . . The

individual mind is important because only the individual mind is the organ of modifications in traditions and institutions, the vehicle of experimental creation.[21]

Dewey's emphasis on the "individual mind," as indicated by the statement above, is a very important feature of his Instrumentalism. Sidney Hook notes the importance of Dewey's concern for individual minds. He tells us that

John Dewey [was] surely the philosopher of the plain man—of the millions who are neither on the top nor on the bottom. . . . Concerned, to be sure with individuals, his interest [was] not in the special case, whether labelled errant genius, or problem child, or the individual, but with conditions and problems that effect multitudes of individuals. For him every individual is a special case.[22]

As we can see from Hook's interpretation, Dewey's concern about individual minds must be a central feature of his Instrumentalism. However, some of Dewey's critics, no doubt, misunderstood his notion of the individual mind and how it relates to Instrumentalism. As an attempt to lay a firm foundation for clarifying Dewey's view of truth, let us pause a moment and try to see how his notion of the individual mind is relevant to his Instrumentalism. Apparently, as Hook's interpretation implies, understanding Dewey's conceptual treatment of them is crucial for correctly comprehending his conception of philosophy. So let's try to clarify Dewey's conceptions, and the employment of his terms.

We noted above how he uses the terms "instrumentalism" and "experimentalism" in his article "The Development of American Pragmatism" (1925). What we will do now is try to elucidate some of the confusion that resulted from his employment of the terms. By exposing some of the critical issues that have arisen concerning his Instrumentalism, perhaps we can clarify the importance that he sees in individual minds. Moreover, by proceeding in this manner, we hope to show how his conception of philosophy evolves from and culminates in his concern about truth.

Research indicates that much of the criticism launched against Dewey's Instrumentalism was instigated by Bertrand Russell, who once provoked Dewey into saying, "You know, he gets me sore," as Sammuel Meyer has noted.[23] Additionally, however, Meyer notes that "Dewey and Russell are undoubtedly the two outstanding figures in Twentieth Century philosophy."[24] Therefore, if we can clarify some distinctions between the views of these "two outstanding figures," perhaps we shall be able to construct a strong foundation for our exposition. Meyer's account, so it seems, provides some useful building material; for he explains why Russell sorely vexed Dewey sometimes. For instance, with respect to Russell's interpretation of Dewey's position, Meyer says that Russell made *no* "serious effort to grasp Dewey's theory of knowledge," but instead, "found in Dewey a handy foil for his fundamental dissatisfaction with the doctrines of pragmatism and instrumentalism."[25] Now in light of Meyer's remark, it seems quite likely that Russell's attitude did indeed vex Dewey.

For present purposes, though, the most significant factor to notice about Meyer's statement is that it refers to John Dewey's instumentalism as a "theory of knowledge." Completely in line with Meyer's reference, we also find Wallace Matson maintaining that "Dewey called his theory of knowledge 'Instrumentalism': [because] concepts are instruments useful in inquiry."[26] Also, Russell indicates the coherence between Matson's and Meyer's reference to Dewey's Instrumentalism as a "theory of knowledge"; he says,

> From the strictly philosophical point of view, the chief importance of Dewey's work lies in his criticism of the traditional notion of 'truth', which is embodied in the theory that he calls 'instrumentalism'.[27]

As Russell's remarks plainly indicate, Dewey's instrumentalism was employed to criticize the traditional notion of truth. However, what is not so clear from Russell's statement is whether we should refer to his instrumentalism as a "theory of truth" or a "theory of knowledge." Judging by Matson's and Meyer's comments, as we have seen, the proper sense of refence should be "theory of knowledge."

What standards should we use to determine the appropriate sense of reference to Dewey's instrumentalism? Norman Melchert seems to provide us with some excellent criteria. He outlines the "four major concerns shared by those we call philosophers," and he cites some "characteristic questions that express each one." They are:

| Metaphysics: | What is the nature of reality? |
| | What kinds of things are there? |
| | Is there a God? |
| | What, if anything, is the soul? |
| | Is free will a possibility? |

Epistemology:    What is knowledge?
                 What—if anything—can we know?
                 Are there different kinds of knowledge?
                 What is truth?

Ethics:          What is good?
                 Are certain actions right or wrong?
                 If so, which?  And why?
                 How should we live?

Human Nature:   What kind of creature is a human being?[28]

As we scrutinize Dewey's method of instrumentalism, let's grant that Melchert correctly defines the "four major concerns shared by those we call philosophers." Apparently Dewey would agree that his list corresponds with "the branches into which philosophy is still conventionally divided."[29] Therefore, let us emphatically notice here that in regard to Melchert's list of philosophical concerns, the words "truth" and "knowledge" are both classified categorically as concerns of epistemology.

Since the words "truth" and "knowledge" are in the category of epistemology, let's get clear on what it means. A rather appropriate analysis of the word "epistemology" is provided by W. B. Williamson, who informs us that

> Basic both to philosophy of religion and doing philosophy in any problematic area of human thought and endeavors is *epistemology*. This ancient branch of philosophy was finally given a name by the nineteenth-century philosopher James F. Ferrier. Ferrier differentiated between the prime metaphysical concern, ontology (the theory of being or existence), and epistemology (the theory or study of knowledge). . . . Epistemology asks "How can we know?" rather than "What is real?" The word is taken from the Greek words *episteme*, meaning knowledge, and *logos*, meaning reason or discourse. *Logos* later was used as a suffix—*logia*—meaning the theory or study of anything.[30]

This brief survey by Williamson seems to clearly describe how the word "epistemology" should be defined, and why the words "truth" and "knowledge" should be classified in that philosophical category. His survey, therefore, shall serve as additional criteria for furthering our scrutiny of Dewey's instrumentalism.

Notice that according to Williamson's survey, which is well in line with Melchert's list, epistemological concerns are clearly distinct from metaphysical and ethical concerns, yet the concerns of all three categories reflect a concern about human beings, as "knowers." So it is in this respect that Dewey's instrumentalism is treated here, and by proceeding in this manner we hope to accomplish two things: (1) Clarify the problem of referring to Dewey's instrumentalism as a "theory of truth," or a "theory of knowledge"; and (2) Show how Dewey sought to employ his instrumentalism as a method that would help get the subject matter of philosophy straight, or clearer.

Russell's criticism of Dewey's instrumentalism seems to shed some light on the problem of reference, as well as Dewey's thematic treatment of metaphysics, epistemology, ethics, and human nature. In other words, Russell's criticism may help us simplify some of the difficulties involved in disclosing Dewey's strategic discussion of these four major branches of philosophy. For instance, as Russell interprets Dewey's position, we may classify the various concerns under a single heading, namely, "Holism." The following statement clearly indicates that Russell thought of Dewey's instrumentalism as a form of holism. He tells us,

> One of the chief sources of difference between philosophers is a temperamental bias towards synthesis or analysis. Traditionally, British philosophy was analytic, Continental philosophy synthetic. On this point, I find myself in the British tradition, while Dr. Dewey belongs with the Germans, and more particularly with Hegel. Instrumentalism his most important doctrine, is, I think, compatible with an analytic bias, but in him it takes a form associated with what General Smuts calls 'holism'.[31]

Is Russell correct in associating Dewey's Instrumentalism with a form of "what General Smuts calls 'holism'"? Is it a legitimate move to categorize Dewey's treatment of the interdependent concerns under the heading of "holism"? In our endeavor to answer such questions, bear in mind that our purpose here is not to contrast Russell's British tradition with Dewey's German idealism, or his American pragmatism. Instead, we just use Russell's bewilderment to try to explain Dewey's "substitution of 'inquiry' for 'truth' as the fundamental concept of logic and theory of knowledge."[32] Moreover, in this respect, Russell's perplexity is quite helful for our consideration of Dewey's assertion that "'warranted assertibility' should take the place of 'truth'."[33] Also we try to understand instrumentalism better by asking why Russell was baffled by Dewey's use of "indeterminate situation."[34] Yet in trying to clarify some of the confusion, the present writer wishes to cast no aspersion on Russell's scholarship. Russell's view, for the most part, is only used as a springboard for addressing some crucial questions concerning references to Dewey's instrumentalism.

A major question about references to Dewey's instrumentalist view of truth, in contrast to Russell's, seems to turn on their different conceptions of the "external world." Now granting that this is so, let us ask ourselves: What did John Dewey think about the problem of the external world? On Dewey's view, is the environment of the human organism its external world? Is the human organism contained within a block universe? With respect to our experience of the universe, or external world, we find the matured Dewey saying,

> The fact that external environing conditions are the causes—and the only causes—of the experiences that occur is just the reason why my theory has emphasized the fact that knowledge, through the intermediary of intelligent action, is the sole means of regulating the existence in experience of values or consumatory objects.[35]

Apparently what Dewey is telling us about the environment, or the world "out there," is that "when we act and find environing things in stubborn opposition to our desires and efforts, the externality of the environment to the self is a direct constituent of direct experience."[36] In other words, Dewey undoubtedly believed that every experience in its direct occurrence is an interaction of environing conditions and an organism.

Dewey advanced this argument in his article "Experience, Knowledge and Value: A Rejoinder" (1939), which was written to help clarify his instrumentalism.[37] Now the pertinent factor to note at this point is that he still was concerned, for the most part, about the "intelligent action," as he puts it, of individual minds. This theme, as we pointed out earlier, was a central feature in his publication of "The Development of American Pragmatism" (1925). On Dewey's notion of individuals, or human organisms in their environment, as we have seen, his instrumentalism "assigns a positive function to thought, that of reconstituting the present stage of things instead of knowing it." An important question that we have not yet addressed, however, is this: How does the human individual reconstitute the "present stage of things," instead of "knowing it"? Seemingly, if we can answer this question sufficiently, it should help make clear some of the terms that Dewey employs in his instrumentalism. Moreover, it should also help explain the sense of reference that distinguishes between a "theory of knowledge" and a "theory of truth," if there are any distinctions to be made.

Sidney Hook's insight helps us here in addressing the previous question. In his effort to explicate Dewey's "theory of truth," as he calls it, Hook discusses a problem that concerns reconstituting the present stage of things, instead of knowing it. He uses a hypothetical case that involves individuals trying to know what has happened in the historical past. He says,

> To begin with, let us suppose we are talking about something which occurred in the past but which has no existential or historical connections with anything observable in the present or future, [for example] . . . like the adventures of the first group of men to cross the Atlantic. . . . What we are trying to determine is precisely what it means to have knowledge about the past. [That is], the past becomes an object of knowledge only when we can tell what present or future it is the past. [Thus] past and present events have different kinds of present and future effects.
>
> The flavor of paradox disappears if we bear in mind that, for Dewey, memory judgments and judgments about the historical past are logically of the same form.[38]

Now with regard to an individual's attempt to reconstitute the present stage of things, instead of knowing it, the unmistakable point that Hook's hypothetical situation illustrates is the fact that thought or "intelligent action" is required. This is why "memory judgments," and "judgments about the historical past," are logically of the same form, for Dewey. Indeed, as he saw things, the logical form of the judgments must be in the form of thoughts. That's why he argued that based on his instrumentalism, "action should be intelligent and reflective, and that thought occupy a central position in life," which is "the reason for our insistence on the teleological phase of thought."

Seemingly, though, Russell was unable to fully understand the central position that "thought" held in Dewey's instrumental method. As we have seen already, the main problem that Russell encountered with Dewey's instrumentalism was his "substitution of 'inquiry' for 'truth' as the fundamental concept of logic and theory of knowledge."

Hook provides several statements that may help us account for Russell's confusion. That is, according to Hook's interpretation of Dewey's logic, "Of all Dewey's contributions, his logical works are the hardest to understand, even for the professional logician."[39] Moreover, says Hook, "Dewey was led to his logical investigations as a result of his attempt to provide a scientific foundation for moral judgments."[40] Could it be the case that Dewey's quest for a scientific foundation for moral judgments baffled Russell?

As an attempt to adequately address this question, let us briefly consider some of Russell's views on "moral judgments." Perhaps the best way to succeed at this endeavor is to first get clear on Russell's notion of truth. He expresses it rather clearly when he says,

> Truth as conceived by most professional philosophers, is static and final, perfect and eternal; in religious terminology, it may be identified with God's thoughts, and with those which, as rational beings, we share with God. The perfect model is the multiplication table, which is precise and free of all temporal dross.[41]

Russell's statement seems to disclose the main difference between his view of truth and Dewey's. Evidently, the key terms divulging their division are disclosed via Russell's caviling associations of "truth" with "God's thoughts," those thoughts that rational beings "share with God." Perhaps it is needless to say that Russell's conception of God certainly seems to smack of the Berkelian theory of immaterialism. Anyway, it is rather clear from Russell's statement that his view of God as a "truth" which is "static and final, perfect and eternal," does indeed clash with Dewey's notion of truth.

What Russell apparently failed to recognize about Dewey's view of truth is his twofold sense of reference. That is, on one hand Dewey would undoubtedly accept Russell's reference to God as a being who is "static and final, perfect and eternal"; and he would concur with him. On the other hand, though, what seems to illustrate the difference between their notions of truth is apparently the universe of discourse in which the word "truth" is taken. For if Russell insists on conceiving of God as a being who exists only in the noumenal realm in which the ancient Greeks had placed him, and if Russell refused to conceive of or talk about truth in any other way, then Dewey would be at odds with Russell's position. Russell's refusal to talk about truth with respect to purely human concerns would indeed mark the diffences in their notions of truth, and disclose his failure to recognize the second sense of reference that Dewey uses to lay his scientific foundation for moral judgments.

As we noted earlier, William James thought of pragmatism as "primarily a method of settling metaphysical disputes that otherwise might be interminable." Moreover, as we have observed in the list of concerns that Melchert cites above, the questions "Is there a God?" and "What is the nature of reality?" are classified as metaphysical queries. Thus it seems safe to say that James's form of pragmatism was designed to deal with the latter kinds of questions. Therefore, an important distinction between James's pragmatism and Dewey's instrumentalism should be made. That is, Dewey focused mostly on sociological problems, while James focused more on cosmological.

As for the reason why Dewey deviated from James's approach, we find that it mostly resulted from confusion about what was meant by the word "pragmatism." With respect to its meaning, for instance, Dewey tells us in the Preface to his *Logic* that

> The word "Pragmatism" does not, I think, occur in the text. Perhaps the word lends itself to misconception. At all event, so much misunderstanding and relatively futile controversy have gathered about the word that it seemed advisable to avoid its use. But in the proper interpretation of "pragmatic," namely the function of consequences as necessary tests of the validity of propositions, *provided* these consequences are operationally instituted and are such as to resolve the specific problem evoking the operations, the text that follows is thoroughly pragmatic.[42]

Now in light of Dewey's explanation regarding the confusion that had gathered about the word "pragmatism," apparently we can feel safe in concluding that the term "instrumentalism" was formulated to offset the definitional problem of reference. Thus Dewey intended for his instrumental method to enable philosophers to discuss the problem of truth in a new or different sense of meaning.

It is quite important to note here, however, that Dewey's new way of thinking about truth did not mean that he stopped dealing with metaphysical issues altogether. For example, in Dewey's article "The Development of American Pragmatism" (1925), which was written more than a decade earlier than his *Logic*, he held that

> Pragmatism . . . has a metaphysical implication. The doctrine of the value of consequences leads us to take the future into consideration. And this taking into consideration of the future takes

> us to the conception of a universe whose evolution is not finished, of
> a universe which is still, in James' term, "in the making," "in the
> process of becoming," of a universe up to a certain point still plastic.[43]

Understanding Dewey's conception of the universe as "not finished" is undoubtedly crucial for recognizing the consistency of his views about metaphysical issues. Moreover, a correct understanding of his view of the universe as unfinished seems to help us understand his logical works, which are the "hardest to read" (as Hook describes them).

In order to get a sufficient understanding of Dewey's logic, which may help us interpret his treatment of metaphysical concerns, it seems that we should consider Peirce's influence on him, as well as James's. By proceeding in this manner, perhaps we shall gain some significant insight into the way Dewey viewed metaphysical questions pertaining to the existence and nature of God. In the same article he explains some of the differences between Peirce's and James's views on metaphysics and truth. Instead of digressing into a discussion of their views here, however, we shall discuss their views later.

For now, though, let's summarize Chapter 2 and make sure we are clear on Dewey's new way of thinking about philosophy and truth. Thus far we have tried to show how he formulated instrumentalism to deal with philosophy's four major areas of concern, but not quite like the earlier pragmatists. Rather than him proceeding completely along their line of thought, trying to resolve seemingly "interminable" metaphysical disputes, he employed another approach. He designed instrumentalism to help expel problematic questions of metaphysics.

For instance, we noted in our analysis of Russell's trouble with Dewey's instrumental method that their notions of truth apparently differ because of the senses of reference that they selected to use. That is, Russell seems to insist on defining truth in a very narrow or restricted way, which poses problematic questions about a highly dubious metaphysical realm of knowledge. On the other hand Dewey seems to restrict his meaning of truth as well. That is to say, he kept his questions about truth confined solely to the phenomenal region, "the territory of opinion, confusion, error," the region of mere "Coming-to-be," the transitory region where humans exist, and experience.

Dewey's notion of truth suggested a new way of philosophizing. The underlying strategy of his instrumentalism, so it seems, was to try to avoid interminable metaphysical disputes altogether. He could therefore direct all of his attention to the problems of being human in this world, where a scientific moral foundation is apparently needed.

Dewey resolutely took a stand against his critics who postulated metaphysical absolutes outside experience. He held that they created unsolvable questions about morals. Five years before he published "The Development of American Pragmatism" (1925), he argued that

> The theory of fixed ends inevitably leads thought into the bog of disputes that cannot be settled. If there is one *Summum bonum*, one supreme end, what is it? To consider this problem is to place ourselves in the midst of controversies that are as acute as they were two thousand years ago.[44]

Dewey expressed this attitude towards metaphysical concerns in his *Reconstruction in Philosophy* (1920). Clearly indicative of his moral stand against those who cling to the classic Greek notion of two orders of existence, Dewey defended his argument by saying,

> The thought of looking ahead, toward the eventual, toward consequences, creates uneasiness and fear. [The pragmatists] disturbs the sense of rest that is attached to the ideas of fixed Truth already in existence. It puts a heavy burden of responsibility on us for search, unremitting observation, scrupulous development of thorough going testing. [Some Idealists and Realists] have slowly grown accustomed in all specific beliefs to identifying the true with the verified. But they still hesitate to recognize the implication of this identification and to derive the definition of truth from it.[45]

Beyond any reasonable doubt, then, in order to understand Dewey's notion of truth, it seems that one needs to understand his attitude towards metaphysical concerns. He expresses his new way of thinking in "Experience, Knowledge and Value: A Rejoinder" (1939). Succinctly stating his position, he tells us that

> In propounding a theory of knowing I have insisted that inquiry itself involves *in its own nature* conditions to be satisfied. The autonomy of inquiry is equalivent to demand for integrity of inquiry. It is this fact that leads to the definition of truth in its intellectual or cognitive sense in terms of fulfilment of conditions intrinsic to inquiry. But the will, the disposition, to maintain the integrity intrinsic to inquiry is a moral matter. In this regard, the operations of evaluation which I have affirmed to be involved in any case of knowing—in choice of

data and hypotheses and experimental operations to be performed—pass into definitely moral valuations whenever the existing habits and character of an inquirer set up obstacles to maintenance of integral inquiry. Reconstitution into a self in some respects new is then not incidental but central. I suggested earlier that the current theory of verification and of cognitive truth of propositions—validity as I call it—suffers from having read into the moral meaning of truth. But whenever the immediate problem in conduct of inquiry for the sake of knowledge involves the will to search for evidence, to weigh it fairly, not to load the dice, to control a preference for one theory over another so that it does not affect the conclusion reached, the category of truth in its *moral* sense is supreme.[46]

Judging from Dewey's own explanation of his strategy for using the term "inquiry," it is evident that he wished to define "truth" with respect to its intellectual or "cognitive sense," as he puts it. No doubt Dewey believed that his new approach to treating metaphysical issues allowed for the possibility of validly grounding valuation propositons. So he had devised instrumentalism to prevent what he describes as "the suicide of scientific knowing, a logical destruction which is not averted by insisting that propositions are inherently true or false."[47]

As we have seen, however, Russell had difficulty understanding Dewey's logic, which led to his misconstrual of instrumentalism. Yet, the question remains whether Meyer is correct and Russell really did not make any "serious effort" to grasp Dewey's theory of knowledge, but instead, found in Dewey a handy foil for his dissatisfaction with the doctrines of pragmatism and instrumentalism. For instance, only three years prior to the publication of the forenamed article, he published "Religion, Science, and Philosophy" (1936), which provides a scrutiny of Russell's book *Religion and Science* (1935).

In Dewey's review we find him candidly expressing what he perceived to be the differences between their approach to defining the word "truth." Once again, as usual, we find that Dewey's concern is mostly about humans struggling to survive in a transistory world of confusion, error, and terror. As he reflects on the human condition, and especially the situation of most Americans, one can hardly help but wonder whether Russell ever really tried to understand Dewey's message. At any rate, Dewey plainly tells us that "most individuals, to be sure, have not enjoyed any participation in the milk and honey of the promised land. But there are few who have not been affected by the lure science in its technical applications has held out."[48]

Following the lead of Peirce's and James's pragmatic method, which emphasized "practical action," Dewey designed instrumentalism to do something about the disparity between the scientific community and ordinary individuals. Why didn't Russell understand his message and his mission? Did he really try to understand Dewey's new way of scientifically thinking about philosophy and truth? It certainly seems that Dewey states his position quite clearly in the review, for he says,

> The need for authority is a constant need of man [and woman]. For it is the need for principles that are both stable enough and flexible enough to give direction to the processes of living in its vicissitudes and uncertainities. . . . The underlying problem of recent centuries is the question of whether and how scientific method, which is the method of intelligence in experimental action, can provide authority that earlier centuries sought in fixed dogmas. The conflict of science and religion is one phase of this conflict.[49]

Dewey goes on to explain further that individuals of a scientific temper are cautious, tentative, and piecemeal in their investigations. Initially, scientists do not imagine that they know the whole truth about their subject matters. They are not even sure that their own knowledge is wholly true. Rather, they know that every doctrine may need revision sooner or later, and that the necessary correction requires freedom of investigation as well as freedom of discussion. Thus we are reminded by Dewey that scientists verify truth by starting "from observed facts, not with fixed general truths from which particular truths can be deductively derived. It [Science] arrives at its general rules through experimental observation of many individual occurrences, and it employs general rules when arrived at as working hypotheses, not as eternal immutable principles."[50]

Although we shall not pause here to try to resolve why Russell misconstrued Dewey's message, it seems that one of the mistakes that he possibly made was putting too much emphasis upon the rational or intellectual aspect of Dewey's method. What we should bear in mind is that Dewey's concern for individuals was not merely for members of the academic arena, but for the "millions who are neither on the top nor on the bottom." Like Hook says, Dewey was concerned about the "conditions and problems that effect multitudes of individuals." So the reader should recognize that this important feature of Dewey's instrumentalism is essential for understanding his logical conception of philosophy and truth.

In concluding, we find that John Dewey's theory of human communication seems to hold the key to comprehending his logic. *Essays in Experimental Logic* (1916), for example, is an apparent attempt to overcome the problem of human communication. In it he tries to free "instrumentalism" from confusion regarding its definition and its method of confirming alleged truth statements scientifically. He tells us,

> In the logical version pf pragmatism termed instrumentalism, action or practice does indeed play a fundamental role. But it concerns not the nature of consequences but the nature of knowing. To use a term which is now more fashionable . . . than it was earlier, instrumentalism means a behaviorist theory of thinking and knowing. It means that the knowing is literally something which we do; and that analysis is ultimately physical and active; that meanings in their logical quality are standpoints, attitudes, and methods of behaving towards facts, and that active experiment is essential to verification.[51]

Despite Dewey's detailed explanation, though, about twenty-three years later we find him yet trying to define his terms, and explain Instrumentalism. This time he says,

> Although the psychological theory involved is a form of Behaviorism, it differs basically from some theories bearing the same name. In the first place, behavior is not viewed as something taking place in the nervous system or under the skin of an organism but always, directly or indirectly, in obvious overtness or at a distance through a number of intervening links, an interaction with environing conditions.[52]

As for this behaviorist account of Instrumentalism, in the following overview a general survey is provided in hope of showing how it applies to his life-career thoughts about philosophy and truth.

# Notes

1. John Dewey, "Philosophy" (1934), reprinted in *John Dewey: The Later Works, 1925-1953*, Vol. 8, Jo Ann Boydston, ed. (Carbondale/ Edwardsville: Southern Illinois University Press, 1989; henceforth abbreviated as *Later Works*). p. 19.
2. John Dewey, "The Experimental Theory of Knowledge" (1906), in *The Influence of Darwin on Philosophy And Other Essays In Contemporary Thought* (New York: Henry Holt and Company, 1910). p. 100.
3. *Ibid.*
4. *Ibid.*, p. 185. Sidney Hook has likewise observed that Dewey "came to regard the form in which the traditional problems of metaphysics were expressed as the result of misinterpretations of the nature of inquiry. His lifework [then] consisted in exploring the possibility that the rationale of scientific inquiry, whose results in some fields had already transformed the face of the globe, could be employed in the solution of all problems of human experience." *John Dewey: An Intellectual Portrait,* (Westport, Connecticut: Greenwood Press, 1939). p. 16.
5. While still corresponding with Arthur F. Bentley, co-author of *Knowing and the Known*, John Dewey ceased his "life-career" and his natural concern about truth. T. Z. Lavine reports that after Dewey had received Bentley's last letter (on December 6, 1951) from Paoli, Indiana, "Dewey died six months later, on June 1, 1952, in his ninety-third year." See Introduction to *Later Works*, Vol. 16, p. xii.
6. John Dewey, "Experience, Knowledge and Value: A Rejoinder" (1939), reprinted in *Later Works*, Vol. 14, p. 6.
7. John Dewey, "Experience, Knowledge and Value: A Rejoinder" (1939), reprinted in *Later Works*, Vol. 14, p. 7.
8. John Dewey, "The Development of American Pragmatism" (1925). Reprinted in *Later Works*, Vol. 2, p. 3.
9. *Ibid.* "Mr. Peirce explained that he took the term 'pragmatic' from Kant, in order to denote empirical consequences," according to Dewey's *Essays in Experimental Logic* (New York: Dover Publications, Inc., 1916). p. 330. For Kant's employment of the term "pragmatic" see his *Critique of Pure Reason,* translated by Norman Kemp Smith (New York: St. Martin's Press, 1965). p. 632.
10. *Ibid.*
11. *Ibid.*, pp. 10-11. Dewey says: "In short, Peirce wrote as a logician and James as a humanist."
12. John Dewey, "The Development of American Pragmatism" (1925). Reprinted in *Later Works*, Vol. 2, p. 14.
13. In contrast to James' definition, one of his interpreters, William B. Williamson, maintains that "William James took Charles Sanders Peirce's criterion for meaning: 'our idea of anything is our idea of its sensible

effects' . . . and developed it into a theory of truth." See *Decisions in Philosophy of Religion* (Columbus, Ohio: Charles E. Merrill Publishing Company, 1976). p. 75.

14. William James, *Pragmatism* (Cambridge, Massachusetts: Harvard University Press, 1978). p. 28.

15. Sidney Hook seems to avoid using the name "instrumentalism" when referring to what he calls Dewey's "theory of truth." It appears that Hook is trying to make a clear distinction between Dewey's theory, as he sees it, and "some other loosely formulated doctrines which are embraced by the generic term 'pragmatism'." Hook's references to Dewey's "theory of truth," no doubt, are illustrative of the need to carefully define Dewey's Instrumentalism and his conception of truth. In any event, according to Hook, "Dewey insists that his theory is a theory of truths—truths of the common garden variety and not of anything that can be called The Truth." *John Dewey: An Intellectual Portrait* (Westport, Connecticut: Greenwood Press, Publishers, 1939). p. 74.

16. James Gouinlock suggests this definition in "Introduction" to *Later Works*, Vol. 2, p. ix.

17. John Dewey, *Experience and Nature* (La Salle, Illinois: The Open House Publishing Company, 1925). p. 135.

18. John Dewey, "The Development of American Pragmatism" (1925). Reprinted in *Later Works*, Vol. 2, p. 13.

19. *Ibid.*, p. 18.

20. John Dewey, "The Development of American Pragmatism" (1925). Reprinted in *Later Works,* Vol. 2, p. 19.

21. John Dewey, "The Development of American Pragmatism" (1925). Reprinted in *Later Works*, Vol. 2, p. 20.

22. Sidney Hook, *John Dewey: An Intellectual Portrait*, p.17.

23. Sammuel Meyer, *Dewey and Russell: An Exchange* (New York: Philosophical Library, Inc., 1985). p. 11.

24. *Ibid.*

25. *Ibid.*, p. 12

26. Wallace I. Matson, *A New History of Philosophy* (San Diego, California: Harcourt Brace Jovanovich, Publishers, 1987). p. 454.

27. Russell, "John Dewey" (1946), in *The Basic Writings of Bertrand Russell*, R. E. Egner and L. E. Denon, eds. (New York: Simon and Schuster, 1967). p. 208.

28. Norman Melchert, *The Great Conversation: A Historical Introduction to Philosophy* (Mountain View, California; Mayfield Publishing Co., 1991). p. xvii.

29. Dewey, "Philosophy," in *Later Works*, Vol. 8, p. 19.

30. William B. Williamsom, *Decisions in Philosophy of Religion* (Columbus, Ohio: Charles E. Merill Publishing Company, 1976). p. 71.

31. Bertrand Russell, "Dewey's New Logic," in *The Basic Writings of Bertrand Russell*, R. E. Egner and L. E. Denonn, eds. (New York: Simon

and Schuster, 1961). p. 192. To find additional details concerning General Smuts' philosophy of holism, see his book *Holism and Evolution* (1924). Also, Jan Christian Smuts Jr. provides a superb interim biography of his father's life and doctrine in *Jan Christian Smuts* (New York: William Morrow Company, Inc., 1952). Smuts, it should be noted, for the most part, derived his philosophy of holism from Hegel's doctrine. In any event, the affinity between the holistic view attributed to Dewey and General Smuts is their view of the Universe, and its entailment of the problem of race. The following quotations, it is hoped, will suffice to help comprehend the relevance of holism to this study. For instance, with regard to holism, Smuts maintains, "The world consists of a rising series of wholes. You start with matter, which is the simplest of the wholes. You then rise to plants and animals, to mind, to human beings, to personality and the spiritual world. This progression of wholes, rising tier upon tier, makes up the structure of the universe" (*Ibid.* p. 258). With respect to the problem of race, young Smuts reports, "my father regularly attended services on Sundays in the Dutch Reformed Church near the Theological College. After services he would hold Bible classes for coloured youths, to whom he expounded the truth of the Books. . . . His love for the Bible he never lost, though his religious feeling for it gradually changed in later life to an interest in it as a panorama of life and a psychological study, and as the supreme classic of the English language" (p. 16). Moreover, when General Smuts delivered the Rhodes Memorial Lectures, speaking on the native problem, he said, "We are concerned today with these racial reactions in so far as they affect Europe and Africa, a small question, but still a very large human question, fraught with immense possibilities for the future of our civilization. . . . What is wanted in Africa today is a wise, far sighted native policy. If we could evolve and pursue a policy, which will promote the cause of civilization in Africa without injustice to the African, without injury, we shall render a great service to humanity. For there is much that is good in the African which ought to be preserved and developed. . . " (pp. 270-275). Rather consistent with Dewey's view, we also find General Smuts saying, "When I look at the world unrest today and the confusion which prevails in science, in philosophy, in religion and our whole human outlook and set-up, I feel more and more that in the concept of Holism we have the key to many a door, and the way to ultimate solutions" (p. 259). Young Smuts, however, points out the difference between their racial problem in Africa and the one Dewey encountered in America. As he puts it, "The native problem in South Africa differs from that in the United States, for there the whites outnumber the Negroes by ten to one. Under those circumstances people can afford to be broadminded and tolerant. In South Africa the white man, at a four to one disadvantage, has to struggle for his existence, and the future of his children is ever uncertain" (*Ibid.*).

32. Russell, "John Dewey," *The Basic Writings of Bertrand Russell,* R. E.
    Egner and L. E. Dennon, eds. (New York: Simon and Schuster, 1961).
    p.206. Dewey explains Russell's argument as follows. "Mr. Dewey
    admits not only that he was once a Hegelian but that Hegel left a permanent
    deposit in his thought; Hegel was a thorough going holist; therefore,
    Dewey uses 'situation' in a holistic sense." See "Experience, Knowledge
    and Value: A Rejoinder," in *Later Works,* Vol. 14, p. 29. In response
    to Russell's accusations, however, Dewey says, "If I held a holistic view,
    his reference to independent causal chains would be highly pertinent.
    But since I do not hold that position I need only remark that Mr. Russell's
    considerations reinforce the point I have made about the logical aspect of
    the matter" (*Ibid.,* p. 54).

33. Bertrand Russell, *An Inquiry into Meaning and Truth* (London: George
    Allen and Unwin LTD, 1940). p. 318.

34. Dewey, *Logic: The Theory of Inquiry* (1938). Reprinted in *Later Works,*
    Vol. 12, p. 160. Perhaps it should be pointed out here that Russell is not
    alone in his perplexity over Dewey's use of "indeterminate situation."
    That is to say, Dewey's 1942 publication of "Inquiry and Indeterminateness
    of Situations" was written in response to D. S. Mackay's article "What
    Does Mr. Dewey Mean by an 'Indeterminate Situation'?" in the *Journal
    of Philosophy,* Vol. xxxix (1942), pp. 141-148. In response to Mackay,
    Dewey writes: "I am indebted to Mr. Mackay for the opportunity to
    correct some wrong impressions about my theory of inquiry. . . ."
    Reprinted in *Later Works,* Vol. 15, p. 34. Dewey also says, "In dealing
    with the difficulty due to vagueness in my idea of indeterminateness, I
    wish first to state that in one point mentioned by Mr. Mackay I was guilty
    of a loose use of language of a kind that readily leads to misunderstanding"
    (p. 38).

35. Dewey, "Experience, Knowledge and Value: A Rejoinder" (1939),
    Reprinted in *Later Works,* Vol. 14, pp. 85, 86.

36. *Ibid.*

37. It is interesting to note R. S. Sleeper's account of Dewey's preparation of
    his article "Experience, Knowledge and Value: A Rejoinder" (1939),
    which is reprinted in *Later Works,* Vol 14. In the Introduction of the
    publication, Sleeper says, "It is unfortunate . . . that the least successful
    entry in this present volume is the most familiar, and that so many of
    Dewey's critics have taken their cue from its content. It is Dewey's
    'Rejoinder' to his critics that first appeared in the initial volume of Paul
    Authur Schilpp's Library of Living Philosophers series. Harried by Schilpp
    to complete the assigned task under a deadline designed to coincide with
    Dewey's eighteth birthday, Dewey rushed its completion in a state of
    exhaustion. Anticipating this condition, Dewey had already decided not
    to attend the New York celebration and went off to his daughter's ranch
    instead." See *Later Works,* Vol. 14, p. xi.

38. Sidney Hook, *John Dewey: An Intellectual Portrait* (Westport, Connecticut: Greenwood Press Publishers, 1939). pp. 84-85.
39. Sidney Hook, *John Dewey: An Intellectual Portrait* (Westport, Connecticut: Greenwood Press Publishers, 1939). p. 88.
40. *Ibid*.
41. Russell, "John Dewey" in *The Basic Writings of Bertrand Russell,* p. 208.
42. Dewey, *Logic: The Theory of Inquiry* (1938), in *Later Works*, Vol. 12, p. 4.
43. Dewey, "The Development of American Pragmatism" (1925), in *Later Works*, Vol. 2, p. 13.
44. Dewey, *Reconstruction in Philosophy* (Boston: The Beacon Press, 1920, 1964). p. 166.
45. *Ibid.*, p. 159.
46. Dewey, "Experience, Knowledge and Value: A Rejoinder" (1939), in *Later Works*, Vol. 14, p. 71.
47. Dewey, "Experience, Knowledge and Value: A Rejoinder" (1939), in *Later Works*, Vol. 14, p. 71.
48. Dewey, "Religion, Science, and Philosophy" (1936), in *Later Works*, Vol. 11, p.459.
49. Dewey, "Religion, Science, and Philosophy" (1936), in *Later Works*, Vol. 11, p. 454.
50. *Ibid.*, p. 457.
51. Dewey, *Essays in Experimental Logic* (New York: Dover Publications, 1916). pp. 331-32.
52. Dewey, "Experience, Knowledge and Value: A Rejoinder" (1939), in *Later Works,* Vol. 14, p. 39.

# Chapter 3

ℰ🙟ℭℛ

# *Dewey's Instrumental Conception of Philosophy and Truth: An Overview*

This third chapter provides a general survey of Dewey's conception of philosophy and his notion of truth. The survey tries to give a comprehensive view of the way John Dewey developed his own philosophy of truth. However, this overview only sets the stage for further elucidating his position. In other words, the main purpose of Chapter 3 is to raise questions and provide some background information for the ensuing chapters.

When *all* of the chapters are viewed as a whole, they show how Dewey's conception of philosophy and his notion of truth originiates and develops during his long life span of 93 years. For it seems quite impossible to understand his thoughts about philosophy and truth without also recognizing how the transitions in his thinking relate to his longevity. In this chapter, therefore, it is suggested that Dewey's intellectual development be divided into three stages, or sections. Accordingly, we shall refer to them in this study as The Early Years, 1859-1890; The Middle Years, 1890-1921; and The Later Years, 1921-1952.

This triadic division of Dewey's life-work, it is hoped, shall enable us to lay a firm foundation for disclosing his conception of philosophy and his notion of truth.  In trying to accomplish this goal, we shall address one of the most perplexing issues of present-day philosophy, which is well formulated by Norman Melchert.

> The issue is whether there is available to us a perspective, a point of view, or a method that will  get us beyond the prejudices and assumptions peculiar  to ourselves as individuals or as members of a culture.  Is there a way to understand the world, ourselves, and human good that is universally acceptable, that is more than just the expression of how we happen to have been brought up or of the peculiarities of our own narrow experience?[1]

In addressing this issue, our survey endeavors to shed some light  on the way Dewey's philosophy of truth provides us with a point  of view, or a method that will get us beyond the prejudices and assumptions peculiar to ourselves, as members of a culture.  It is argued here that Dewey furnishes us with a way to understand the world, and human good, that could be acceptable universally.  Indeed, our survey tries to show that Dewey's philosophy of truth can get us beyond the "peculiarities of our own narrow experience."

Within rather recent times, however, there have been marked differences of opinion concerning the value of Dewey's philosophy. For instance, on one hand we find Melchert telling us,

> In my judgment, Wittgenstein and Heidegger are the major players in the two main philosophical movements of our century.[2]

On the other hand we find the sagacious John J. McDermott saying,

> I can think of no person other than John Dewey to whom I would rather turn for wisdom as to the amelioration of our present plight and as a beacon of intelligence for our future.[3]

Is McDermott or Melchert correct?  Has Wittgenstein's influence on language analysis and Heidegger's influence on the existential and phenomenological movement surpassed the importance of Dewey's influence on pragmatism?  Should Dewey no longer be considered as a major player in the main philosophical movements of our century?

Before we try to answer the latter questions, let us consider a very pertinent observation that has been made by T. Z. Lavine. As for the main philosophical movements of our century, Lavine says,

> It is plausible that "seen through American eyes, the converging themes of the entire movement of contemporary Western Philosophy"—phenomenology, Marxism, hermeneutics, deconstruction—"are decidedly pragmatist in cast." [Thus] In the course of the development of American pragmatism, the richly complex philosophies of Dewey and Bentley played their major roles.[4]

Is Lavine implying that John Dewey's philosophy no longer has a major role to play in contemporary Western philosophy? Does Lavine, like Melchert, think that Wittgenstein and Heidegger should be the major players in the main philosophical movements of our century?

Now our survey makes no attempt to determine whether Lavine would agree or disagree with Melchert's opinion about Wittgenstein and Heidegger; but the survey does endeavor to show why Dewey's philosophy should have a more important role to play than ever before. That is to say, in agreement with McDermott, the present writer thinks that we should turn to Dewey's philosophy for wisdom as to the amelioration of our present plight, and as a beacon of intelligence for our future. In any case, as we noted in Chapter 1, Melchert provides some excellent criteria for judging Dewey's view of truth; and perhaps it will help us determine the value of his view above the others.

We've seen already that the criteria is in line with traditional Western philosophy. For as we noted earlier, Melchert cites four major concerns shared by philosophers.[5] The branches of concern are metaphysics, epistemology, ethics, and human nature.[6] Also, granting that Melchert correctly defines the four major concerns, we've presupposed that Dewey would agree with his list as "the branches into which philosophy is still conventionally divided."[7] Our survey, however, does not focus on metaphysics, epistemology, ethics, and human nature as four independent topics of discussion. Instead, what we shall do is examine Dewey's thematic treatment of the topics in a more systematic manner. That is, our survey treats the four major concerns as one interrelated problem of philosophy. While each branch may be discussed as a separate subject, our study treats them all in a holistic manner, as Dewey seems to do.

It should be understood, however, that there has been and still is some debate concerning Dewey's holistic doctrine. Though we will not stop to defend his ideas about holism, let us pause here to clarify and sustain our manner of procedure. We will follow the lead of R. S. Sleeper, who displays a fine understanding of Dewey's holism, and recognizes the importance of his doctine. For example, Sleeper says,

> Dewey's system is wholly original. It is a system that is wholly in process, movement, and change—as nature itself is—and that grows, emerges, and evolves.[8]

As we can see, Sleeper recognizes the originality of Dewey's holistic doctrine. What is more important, though, Sleeper also stresses how vital it is, if one wishes to grasp Dewey's doctrine and get a true "sense of the whole." "Without it," says Sleeper, "we risk missing, as so many of his critics did, the whole point."[9] So, let's follow Sleeper's advice, and consider the "whole point."

It should be understood that Dewey's system of holism sought to avoid "apart thought," which for Dewey, "meant the bifurcation of reason from nature and the distinction of the 'analytic' from the 'synthetic' in logical discourse."[10] Sleeper argues that on Dewey's view of "apart thought," it meant the "dualism of the mind and body problem" that he tried to overcome in his 1896 essay "The Reflex Arc Concept in Psychology."[11] What is more significant, though, Sleeper also says of Dewey's approach,

> This "holistic" theme was then developed further in Dewey's contribution to . . . *Studies in Logical Theory* in 1903, reiterated in the *Essays in Experimental Loigic* in 1916, and received its most thorough elaboration in the 1938 *Logic.* It is there that it was detected by Russell as a feature of Dewey's conception of scientific method.[12]

As for Russell's interpretation of Dewey's holism, Sleeper seems to think that *Later Works,* Vol. 14, "contains an essay by Dewey that sets the whole matter of his 'holistic' aproach in perspective."[13] Sleeper holds that the essay "Nature and Experience" (1939) is a "model of clarity and responsiveness." "Patiently put together in reply to M. R. Cohen and W. E. Hocking," says Sleeper, "Dewey lays bare in simple terms what counts as his 'first philosophy' and explains what his 'holism' amounts to."[14] Moreover, as Sleeper has interpreted him, "It is perhaps [Dewey's] clearest statement of why it is that metaphysics does not play the foundational role for him that it had regularly played for his predecessors."[15] But why is it that metaphysics did not play the same foundational role for him that it had regularly played for his predecessors?

Have critics such as Cohen, Hocking, and Russell misunderstood Dewey's different way of dealing with metaphysic? Isn't it obvious that some of his critics have misconstrued his notion of metaphysics? The present writer certainly thinks so. Moreover, they apparently have not seen how metaphysics, for Dewey, entails epistemology, ethics, and human nature as one interrelated problem of philosophy. Yet grasping his notion of this entailment, so it seems, is crucial for understanding his thematic treatment of those four major concerns.

Seemingly, Sleeper sees how Dewey's handling of the various problems and their various hypotheses create a coherent system. For he says, "It is a system that hangs together because it all comes from a 'perspective determined from a definite point of view'."[16] As we mentioned earlier, though, it is John Dewey's perspective from a "definite point of view" that this survey tries to make clear. Hence, we can see that Sleeper definitely emphasizes the importance of Dewey's unique view of philosophy; for Sleeper explicitly says, "It is this perspective that brings coherence to the whole, an *elenchus* that distinguishes it most sharply from the systems of his predecessors from Plato to Peirce."[17] How? and Why? When *all* the chapters of this study are considered synoptically, it may be easier to see how Dewey's system compares to the "systems of his predecessors from Plato to Peirce," as well as his younger contemporaries, such as Russell, Wittgenstein and Heidegger.

For now, though, let's examine his conception of philosophy and his notion of truth in greater detail, and perhaps that will help clarify the "value" of his perspective. First of all, let us consider Dewey's "Foreword" to *The Story of Philosophy* (1926); it furnishes some important insight concerning the increasing complexity of the discipline. In this particular work Dewey takes care to remind us that "philosophic writing is often so specialized and technical that even educated readers, unless professionally trained, are repelled rather than attracted."[18] He regarded this, of course, as an inept turn of events for philosophy. What is more significant for our discussion, though, is the fact that Dewey was still battling with the same problem more than twenty-one years later.

At that time he published "The Future of Philosophy" (1947), and woefully says,

> The most discouraging thing in philosophy is neo-scholastic formalism, . . . . It is form for its own sake, in so many cases. A form of forms, not forms of subject matter. But the subject matter is so chaotic and confused today in the world that it is difficult to handle. This is how I would explain this retreat from work in the facts of human life into purely formal issues—I hesitate to call them issues because nothing ever issues except more form! It's harmless for everyone except philosophers. This retreat accounts for the growing disinterest of the general public in the problems of philosophy.[19]

Dewey's statement seems to clearly indicate his desire to get the "general public" involved in the problems of philosophy. Moreover, it is also clear that he considered "neo scholastic formalism" to be hazardous for the future of philosophy. But why? Apparently, as Dewey has observed, it creates chaos and confusion about the subject matter of philosophy by fostering the problem of definition. However, as his article "Philosophy" (1934) bears witness, he had been struggling with the philosophical problem of definition for quite a while; at that time he held that, "Definitions of philosophy are usually made from the standpoint of some system of philosophy and reflect its special point of view."[20]

As for Dewey's "special point of view," he apparently believed that we may avoid the definition problem by "defining philosophy from the point of view of its historical role within human culture."[21] This feature of Dewey's perspective sharply distinguishes his system of philosophy from his predecessors, and his contemporaries. Characteristic of the mature John Dewey, he repeatedly argued that "cultural causes have produced the main changes in the direction and content of philosophic systems."[22] Undoubtedly this is why he kept suggesting that we define philosophy from the perspective of its historical role within human culture.

Explaining his view of philosophy's historical role, Dewey says,

> Such a historical survey shows the necessity of defining philosophy from the standpoint of value, since the changes of philosophy are all inherently bound up with problems that arise when new emphases and new redistributions in the significance of values take place.[23]

In other words, his concept of "value" apparently conditioned his view of philosophy's historical role within human culture. No doubt this is why he thought that our varying judgments or opinions about value have created the cultural causes that have produced the main changes in the direction and content of philosophic systems. Yet, the question remains: Can philosophers do anything about it?

In hope of providing some insight for addressing this question, let us consider "The Basic Values and Loyalties of Democracy" (1941). The article divulges Dewey's view of "values" and the historical role that our philosophies ought to play within human culture. He quite candidly reminds us that

> Our anti-democratic heritage of Negro slavery has left us with habits of intolerance toward the colored race—habits which belie profession of democratic loyalty. [Then too] The very tenets of religion have been employed to foster antisemitism. [Hence] There are still many, too many, persons who feel free to cultivate and express racial prejudices as if they were within their personal rights, not recognizing how the attitude of intolerance infects, . . . as the example of Germany so surely proves . . . .[24]

As indicated by the foregoing statement, and as this study attempts to show, Dewey's unbiased attitude sets his perspective apart from his predecessors, and also his contemporaries (Russell, Wittgenstein, and Heidegger). In contrast to them, one distinct factor accounts for Dewey's highly evolved conception of philosophy's value. He had inherited America's racial problem. Dewey was heir to a unique American experience. In other words, unlike Dewey, none of them could legitimately claim to be American born and bred.

From his viewpoint as a U. S. citizen, Dewey says, "In theory democracy has always professed belief in the potentialities of every human being, and all the need for providing conditions that will enable these potentialities to come to realization."[25] Of course this is only theoretical. For he says, "The attempt to identify democracy with economic individualism as the essence of free action has done harm to the reality of democracy and is capable of doing even greater injury than it has already done."[26] Nevertheless, Dewey believed that philosophy could and should do something about the problem of "economic" values, which seems to be a major threat against the opportunity for some individuals to develop their potentialities. After making his own survey of philosophy's historical role in human culture, Dewey was well aware that

> In Plato and Aristotle economics is definitely subordinated to politics; and politics is a branch, the most important branch of ethical theory. Upon the whole this conception remained dominant into the seventeenth century. . . . The philosophical psychology associated with classic political and legal theory had set up ideas as the ruling factors in man. The theory of human nature which philosophy of economics brought forward treated wants as fundamental and ideas as subordinate. "Reason" was merely the power of calculating the means by which desires could be satisfied economically and effectively.[27]

It was the latter view of economics that repelled Dewey; he opted instead to follow Plato's approach, or philosophical psychology. It is in this sense that Dewey, like Plato, thought that both economics and politics are entailed by ethics. For instance, Dewey says,

> When I have touched upon economic and political problems in writing upon social philosophy I have held that all such problems are problems of valuation in the moral sense. It is in this context that I have dwelt upon *intelligent action* as the sole and supreme method of dealing with economic and political issues, and have tried to take that statement out of the region of innocuous truisms. . . . [Consequently] We are thus brought back to that instrumental view of attained knowledge which has given so much trouble to some of my critics.[28]

Why did his critics have so much trouble with the entailment of his ethics? One of his most vexing critics, Bertrand Russell, really had trouble trying to understand how Dewey's notion of ethics entails economics and politics. Fortunately, though, in his article "The Development of American Pragmatism" (1925), he provides us with some insight into the gross misreadings of Russell. As Dewey saw the problem, Russell had misunderstood William James's employment of "cashed in."

Instead of seeing "cashed in" as a metaphor referring to specific consequences of any concrete observations, Dewey noted that one reason for Russell's mistake was,

> For those who are not familiar with American idioms, James' formula was taken to mean that the consequences themselves of our rational conceptions must be narrowly limited by their pecuniary value. Thus

Mr. Russell wrote recently that pragmatism is merely a manifestation of American commercialism.[29]

Evidently, then, Russell's errant view of American pragmatism was largely due to his non-American upbringing, or not understanding "American idioms." Thus Dewey defended James's metaphor against Russell's misconstrual. As Dewey points out, "It is not true therefore to say James treated reason, thought and knowledge with contempt, or that he regarded them as mere means of gaining personal or even social profits."[30]

Just as he came to James's defense, however, John Dewey also championed Peirce's theory of pragmatism, or pragmaticism. He held that Peirce's theory was "far from being that glorification of action for its own sake which is regarded as the peculiar characteristic of American life."[31] In fact, we are informed by Dewey that Peirce's theory was "strongly opposed to the idea that reason or thought should be reduced to being a servant of any interest which is pecuniary or narrow."[32] So we can see that Dewey tried to free the pragmatists's claims from non-American philosophers like Russell, who missed their meaning by insisting upon defining "truth" too narrowly.

Of course Dewey tells us *why* some philosophers tend to view truth from a narrow perspective, instead of broadly. He says,

> In considering a system of philosophy in its relation to national factors it is necessary to keep in mind not only the aspects of life which are incorporated in the system, but also the aspects against which the system is a protest.[33]

The apparent implication of Dewey's assertion is that we all must face the age-old problem of Protagorean relativism when we judge other systems of philosophy and their truth criteria. For he tells us,

> There never was a philosopher who has merited [that] name for the simple reason that he glorified the tendencies and characteristics of his social environment; just as it is also true that there never has been a philosopher who has not seized upon certain aspects of the life of his time and idealized them.[34]

Apparently Dewey's latter statement implies that *all* philosophers *must* do philosophy, or philosophize, from a relativistic perspective.

Dewey further elucidates the issue in "Philosophy" (1934), where he gives the subject a more systematic treatment. His brief historical survey shows that the problem of relativism has persisted down through the ages. For instance, as he puts it,

> In spite of the distance that separated the territorial national state of the nineteenth century from the small city-state of antiquity, Hegel and his followers employed the political philosophy of Plato and Aristotle to interpret and justify the structure of the European states of their day.[35]

In other words, we can see that Dewey was well aware that it was Plato who first devised a system of philosophy to combat the problem of Protagorean relativism; and subsequent philosophers like Hegel just followed Plato's lead. What is more important for our present purpose, however, is the fact that John Dewey also espoused Plato's method of combating the age-old problem of relativism; and he suggests that we do so.

Consider "From Absolutism to Experimentalism" (1930). We are informed by McDermott that it "yields a number of judgments by Dewey which are crucial to any understanding of his life and work."[36] Hence, it is in this article that Dewey suggests, or tells us,

> Nothing could be more helpful to present philosophizing than a "Back to Plato" movement; but it would have to be back to the dramatic, restless, co-operatively inquiring Plato of the Dialogues, trying one mode of attack after another to see what it might yield; back to the Plato whose highest flight of metaphysics always terminates with a social and practical turn, and not to the artificial Plato constructed by unimaginative commentators who treated him as the original university professor.[37]

Seemingly, though, too few philosophers have understood Dewey's proposal that we follow Plato. Apparently they have not recognized that Dewey's idea of "truth," like Plato's, is designed to combat the problem of relativism.

In any event, as our study tries to show, we must understand *why* he suggests that we use Plato's method of doing philosophy, if we wish to comprehend Dewey's notion of truth. Also, of course, it would be helpful to understand how American pragmatists such as Peirce, James, and Meade influenced his thoughts about truth; but he mainly follows Plato's lead.

For example, the following statement seems to clearly indicate his deep appreciation of Plato; and it seems to bestow the highest of accolade upon him. Dewey informs us that

> Were it possible for me to be a devotee of any system, I still should believe that there is greater richness and greater variety of insight in Hegel than in any other single systematic philosopher—though when I say this I exclude Plato, who still provides my favourite philosophic reading.[38]

So indeed, it should be understood that Dewey mostly follows Plato's system; and he came to regard Hegel's as deficient, because Hegel's "highest flight of metaphysics" *did not* always terminate with a "social and practical turn."

Neil Coughlan has noted Hegel's delimited influence upon Dewey; for the latter came to believe that Hegel "had to be made practical."[39] Yet we are assured by Dewey that his acquaintance with Hegel had, as he puts it, "left a permanent deposit in my thinking."[40] As for the "permanent deposit," however, Sleeper contends that, "Hegel's refusal to draw a hard and fast line between 'theory' and 'fact' was the one feature of Hegelian logic that Dewey wanted to save."[41] Now either way we consider Dewey's view, whether it is in light of Sleeper's or Coughlan's interpretation, the important factor to bear in mind is that John Dewey, like Hegel and Plato, employs a holistic method. But because of his American upbringing, no doubt, Dewey's method is more unbiased than theirs. For Dewey's holistic perspective offers us a unique practical approach for getting pass the relativism of our own "narrow experience."

John Dewey was brought up in the tradition of the Andover Liberals, and accordingly, cultivated his view of philosophy in light of their influences.[42] As he had interpreted the meaning of the term "liberal," he informs us that

> The word has never been associated in this country with *laissez-faire* economics and hands-off governmental action, as it has been in England and especially on the continent of Europe. [In America] It has been used in connection with what is vaguely called a forward-looking and progressive attitude. . . . [43]

This "forward-looking and progressive attitude" characterizes his view of the liberals. For indeed, the association of "liberalism" with "liberty," as he conceived it, "points to an open mind, to emancipation from bigotry and from domination by prejudice."[44]

The meaning of "liberalism," says Dewey, "consists in quiet and patient pursuit of truth," which is marked by the will to "learn from every quarter." Liberalism is "humble and persistent," according to Dewey, yet it is "strong and positive in its faith that the intercourse of free minds will always bring to light an increasing measure of truth."[45] Hence it is along this line of thought that he develops his own liberal philosophy to combat the problem of relativism.

Dewey vehemently upheld the liberal attitude of the pragmatists who emphasized "collectivism" as the best way of determining truth. One of his clearest distinctions between the pragmatic method of collectivism and the old sophist method of relativism may be found in his "Logic" (1933). This publication clarifies Plato's claim that "the method of the sophist was one of sham . . . [because] it was the art of appearing wise, not of being so. It aimed not at truth but at persuasion by whatever specious arguments would silence an opponent."[46] On the other hand, as for Plato's notion of a "true method," Dewey maintains that it involves a "cooperative search, assuming an objective unity beneath all divisions of opinion and belief and terminating in the production of a common understanding sustained by grasp of the one relevant objective truth."[47] Moreover, says Dewey, "Plato called his method dialectic, a term obviously derived from the dialogue of those engaged in the exchange of ideas."[48] To be sure, it is Plato's emphasis upon the "exchange of ideas" that Dewey regards as congenial with the pragmatists method of collectivism. He believed that their liberal approach could combat the age-old problem of relativism, especially if the intercourse of "free minds" will *always* bring to light an increasing "measure of truth."

Apparently, though, not enough philosophers have followed this liberal approach, or "true method," and as an unhappy result,

> We now oscillate between a normative and rationalistic logic in morals and an empirical, purely descriptive method in concrete matters of fact. Hence our supposed ultimate ideals and aims have no intrinsic connection with the factual means by which they must be realized, while factual data are piled up with no definitely recognized sense of their bearing on the formation of social policy and the direction of social conduct.[49]

Of course six decades have passed since those observations were made, but as our study tries to show, the problem that he addressed is yet extant today. Why? Because we have not exploited Dewey's pioneering work in this area.

With regard to his effort to deal with the problem, for example, he additionally informs us that

> Consciousness of this situation has been a main factor in a new attempt to generalize the experimental side of natural science into a logical method which is applicable to the interpretation and treatment of social phenomena.[50]

What influenced Dewey's "consciousness of this situation," and the horizon from which his "new attempt" had emanated? Dewey gives us the answer to the latter question himself, when he acknowledges his debt to the pragmatists; for he says, "So far this recent movement remains almost entirely American in character. It was initiated by Charles S. Peirce and carried out especially in morals and religion, under the name of pragmatism, by William James."[51]

One of the big problems that Dewey encountered, of course, was the fact that some philosophers misconstrued their meanings, and his in particular. It is hoped, however, that we can help clarify Dewey's conception by showing why he attempted to develop a "logical method" based upon the pragmatists's meaning of truth, which is applicable to the interpretation and treatment of social phenomena, and which follows Plato's "true method." Perhaps the best way to go about accomplishing this goal is to first get clear on Dewey's view of Plato's treatment of social phenomena. Proceeding in this manner may enable us to see the role that philosophy plays for both Plato and Dewey.

An important point that needs elucidating, so it seems, is Dewey's interpretation of Plato's holistic approach, or his notion of "entailment." We have already noted Dewey's belief that, "In Plato and Aristotle economics is definitely subordinated to politics," which is "the most important branch of ethical theory." However, what one should understand is that ethics or ethical theory is only at the third level of Dewey's hierarchical entailment. That is, as indicated by Melchert's list above, ethics entails the fourth of the major concerns, which is human nature. But on the other hand, when the hierarchy is viewed from the top and then downward, it should be arranged so that metaphysics entails epistemology, which in turn, entails ethics.

As the subsequent chapters of this study unfold, it is hoped that Dewey's notion of the entailment shall become much clearer. For present purposes, though, perhaps one of the best ways to clarify the hierarchial arrangement is to see it in light of Plato's explanation. In his dialogue *Timaeus,* Plato makes the character Timaeus say:

> A man may sometimes set aside meditations about eternal things, and for recreation turn to consider the truths of generation, which are probable only; he will thus gain a pleasure not to be repented of, and secure for himself, while he lives, a wise and moderate pastime.[52]

If a person can come to understand the "truths of generation," then maybe Plato's and Dewey's notion of the entailment shall be grasped. That is to say, when we spend enough time *wondering* about how things come to be by "generation," we may discover a great chain of causes that are quite contingent upon each other. Analogously speaking, for example, we could say that if there were no Tennessee, then there could be no cities or towns within it; and if there were no America, for instance, there could be no states within it, or constituting it. Moreover, if there were no world there could be no states or countries in it; and if there were no Universe, then there could be no world; if there were no people, then there could be no humans to speak, think, or write words. Also, if there were no God, could there be a universe or a world, with words, people, places, and things in it, where subjects such as metaphysics, epistemology, and ethics are discussed?

What would the world or the universe be like without a word, or words to explain one's experience(s), or ours? One bold writer takes the position that:

> In the beginning was the Word, and the Word was with God, and the Word was God. [Jesus] was in the beginning with God. All things were made by him; and without him was not anything made . . . .[53]

Did John Dewey believe this, or take the same position? Did Dewey employ his "words" with this sense of meaning, or reference? The present writer thinks he did; and the following chapters, it is hoped, shall sustain his position.

Our triadic survey of Dewey's long life-span indicates that he firmly fixed his belief(s) about God in his early years. During his youth, for example, he believed that

In no way can the individual philosophize about a universe which has not been realized in his conscious experience. The universe, except as realized in an individual, has no existence. In man it is partially realized, and man has a partial science; in the absolute it is completely realized, and God has a complete science.[54]

When Dewey made the latter statement, he apparently thought that the term "God" was a legitimately scientific word that could and should be employed in philosophic discourse.

However, in his middle and later years, when his concept of God as Absolute changed so dramatically, it seems that some of his interpreters misconstrued his ideas about God as an absolute being, or the Absolute. Undoubtedly they were somewhat baffled by the transitions in Dewey's thinking; because in his early years he argued that

There is an absolute self-consciousness. The science of this is philosophy. This absolute self-consciousness manifests itself in the knowing and acting of individual men. The science of this manifestation, a phenomenology, is psychology.[55]

Young Dewey held that the "whole course of philosophic thought," as he saw it, "has consisted in showing that any distinction between the form and the matter of philosophic truth, between the content and the method, is fatal to the reaching of truth."[56] Indeed, from his youthful perspective, he held that "Self-consciousness is the final truth, and in self-consciousness the form as organic system and the content as organized system are exactly equal. . . . Psychology, as the account of this self-consciousness must necessarily fulfill all the conditions of true method."[57] As young Dewey began to mature, however, instead of him continuing to champion Psychology as a method of philosophy, he moved beyond this stage of thought in significant ways; and his transition still seems to be baffling some of his interpreters.

In his later years, for instance, while continuously trying to elucidate the subject matter of philosophy, Dewey desired to end the dispute and disunity between those philosophers who assert that Mind or Spirit is all embracing, and those who counter the claim by asserting the same thing about Matter. For he had come to believe that as long as philosophers try to resolve the problem of truth by looking exclusively to either one of the two schools of thought, they would be looking in the "wrong direction." Therefore, as he reflected on the "future of philosophy," he offered the following proposal as an attempt to help clarify philosophy's subject matter. Dewey says,

> The aim is to suggest that it [philosophy's subject matter] has been looked for in the wrong direction so that it is worth while to try the experiment of turning around and about the direction in which what is comprehensive is to be looked for. . . . The traditional direction of search is fortunately not hard to identify. That which has been given such names as Being, Reality, The Universe, Nature at Large. and so forth. These names have been supposed to designate that which is inherently marked off from everything else as partial.[58]

Instead of continuing to search for truth in the "traditional direction," he held that any "search" that is philosophical should be "directed towards what is most comprehensive *within* human affairs and occupations, not towards that which is completely independent of concerns nd occupations that are distinctively human."[59] As for his reference to those distinctively human things, perhaps it is rather unfortunate that an awkward result seems to occur.

When Dewey suggests that we try his method of experiment to "turn around and about" the direction of philosophic discourse, he tends to allow room for himself to be misinterpreted as a proponent of materialism. Apparently this happened because he says,

> Our "other way around and about" is contented to leave the eternal and immutable alone in their solitude so as to be in accord with what is legitimately scientific, since the latter always deals with what is located in time and space.[60]

Is Dewey telling us that we should no longer direct our search for truth towards an eternal and immutable God? Is Dewey saying that God has nothing to do with anything legitimately scientific?

As our triadic survey tries to show, Dewey was not attempting to alleviate the term "God" from philosophic discourse. Instead, he was proposing a method for rectifying the classic Greek notion of "two orders of existence," which for him, represented an appalling form of dualism. In other words, Dewey only wished to dispel the traditional notion of a dichotomous universe.

To fully understand what he was attempting to do, however, one should recognize that he was following Plato's holistic method. During Dewey's later years, for example, he argued that

If the Platonic theory of universals had been a logical theory, instead of an ontological one, it would be logically more correct than the Aristotelian.[61]

Only two years before this statement was made, Dewey had been trying to get his audiences to read Plato correctly. With respect to his own interpretation of Plato's ontological view, Dewey says,

Being with Plato always has the connotation of the stable, the dependable, while change imports instability and variation—departure from a standard which is fixed. In a similar way his distinction of universal and particular is not merely logical or merely metaphysical, but is concerned with the relation of law—which is legislative and normative—to application to the individual in judicial decision and administration. Such points are . . . examples of the interpenetration of the politico-moral with the logical and metaphysical, which is evidenced on a larger scale in his most systematic work, the *Republic*, since this is at once a treatise on metaphysics, theory of knowledge, politics, and education.[62]

According to Dewey's interpretation, Plato gave meaning to philosophy as the "search for wisdom"; but unfortunately, it could not long be maintained as he set it forth. Why? We are informed by Dewey that "Philosophy was in a condition of unstable equilibrium with respect to the various factors in it. To Plato it seemed still possible, at least as an intellectual and moral aspiration, to reform and preserve the city-state."[63] But after Aristotle became tutor of Alexander the Great, as Dewey points out, this seems to clearly indicate that the "failure of [Plato's] dream was imminent and consequently a redistribution of the whole inevitable."[64]

In other words, although Aristotle has made a great contribution to philosophy, his "redistribution of the whole" has only created more problems for the discipline. Accordingly, Dewey says that Aristotle "gave philosophy as a whole a radically different turn and form." Aristotle's terminology, that is, "enabled him to distinguish, define, and classify in a way not open to Plato, since the latter's problem was to institute actual connection between matters assigned by Aristotle to different classes or realms."[65] Yet, as we've seen already, Dewey opposed their dualism of realms.

To counter this problem of dualistic realms, just as Plato's highest flight of metaphysics had always terminated with a social and "practical turn," so had Dewey desired to employ his literature in such a manner. No doubt that is why he says that

The problem of the organization and direction of personal and community conduct was still uppermost with Plato, although he took steps which led to an apparent relegation of that issue to a secondary position, a fact that has frequently caused his modern interpreters to place him in a perspective foreign to his own intent.[66]

As we can see, then, a correct reading of Plato is important for gaining a clear understanding of the way Dewey employs his own literature. Moreover, as he reminds us, "philosophy occupies a peculiar position with respect to literature."[67] To clarify his own positon, Dewey goes on to explain that

Although few philosophers have found a significant aesthetic form of expression for their ideas, when expression is judged by the criterion of literature, nevertheless philosophy performs for some exactly the same office that the fine arts perform for others. There is a kind of music of ideas that appeals, apart from any question of empirical verification, to the minds of thinkers, who derive an emotional satisfaction from an imaginative play synthesis of ideas obtainable by them in no other way.[68]

This is evidently why Dewey used his literature as he did. Indeed, he says, "The positive cause which accounts for recent comparative decline of the prestige of philosophy is found in the tremendous multiplication of specialized knowledge and in the irreconcilable divergencies among social tendencies characteristic of the present time."[69] Therefore, to counter this problem, he wished to use "art."

With these observations in mind, let us turn to our triadic survey and scrutinize the way he employed his literary skills in dealing with the "tremendous multiplication of specialized knowlege." Let's give due consideration to his perspective and see how he tries to provide us with a point of view, or a method that will get us beyond the prejudices and assumptions peculiar to ourselves as individuals, or as members of a culture. Let's see if Dewey provides us with a way to understand the world, ourselves, and human good—one that can be acceptable "universally," one that is more than just the expression of how we happen to have been brought up.

Let's see if Dewey's conception of philosophy and truth can help us get beyond the peculiarities of our own narrow experience. As we turn to our investigation, let's bear in mind what Sleeper says about Dewey's perspective; for he tells us, "It is a perspective that brings coherence to the whole, an *elenchus* that distinguishes it most sharply from the systems of his predecessors from Plato to Peirce." Is this correct? Let's look and see. Let us start with his earliest encounters with the problems of philosophy and truth; then, in turn, we shall scrutinize his middle and later years to try to determine the "value" of his mature conception of philosophy and his notion of truth.

Did Dewey consider the "truths of generation" in the same sense as Plato? Maybe this is why Dewey argued in his later years that "the generative ideas of future science will appear first in a speculative or philosophical form."[70] Let's examine further and see.

# Notes

1.  Norman Melchert, *The Great Conversation: A Historical Introduction to Philosophy* (Mountain View, California: Mayfield Publishing Co., 1991). p. xvii.
2.  Melchert, *The Great Conversation*, p. xiii. With respect to Melchert's opinion, it is interesting to note a suggestion made by Stephen Toulmin. In his superb Introduction to the *Later Works,* Toulmin suggests that we may increase our understanding of Dewey by comparing his achievements with those of his "younger contemporaries, Ludwig Wittgenstein and Martin Heidegger" (Vol. 4, p. ix).
3.  McDermott, "Introduction" to *Later Works*, Vol. 11, p. xxxii.
4.  T. Z. Lavine, "Introduction" to *Later Works*, Vol. 16, p. xxxviii.
5.  Melchert, *The Great Conversation,* p. xvii.
6.  *Ibid.*
7.  Dewey, "Philosophy," in *Later Works,* Vol. 8, p. 19.
8.  Ralph W. Sleeper, "Introduction" to *Later Works*, Vol. 14, p. x.
9.  *Ibid.*, p. xi.
10. *Ibid.*, pp. xi-xii.
11. *Ibid.*, p. xii.
12. Ralph W. Sleeper, "Introduction" to *Later Works*, Vol. 14, p. xii.
13. *Ibid.*
14. *Ibid.*
15. *Ibid.*
16. Ralph W. Sleeper, "Introduction" to *Later Works,* Vol. 14, pp. ix-x.
17. Ralph W. Sleeper, "Introduction" to *Later Works,* Vol. 14, p. x.
18. Dewey, "Foreword" to *The Story of Philosophy* (1926), reprinted in *Later Works*, Vol. 2, p. 387.
19. Dewey, "The Future of Philosophy" (1947), reprinted in *Later Works*, Vol. 17, p. 469.
20. Dewey, "Philosophy" (1934), reprinted in *Later Works,* Vol. 8, p. 19.
21. *Ibid.*
22. *Ibid.*, p. 25.
23. *Ibid.*
24. Dewey, "The Basic Values and Loyalties of Democracy" (1941), reprinted in *Later Works*, Vol. 14, p. 277. With respect to the Aristocentric or egocentric predicament that we find ourselves in, it is interesting to note John Dewey's views on Aristocentrism; he tells us that, "Some old Greek philosophers held that it is necessary that there should be a large class, intellectually undeveloped, in order to support the few, and to give the minority the leisure that would enable them to have a free intellectual and highly developed life. Perhaps they were right, under the limited conditions of production in the ancient world. With the modern machine and modern inventiveness, with present command of raw material and

technical skill, the reason for separation between culture of an aristocratic few and the absence of culture from the great mass, no longer holds." See Dewey's "Politics and Culture" (1932), in *Later Works*, Vol. 6, pp. 46-7). During the same year, in an article entitled "Human Nature," Dewey pointed out that, "Classic Greek thought is based upon belief in the natural and inherent inequality of men. The most widely known expression of this point of view is Aristotle's statement that some men are slaves 'by nature' and hence are to be ranked with tools and domestic cattle as means of production. . . . Women were also ranked as constitutionally inferior and hence as properly subject to fathers and husbands. . . " (*Ibid.*, pp. 32-33). Eight years later, we still find him holding to this same line of thought, for he said: "Today the argument that something is 'contrary' to nature tends to take the form of contrary to *human* nature. In the past, changes in institutions, that is in fundamental customs, have opposed on the grounds that they were contrary to Nature in its most universal sense, and hence to the will and reason of God as the Founder of Nature. One has only to go back to the arguments advanced against the abolition of slavery to see that such was the case. [Moreover] . . . many opponents of the idea of enfranchising women used the argument that it was contrary to the very laws of Nature and of Nature's God." See Dewey's "Contrary to Human Nature" (1940), in *Later Works*, Vol. 14, p. 259.

25. Dewey, "The Basic Values and Loyalties of Democracy" (1941), reprinted in *Later Works*, Vol. 14, p. 276.

26. *Ibid.*, p. 277.

27. Dewey, "Philosophy," in *Later Works*, Vol. 8, p. 36.

28. Dewey, "Experience, Knowledge and Value: A Rejoinder" (1939), in *Later Works*, Vol. 14, p. 74.

29. Dewey, in *Later Works*, Vol. 2, p. 13. See Note 8. In regard to Russell's misconstrual of Dewey's holistic method of pragmatic instrumentalism (ethics, for example, entailing economics and politics) Russell argued that, "Dr. Dewey has an outlook which, where it is distinctive, is in harmony with the age of industrialism and collective enterprise. It is natural that his strongest appeal should be to Americans, and also that he should be almost equally appreciated by the progressive elements in countries like China and Mexico." But in reply to his comments, he tells us that Dewey's response was: "Mr. Russell's confirmed habit of connecting the pragmatic theory of knowing with obnoxious aspects of American industrialism . . . is much as if I were to link his philosophy to the interests of the English landed aristocracy." However, despite Dewey's persistent defense of his method, Russell still concluded that: "Dr. Dewey's world, it seems to me, is one in which human beings occupy the imagination. . . . His philosophy is a power philosophy, though not, like Nietzsche's, a philosophy of individual power; it is the power of the community that is valuable. It is this element of social power that seems

to me to make the philosophy of instrumentalism attractive to those who are more impressed by our new control over natural forces than by the limitations to which that control is still subject." See *A History of Western Philosophy*, reprinted in *The Basic Writings of Bertrand Russell*, R. E. Egner and L. E. Dennon eds. (New York: Simon and Schuster, 1961). pp. 213-14. Perhaps it should also be mentioned here that Russell, as Samuel Meyer interprets his position, made no "serious effort to grasp Dewey's theory of knowledge," but instead, "found in Dewey a handy foil for his fundamental dissatisfaction with the doctrines of pragmatism and instrumentalism." See Meyer's *Dewey and Russell: An Exchange* (New York: Philosophical Library, Inc., 1985). p. 12.

30. Dewey, "The Development of American Pragmatism" (1925), in *Later Works*, Vol. 2, p. 13. Perhaps it should be noted here that even though Dewey was an ardent defender of the American pragmatists, we are reminded by Stephen Toulmin that it is quite important for us to recognize how "misleading it can be to lump them all together, as the single school of 'pragmatists.'" See Toulmin's superb Introduction to *The Quest for Certainty*, in the *Later Works*, Vol. 4.

31. Dewey, "The Development of American Pragmatism," in *Later Works*, Vol. 2, p. 5.

32. *Ibid*.

33. *Ibid.*, p. 6. When a person is "considering a system of philosophy in its relation to national factors," there always seems to be a problem of "relativism" involved. A very good example can be seen in the work of Rene Descartes. In the *Discourse,* where he tells us about his undertaking to discover a "method" for determining "truth," he says quite candidly: "In order to live as happily as I could during this time, I formed for myself a provisional moral code consisting of just three or four maxims. . . . The first was to obey the laws and customs of my country, . . . . For I had begun at this time to count my own opinions as worthless, because I wished to submit them all to examination, and so I was sure that I could do no better than follow those of the most sensible men. And although there may be men as sensible among the Persians or Chinese as among ourselves, I thought it would be most useful for me to be guided by those with whom I shall have to live." Reprinted in *The Philosophical Writings of Descartes,* Vol. 1. Translated by J. Cottingham, R. Stoothoff, and D. Murdock (New York: Cambridge University Press, 1985). p. 122.

34. Dewey, "The Development of American Pragmatism," in *Later Works*, Vol. 2, p. 6.

35. Dewey, "Philosophy" (1934), in *Later Works,* Vol. 8, p. 32. Perhaps we should note Norman Melchert's observation here; for he maintains that: "Plato [was] occupied, one might even say obsessed, with the problem of refuting Protagorean relativism and skepticism. This [was] terribly important to him. . . . [But] To that problem Aristotle seems almost

oblivious, as though it was not on his horizon at all. The explanation may be partly that he believes Plato has succeded in refuting the skeptics, so it doesn't have to be done again." See *The Great Conversation,* pp. 142-43.

36. McDermott, *The Philosophy of John Dewey,* p. 1.

37. Dewey, "From Absolutism to Experimentalism" (1930), reprinted in *Later Works*, Vol. 5, p. 155.

38. *Ibid.,* p. 154. With respect to Dewey's own system of philosophy, in comparison with the great accomplishments of Plato, Dewey clearly admits that, "Although I have not the aversion to system as such that is sometimes attributed to me, I am dubious of my owm ability to reach inclusive systematic unity. . . " (p.9). It is interesting to note that in 1939, however, Sidney Hook said: "Even [Dewey's] critics grant that his most recent books have constituted his weightiest and most systematic statement of the philosophy of experimentalism." Yet Hook also tells us, "John Dewey has always denied that his philosophy constituted a system." Thus, in defense of Dewey's position, Hook explains that, "A philosophy, however, may have a systematic quality without being a system. . . . [For example] An empirical investigation of mind in a particular field which leads to conclusions that reappear when fresh investigations of other fields are conducted gives a systematic theory of mind. It is in this last sense that I believe John Dewey's philosophy is systematic." So Hook holds that, "In Dewey's philosophy we have a sustained and systematic attempt to take the pattern of scientific inquiry as a model for knowledge and action in all fields." See Hook's *John Dewey: An Intellectual Portrait,* pp. 26, 27, 233, respectively. Since we shall not debate the issue of Dewey's systematism in this paper, let it suffice here to note that Jo Ann Boydston has described Hook as "John Dewey's most illustrious protege, supporter, and interpreter," yet in contrast to Hook's interpretation, when she refers to "the first twelve authors whose works were edited by the standards of the Modern Language Association Center for Editions of American Authors," she additionally informs us that "Dewey is the only systematic philosopher represented in this list of literary figures. . . ." See *Later Works,* Vol. 17, p. xxxiv.

39. Coughlan, *Young John Dewey* (Chicago: University of Chicago Press, 1975). p. 83.

40. Dewey, "From Absolutism to Experimentalism," in *Later Works,* Vol. 5, p. 154.

41. Sleeper, "Introduction" to *Later Works,* Vol. 14, p. xi. Sleeper's interpretation seems to be clearly sustained by Dewey's "Logic" (1933), in *Later Works,* Vol. 8, where Dewey provides some additional insight concerning his own reading of Hegel; for Dewey says, "The technical transformations wrought by Hegel in logical theory, with his dialectic movement of thesis, antithesis and synthesis, lie beyond the scope of this article. In substance it may be said, however, that Hegel sought a logic which would avoid the abstract, non-historical character of the earliest

semimathematical rationalism. He wished in effect to make the movement of history the supreme rational manifestation. If philosophical and terminological technicalities are ignored, his work may be characterized as an attempt at a logical apotheosis of the historical method; indeed it was largely through his influence that the historical method was in the first half of the nineteenth century brought to consciousness in the fields of law, politics, morals, language, religion and political economy. Hegel piously retained the rationalistic idea of the supremacy of reason and absolute mind in history" (pp. 9-10). Then too, we can see that Sleeper's interpretation is further sustained by the article "Philosophy" (1934), where Dewey additionally exhibits his degree of agreement with Hegel's system. Dewey tells us that, "Hegel, for example, treated the doctrines and institutions of Christianity; their rational meaning was sound, but their garb was that of the pictorial imagination. Since his interpretation excluded acceptance of the supernatural in its received sense, the effect was 'revolutionary' as far as popular belief was concerned" (*Ibid.*, p. 31).

42. As for Dewey's affiliation with the Andover Liberals, or Congregational progressives, Bruce Kuklick says in *Churhmen and Philosophers* that: "Three themes of the new theology structured Dewey's thought throughtout his life. Like Andover, Dewey heralded science as the method of philosophy. With the new theologians he also controverted the dichotomies between God and man and between the natural and the supernatural. For him, God was incorporated in humanity, and spirit in nature. An emphasize on science and a concern to deny these two distinctions essentially characterized Dewey's thought through the eighties and early nineties. He wanted a more genuine philosophy of immanence, and, . . . a speculative spine for Progressive Orthodoxy" (p. 233).

43. Dewey, "The Meaning of the Term: Liberalism" (1940), reprinted in *Later Works*, Vol. 14, p. 252.

44. *Ibid.*, p. 253.

45. *Ibid.*, p. 254.

46. Dewey, "Logic" reprinted in *Later Works*, Vol. 8, p. 4.

47. Dewey, "Logic" reprinted in *Later Works*, Vol. 8, p. 4.

48. *Ibid.*

49. *Ibid.*, p. 11.

50. Dewey, "Logic" reprinted in *Later Works*, Vol. 8, p. 11.

51. Dewey, "Logic" reprinted in *Later Works*, Vol. 8, p. 11. As for the "almost entirely" American character of pragmatism during that time, it is interesting to note Dewey's "Tribute to F. C. S. Schiller" (1937), reprinted in *Later Works*, Vol. 11. With respect to the work that Schiller did in Great Britain and this country to loosen "the strait jacket in which Aristotelian logic had confined science," as Dewey puts it, "He was one of the first [Europeans] to insist upon intimate connection of logic with actual scientific work. He was a pioneer in insisting upon the central

place of *meaning* and its primacy over the conception of truth" (p. 157). Quite opposed to some of his fellow logicians, Dewey notes Schiller's belief that, "pure form is meaningless; . . . [since] form is always the form of a subject-matter. . . . purely formal logic is condemned to inconsistency since it defines judgment and propositions in terms of truth-falsity while 'truth' and 'falsity' are meaningless apart from subject-matter" (p. 156). As for Dewey's own interpretation of Schiller, however, we are told that, "There were two main considerations, I think, which attracted Schiller to James. One was the freedom of the latter from the conventions which limited philosophy. . . . The other and more definitely philosophical moving force was the emphasis James placed upon the purpose and upon practical ends in determining all intellectual operations" (p. 156).

52. Plato, *Timaeus*, reprinted in *Plato:The Collected Dialogues*, Edith Hamilton and Huntington Cairns, eds. (New Jersey: Princeton University Press, 1961). p. 1185.

53. *St. John* 1: 1-2 (King James Version).

54. Dewey, "Psychology as a Philosophic Method" (1886), reprinted in *John Dewey: The Early Works, 1882-1898*, Jo Ann Boydston, ed. (Carbondale: Southern Illinois University Press, 1969). Vol. 1, p. 149. Henceforth it is referred to as *Early Works*. With respect to the forenamed artitle, it is interesting to note that Dewey used it to criticize idealists such as Edward Caird, who's arguments about metaphysics (or God) sought to "determine the unconditioned whole, self-consciousness, by that which has no existence except as a conditioned part of this very whole" (*Ibid.*, p. 146).

55. Dewey, "Psychology as a Philosophic Method" (1886), reprinted in *Early Works*, Vol. 1, p. 156.

56. *Ibid.*

57. Dewey, "Psychology as a Philosophic Method" (1886), reprinted in *Early Works*, Vol. 1, p. 156.

58. Dewey, "Has Philosophy a Future?" (1949), reprinted in *Later Works*, Vol. 16, p. 358.

59. *Ibid.*, p. 359.

60. Dewey, "Has Philosophy a Future?" (1949), reprinted in *Later Works*, Vol. 16, p. 359.

61. Dewey, "What Are Universals? (1936), reprinted in *Later Works*, Vol. 11, p. 107.

62. Dewey, "Philosophy" (1934), reprinted in *Later Works*, Vol. 8, p. 23.

63. *Ibid.*

64. Dewey, "Philosophy" (1934), reprinted in *Later Works*, Vol. 8, p. 23.

65. *Ibid.*, p. 24.

66. Dewey, "Philosophy" (1934), reprinted in *Later Works*, Vol. 8, p. 22.

67. *Ibid.*, p. 26.

68. Dewey, "Philosophy" (1934), in *Later Works*, Vol. 8, p. 38.
69. *Ibid.*, pp. 38-39. It is interesting to note Dewey's argument that "Even ignorance or lack of specialized knowledge may be an aid in freeing imagination and permitting the generation of ideas that give a new direction to interest and intention" (*Ibid.*, p. 34).
70. Dewey, "Philosophy" (1934), reprinted in *Later Works*, Vol. p. 34.

# Chapter 4

ഇരbirths

## Young Dewey's Conception of Philosophy and Truth: His Early Years, 1859-1890

In regard to the task of surveying and explaining John Dewey's early conception of philosophy and his notion of truth, the scholarly research of J. J. McDermott is quite helpful. Fortunately, he provides a very concise chronology of Dewey's longevity. His early years are outlined by McDermott as follows.

| | |
|---|---|
| 1859 | Born on October 20, in Burlington, Vermont |
| 1879 | Graduates from the University of Vermont |
| | Begins teaching high school at Oil City, Pennsylvania |
| 1881 | Teaches in Charlotte, Vermont, and studies philosophy with H. A. P. Torrey |
| 1882 | Graduate student, Johns Hopkins University |
| 1884 | PhD, Johns Hopkins University |
| | Begins teaching philosophy at the University of Michigan, 1884-88 |

1886    Marries Alice Chipman
1888    Professor of philosophy, University of Minnesota
1889    Professor of philosophy, University of Michigan,
        1889-94[1]

As we can see, McDermott does provide a rather succinct account of Dewey's first thirty years. He plainly notes the place and the date of Dewey's initial arrival into the world. He tells us about the academic concerns of Dewey—his study of philosophy, for instance, and his teaching career. McDermott also tells us about Dewey's social interest, and about his marriage to Alice Chipman.

What McDermott's outline omits, however, is information about one of the most important ingredients for understanding Dewey's philosophy of truth. He does not mention John Dewey's religious disposition, nor affiliations. But as we shall see, throughout his entire life-career Dewey shows deep concern about the problem of religion, for it is a recurring theme in his writings. Therefore, in view of McDermott's omission, our procedure supplements the outline by giving due consideration to Dewey's thoughts about religion.

For the most part, during his early years, Dewey clearly states his views on religion; and there is ample evidence to support the latter interpretation. Dewey even confirms it himself. On one occasion, for instance, near the age of seventy-one, we find Dewey recollecting his early years, and he tells us,

> I was brought up in a conventionally evangelical atmosphere of the more "liberal" sort; and the struggles that later arose between acceptance of that faith and the discarding of traditional and institutional creeds came from personal experiences and not from the effects of philosophical teaching . . . Of Hegel I was then ignorant. My deeper interests had not yet been met, and in the absence of the subject-matter that would correspond to them, the only topics at my command were such as were capable of a merely formal treatment. I imagine that my development has been controlled largely by a struggle between a native inclination toward the schematic and formally logical, and those incidents of personal experience that compelled me to take account of actual material. . . . During the time when the schematic interest predominated, writing was comparatively easy; there were even compliments upon the clearness of my style. Since then thinking and writing have been hard work.[2]

In the preceding discussion, Dewey takes care to inform us that he was "brought up in a conventionally evangelical atmosphere." That atmosphere existed in the late 1870s, he says, "in the smaller New England colleges," while he was an undergraduate.[3] Also, in describing that evangelical atmosphere, Dewey tells us, "Teachers of philosophy were at that time, almost to a man, clergymen; the supposed requirements of religion, or theology, dominated the teaching of philosophy in most colleges."[4] However, during this stage of Dewey's development, he was not effected too deeply by the "requirements of religion, or theology." This latter interpretation is sustained, no doubt, as Dewey says,

> While the conflict of traditional religious beliefs with opinions that I myself honestly entertain was the source of a trying personal crisis, it did not at any time constitute a leading philosophical problem. . . . [However] any genuinely sound religious experience could and should adapt itself to whatever beliefs one found oneself intellectually entitled to hold—a half unconscious sense at first, but one which ensuing years have deepened into a fundamental conviction. In consequence, while I have, I hope, a due degree of personal sympathy with individuals who are undergoing the throes of a personal change of attitude, I have not been able to attach much importance to religion as a philosophic problem; for the effect of that attachment seems to be in the end a subordination of candid philosophic thinking to the alleged but factitious needs of some special set of convictions.[5]

In the subsequent chapters we shall examine some of the reasons for the changes in Dewey's attitude toward religion. Meanwhile, though, let us try to clarify the religious views he held during his early years.

Before he became overwhelmed by "philosophical teaching," as noted above, Dewey thought that "writing was comparatively easy"; and so expressing his views didn't seem very difficult. The ease that he wrote with then was evidently due to his Christian upbringing, or his Congregationalism. That is, prior to his philosophical teaching, Dewey led the simple life of a Congregationalist. A scrutiny of his religious background apart from his academic training clearly trace his steps to the First Congregational Church of Burlington, Vermont. Moreover, as Bruce Kuklick points out, we find that John Dewey "regularly went to services and often taught Bible classes at the Congregational church of which he was a member."[6]

In addition, after receiving his doctorate from Johns Hopkins University in 1884, we are told that Dewey spent the next ten years teaching almost exclusively at the University of Michigan. And while at Ann Arbor, he was active in the local Congregational church, busy defending religion against materialism. But for some strange reason, he began distancing himself from Congregationalism. According to Kuklick's account, "Dewey's church affiliation lapsed. . . after he left Ann Arbor: his children did not attend Sunday school, his attention to student religion stopped; and he increased his commitment to social reform."[7] What was his conception of philosophy at that point? What happened to Dewey's religious beliefs about truth?

Let's look back at his early years and see. Accordingly, we find that one of the persons who mostly influenced young Dewey's beliefs about religion was the woman who helped bring him into the world, Lucina Rich Dewey. Apparently she was primarily responsible for inculcating an ardent and devoted piety into her sons. Young John's biological father, Archibald Sprague Dewey, was nearly 48 years old when the former was born, and twenty years older than his wife. What is more important, however, during the War between the States, long periods of absence were spent away from his family. Therefore, Archibald apparently did not have much time to strongly influence young John's intellectual development.

In other words, Archibald could hardly compete with Lucina's convictions about raising their sons. Lucina seems to have reflected an intense inner feeling, which manifested itself in a healthy concern for the well-being of others; and this especially seems to be true regarding her sons and their spiritual relationship with God. Her own religious upbringing reflected the liberalizing theology of Andover's Progressive Orthodoxy, which resulted from the New England theology that Jonathan Edwards initiated. Though she started John in the family's church, she was cautious about the kind of Calvinism that was promoted there. In other words, Burlington's First Congregational Church, under the leadership of Reverend Lewis O. Brastow, was not the fiery type of Edwards evangelicism that had converted her. Evidently Brastow did preach an evangelical religion of the Bible, but it was a more subdued or refined liberal sort; he apparently placed more emphasis on the intellectual than on the experiential.[8] Yet it was at Lucina's urging that, by age eleven, he became a member of the First Congregational Church at Burlington.[9]

As we can see, then, it was John Dewey's mother that first instilled in him a deep religious concern. It was his mother who taught him his childhood prayer, and read Biblical narratives to him. It was his mother who was mainly responsible for seeing that he regularly attended worship services, and Sunday school; she was the one who primarily nurtured young Dewey's spiritual growth. And, most likely, he was thinking about her when he explained to us that

> Religious feeling is unhealthy when it is watched and analyzed to see if it exists, if it is right, if it is growing. It is as fatal to be forever observing our own religious moods and experiences, as it is to pull up a seed from the ground to see if it is growing. We must plant the seed and nourish it, and leave the rest where it belongs—to God.[10]

It was only after entering the University of Vermont that Dewey began to consider philosophy as a way to resolve some of his questions about religion. His initial philosophic awakening occurred as follows. Though the study of philosophy was still in its infancy stage during the formative years of American universities, as he remembers those days, he says,

> There was, however, one course in the previous year that had excited a taste that in retrospect may be called philosophical. That was a rather short course, without laboratory work, in Physiology, a book of Huxley's being the text. . . . I got great stimulation from the study, more than from anything I had had contact with before; and as no desire was awakened in me to continue that particular branch of learning, I date from this time the awakening of a distinctive philosophic interest.[11]

In addition, he tells us, "The University of Vermont rather prided itself upon its tradition in philosophy."[12] Looking back at those days, Dewey says that H. A. P. Torrey was the first professor of philosophy he met, and

> His interest in philosophy . . . was genuine, and not perfunctory; he was an excellent teacher, and I owe him a double debt, that of turning my thoughts definitely to the study of philosophy as a life-pursuit, and of a generous gift of time to me during a year devoted privately under his direction to a reading of classics in the history of philosophy and learning to read philosophic German.[13]

Moreover, says Dewey, "During that year of private study, . . . I decided to make philosophy my life-study, and accordingly went to Johns Hopkins the next year (1884) to enter upon that new thing, 'graduate work'."[14] However, "It was something of a risk," as he puts it, since "the work offered there was almost the only indication that there were likely to be any self-supporting jobs in the field of philosophy for others than clergymen."[15] Yet, despite the problem of "jobs in the field of philosophy," he kept his pursuit, earning his Ph. D. in 1884.

While doing his graduate work at Johns Hopkins University, however, Dewey became disenchanted with Torrey's philosophy, which was merely "schematic and formally logical." Thus, because his own "formal interest persisted," as he puts it, "there was an inner demand for an intellectual technique that would be consistent and yet capable of flexible adaptation to the concrete diversity of experienced things."[16] Thus it seems that Torrey's philosophy had left him unable to intellectually resolve his problem with dualisms. For as Dewey reflects on those early years, he tells us,

> It is hardly necessary to say that I have not been among those to whom the union of abilities to satisfy these two opposed requirements, the formal and the material, came easily.[17]

Evidently it was not until Dewey came under the influence of George Sylvester Morris that his intellectual confidence increased, and his optimism about jobs in the field of philosophy began to look brighter. Moreover, while it is rather difficult to say which direction Dewey's philosophic thought was heading under the influence of Torrey, Morris's Hegelian influence leaves us with no doubts about it.

As for Torrey's influence on his intellectual growth, however, Dewey says that while he was a student at the University of Vermont "the teaching of philosophy had become more restrained in tone, more influenced by the still dominant Scotch school," even though "its professor, Mr. H. A. P. Torrey, was a man of genuinely sensitive and cultivated mind."[18] But, did Dewey clearly understand Torrey' s view of philosophy? Seemingly there is a problem here! Lewis Feuer, for example, points out a possible inconsistentency of Dewey's recollection of his early years. Feuer informs us that "all available evidence indicates that Dewey erred, that Torrey indeed was from beginning to the end of his philosophic career Kantian in his inclinations."[19] On the other hand, however, Neil Coughlan interprets Torrey's position and tells us "it is probable that he was both a Kantian and an intuitionalist."[20] So we can see the problem of determining the degree of influence that Torrey might have had upon young Dewey's thinking; but we will not try resolving it here.

Instead, let us turn to a more fruitful survey of Morris's Hegelian influences. Telling us about the impact that Morris had upon his intellectual growth, Dewey reminiscently says,

> I have never known a more single-hearted and whole-souled man— a man of a single piece all the way through; while I long since deviated from his philosophic faith, I should be happy to believe that the influence of the spirit of his teaching has been an enduring influence.[21]

Why had Dewey turned away from Morris's "philosophic faith"? Apparently one of the faults that Dewey found with Morris and his doctrine was that, "[Morris] retained something of his early Scotch philosophical training in a common sense belief in the existence of the external world." Moreover, says Dewey, "He used to make merry over those who thought the *existence* of this world and of matter were things to be proved by philosophy. . . . [Of course] his idealism was wholly of the objective type."[22]

On the other hand, though, what Dewey evidently liked most about the teachings of Morris, was that the latter introduced him to Hegel. Dewey was quite impressed, no doubt, by the way Morris approached the study of Hegel. For instance, the account that Dewey gives of Morris is that, "He came to Kant through Hegel instead of to Hegel by way of Kant, so that his attitude toward Kant was the critical one expressed by Hegel himself."[23] Thus, Dewey readily admits that because of Morris' teaching on Hegel, some tenable answers to many of his questions about religion had been found.

After finding Hegel's work Dewey must have felt that his quest for truth had all been worthwhile. Reminiscing Hegel's influence upon him, he says,

> There were . . . "subjective" reasons for the appeal that Hegel's thought made to me; it supplied a demand for unification that was doubtless an intense emotional craving, and yet was a hunger that only an intellectualized subject-matter could satisfy. . . . [Moreover] as a consequence of a heritage of New England culture, divisions by way of isolation of self from the world, of soul from body, of nature from God, brought a painful oppression—or, rather, an inward

laceration. . . . [But] Hegel's synthesis of subject and object, matter and spirit, the divine and the human, . . . operated as an immense release, a liberation. Hegel's treatment of human culture, of institutions and the arts, . . . had a special attraction for me.[24]

Though Dewey thought that Hegel had truly helped him answer some of his many questions, evidently he believed that something was still lacking. In other words, he later informs us that

I drifted away from Hegelianism in the next fifteen years; the word "drifting" expresses the slow and, for a long time, imperceptible character of the movement, though it does not convey the impression that there was an adequate cause for the change.[25]

Why had Dewey "drifted" away from Hegelianism? It appears that Neil Coughlan correctly cites the main reason when he notes Dewey's belief that Hegel, as he puts it, "had to be made practical."[26] So, our survey tries to show why Dewey thought that Hegel's philosophy lacked practical application; and we hope to show why he felt that this lack provided an adequate cause for his change, or drifting.

Though Dewey did drift away from Hegelianism as an attempt to make it practical, bear in mind that he never did break completely away from Hegel. Remember, Dewey explicitly acknowledges that: "Hegel has left a permanent deposit in my thinking."[27] For present purposes, though, we need not further discuss Dewey's drift away from Hegel. It may be more fruitful here, so it seems, to mention Dewey's espousal of Plato's system of philosophy, instead of Hegel's.

What we should keep in mind is Dewey's assertion that Plato continuously provided him with his "favourite philosophic reading."[28] However, apart from Plato's influence and the strong impact that the philosophies of Hegel and Morris had on Dewey, we also should take into consideration the influence that Peirce had on the development of his conceptions of philosophy and truth during those early years. So before we turn to our survey of his middle years, perhaps it will be helpful here if we examine how Peirce possibly influenced his earlier writings. After considering the feasibility of Peirce's effect on him, then our approach may very well put us in a better position to comprehend the transitional phases in Dewey's thoughts regarding the "true method" of Plato's philosophy.

Though a detailed study of Peirce's influence is not given here, we nevertheless try to clarify his possible impact on Dewey's views. Apparently Peirce effected his view of human communication rather immensely, even though the influences possibly occurred indirectly. Morris Eames, for instance, raises some serious questions about the degree of influence that Peirce had on Dewey's early years. He says,

> During this period Dewey published six articles and reviews in the field of logical theory, and some of these show the slowly developing, perhaps unconscious, influence Charles Sanders Peirce, with whom Dewey had studied logic at Johns Hopkins. . . . Peirce had maintained that logic had made no progress for two hundred years, . . . .[29]

Now judging from Eames's observation, we need to clarify, if possible, some distinctions regarding the historical context in which Dewey's conceptions of philosophy and truth developed during the different stages of his writings.

For example, with respect to some of his early writings, "Is Logic a Dualistic Science?" (1890) and "The Present Position of Logical Theory" (1891), it seems that several perplexing questions need answering. For instance, Eames informs us that

> These early essays set a problem for Dewey on which he worked until the end of his life, the problem of overcoming the dualism which had developed between logic and science. His proposal in these early writings is similar to Peirce: Logical forms must be set inside a general pattern of scientific inquiry where a working harmony and unity of all procedures can be effected, and logic must be concerned with the pursuit of truth, which is the goal of all scientific inquiry.[30]

As we can see from Eames's interpretation, Peirce may have swayed Dewey's thinking about logic, science, and the pursuit of truth.

Somewhat in line with Eames's view, Morton White points out that "Perhaps the most fortunate thing for Dewey's development is that he decided to study at Johns Hopkins. . . . Its members, at the time, were Charles Peirce, George S. Morris, and G. Stanley Hall."[31] White informs us that Hall, Morris, and Peirce influenced Dewey. Accordingly, White says, "Peirce's greatness becomes more evident as more of his works are read. Hall founded the first laboratory for experimental psychology in America. And Morris—the man people know least about today—was the teacher who had the greatest influence on Dewey."[32] When reflecting back on Dewey's early years, White reports that

In restrospect this almost total attachment to Morris among the philosophical faculty at Johns Hopkins can very well be regarded as unfortunate. For Peirce had already formulated the outlines of a position which Dewey came to regard as brilliant—but Dewey's discovery of Peirce came twenty years later. Dewey seems to have regarded Peirce as entirely devoted to formal logic.[33]

White additionally tells us that

Although Peirce had no influence on Dewey in these early years, Hall did. . . . He shared the contempt for Hegel that James expressed in his paper on Hegelianism. Hall's lectures seem to have led Dewey to study experimental psychology. The emphasis is upon the word "study," for Dewey never really became an experimental psychologist in the way other students of Hall did.[34]

So how much impact did Peirce have on Dewey's early years? Kuklick provides some additional insight regarding this matter. His research tends to support parts of White's report, but it raises some further questions concerning Peirce's influence on Dewey. He says,

Dewey's early career suggested how far his thought  was from the Cambridge pragmatism emerging in the work of Hall's mentor William James and Hall's colleague at Hopkins, Charles Peirce. When Dewey's text, *Psychology*, appeared in 1887, Hall and James poked fun at it. Both men adopted "naturalistic" psychologies that commentators have identified with pragmatic themes, and both deprecated Dewey's Hegelianism. Critics have also noted that Peirce did not influence Dewey at Hopkins, but have taken at face value Dewey's after-the-fact statement that he later saw the value of Peirce's thought. But at Hopkins Peirce represented a pervasive philosophical error. The logic he taught exemplified the formalism Dewey detested. . . . Dewey did appreciate James' *Principles of Psychology* published in 1890, but by that time his ideas were formed. When he wrote *Logic: The Theory of Inquiry* (1938) his conception of logic still differed dramatically from Peirce's.[35]

So how much did Peirce influence Dewey during his early years? Judging from the accounts of Kuklick and White, undoubtedly the answer should be: None!

As we have seen already, White maintains that "Peirce had no influence on Dewey in these early years," and likewise Kuklick says,

"Critics have also noted that Peirce did not influence Dewey at Johns Hopkins." Although we shall not try to resolve this issue here, it should be understood that in contrast to Kuklick and White, the present writer thinks that Peirce did influence Dewey during his early years. Peirce and James, so it seems, were mostly responsible for Dewey's diminishing references to "God" in his writings.

Perhaps the present writer's interpretation can be confirmed by noting an explanation of Sidney Hook, whom Jo Ann Boydston describes as "John Dewey's most illustrious protege, supporter, and interpreter."[36] Accordingly, he takes the position that

> At Johns Hopkins, Dewey listened to Charles Peirce but did not come under his direct influence. Years later, after he had developed his own distinctive ideas, Dewey was to return to the writings of Peirce to find independent support for his philosophy of experimentalism.[37]

As we can see from Hook's explanation, "Dewey listened to Charles Peirce," even though he *did not* come under his "direct influence." Now isn't listening to someone, and observing their actions, just as influential (sometimes) as it is to read their work? The present writer thinks so; and he thinks that this is what happened with Peirce and Dewey. Of course Peirce's writings were read by Dewey, no doubt, and gave him "independent support" for his philosophy.

Granting that Peirce did influence Dewey in his early years, let us ask ourselves: What doctrine was Peirce teaching, if it led Dewey to decrease his references to "God" in his writings? To answer this question, let us consider a suggestion that Peirce makes in his classifications and semiotic. Peirce's proposal seems to indicate how he might have influenced Dewey to use the term "God" less frequently in subject matters of scientific discourse.

Peirce believed that philosophers could make some great progress in the science of semiotic, or logic, by employing a process of abstraction, which is a "sort of observation," to use his suggested terminology. "Abstraction," as he calls it, is not a very difficult process to understand; for as he says himself,

> The faculty which I call abstractive observation is one which ordinary people perfectly recognize, but for which the theories of philosophers sometimes hardly leave room.[38]

Now the question is: How can philosophers—like ordinary people—recognize and utilize "abstractive observation"? Peirce gives the following explanation.

> It is a familiar experience for every human being to wish for something beyond his present means, and to follow that wish by the question, "Should I wish for that thing just the same, if I had ample means to gratify it?" To answer that question, he searches his heart, and in doing so makes an abstract observation. He makes in his imagination a kind of skelton diagram, or outline sketch, of himself, considers what modifications the hypothetical state of things would require to be made in that picture, and then examines it, that is, observes what he has imagined, to see whether the same ardent desire is there to be discerned. By such a process, which is very much like mathematical reasoning, we can reach conclusions as to what would be true of signs in all cases, so long as the intelligence using them was scientific. [Therefore] the modes of thought of a God, who should possess an intuitive omniscience superceding reason, are put out of the question. . . . [because] the whole process of development among the community of students of those formulations by abstractive observation and reasoning of the truths which must hold good of all signs used by a scientific intelligence is an observational science, [which is strictly for human beings] . . . .[39]

So it is apparent that Peirce's notion of abstractive observation, or imagination, might have influenced Dewey's use of the term "God." As our study tries to show, Peirce's suggestion was quite compatible with Dewey's later desire to direct philosophic discourse away from the theological idea of creation; and it was also congenial with his desire to overcome dualisms.

As for the fixation of Dewey's religious beliefs during those early years, it is difficult to specify how much Peirce influenced him. Nevertheless, a scrutiny of his early writings seem to furnish ample evidence of Dewey's religious convictions. For example, with respect to the problem of overcoming dualisms, the young Dewey leaves us with no doubt about his position. Consider his 1886 article entitled "What Is the Demonstration of Man's Spiritual Nature?" As he replies to H. S. Swift's "The Revival of the Soul," Dewey says,

> I am inclined to suspect that there is more of sympathy than of difference between my critic and myself, because, if I understand him, he takes the position that the teaching and life of Jesus overcame

the dualism of spirit and matter, and reconciled them in a perfect unity, and that this teaching is in complete conformity with reason. And in this position I fully concur, . . . The teaching of Jesus is that the kingdom of God is within; that we are not to say, lo here, nor, lo there, nor to run about expecting to find it in this or that quarter. It is the teaching of Jesus that the kingdom of God is a spiritual kingdom, and its life one of the spirit. The sole requirement of Christianity is faith in the supreme reality of spirit, and complete devotion to it. That there is no dualism between spirit and nature, the soul and flesh, follows from this; for reality is one, not two.[40]

Clearly, then, young Dewey thought that the answer to the problem of dualisms could be found in the Christian religion, or the teachings of Christ. Moreover, Dewey held that, "Theology or philosophy has reflectively to show that the pre-suppositions of religion, namely of the reality of spirit and of the relations of the human spirit and the divine, are the ultimate truths of experience when experience is thoroughly interpreted."[41]

In "The Psychological Standpoint" (1886), Dewey expresses his beliefs about the "ultimate truths of experience," and argues that as philosophers we are on scientific ground if we candidly admit that "the origin of knowledge and experience cannot be accounted for."[42] Young Dewey argues that "a sensation is not prior to consciousness or knowledge"; instead, it is only "one element in an organic whole."[43] Thus, strongly opposing any person who thinks that he can account for the experience(s) of initial consciousness, Dewey argues that

. . . he is not accounting for the origin of consciousness or knowledge as such at all. He is simply accounting for the origin of an individual consciousness, or a specific group of known facts, by reference to the larger group of known facts or universal consciousness. Hence also the historic impotence of all forms of materialism.[44]

As we can see, Dewey explains his view of human experience and the origin of consciousness; and he rejects all forms of materialism.

Apparently being candid in communicating his ideas about the way humans actually experience things, young Dewey goes on to say, "If we actually believe in experience, let us be in earnest with it, and believe also that if we only ask, instead of assuming at the outset, we shall find what the infinite content of experience is. How experience became we shall never find out, for . . . experience always is."[45] Now if we consider Dewey's reference to "experience" in the context of his youthful Christian convictions, no doubt this latter statement can be interpreted as a reiteration of Christ's teachings; for he allegedly said,

> Ask, and it shall be given you; seek, and ye shall find . . . For everyone that ask[s] receive[s]; and he [or she] that seek[s] find[s] . . . .[46]

In light of Dewey's own youthful religious experiences, however, it should come as no surprise to find that he frequently paraphrased biblical scripture during those early years. Perhaps it is somewhat unfortunate, though, that he hardly ever documented or recorded the sources of those references.

For example, the preceding year he published an article titled "The Revival of the Soul" (1885) in which he paraphrases scripture, or so it seems. For when discussing the "essence of the religious life," as he refers to it, we find him asserting that, "It is as true now as ever it was that the just shall live by faith."[47] This latter statement seems to be a resonance of the Apostle Paul's alleged message to the Romans, where he contends that, "The just shall live by faith."[48] At any rate, sometimes it is not too difficult to detect the various scriptural paraphrases among Dewey's philosophic writings, as the last statements seem to show.

With regard to the latter article, however, we find that Dewey makes a common sense distinction between philosophy and science which he apparently maintained throughout his philosophic career. In distinguishing between the two disciplines, Dewey argues that

> Once for all, it should be said that it is absolutely impossible for science to settle any religious question. Religion would see the world as a whole, and would find that whole beating with love, pregnant with intelligence and vital with will. Science has nothing to do with wholes, nor with love, intelligence and will.[49]

The apparent distinction to be drawn is that philosophy, if it is defined by philosophers as the "love of wisdom," then it must be *about* "love." On the other hand, as for science,

> It discovers only connections between facts. It establishes only certain relations of coexistence or sequence among phenomena, and to these relations it gives the name law. Beyond these phenomenal connections into the realm of absolute truth and reality it cannot pierce.[50]

Apparently, then, judging from the common sense distinctions that Dewey makes between philosophy and science, the major difference is that the latter is much more limited than the former. Of course when Dewey made these distinctions he still was under the influence of Morris's Hegelianism. Nevertheless, with respect to the "inward laceration" that he had previously experienced in the evangelical atmosphere of New England, we can see that he had fixed his religious beliefs firmly during those early years. While defending Idealism he believed that God is Absolute Consciousness. In "Psychology as Philosophic Method" (1886), he maintains that

> There is an absolute self-consciousness. The science of this is philosophy. This absolute self-consciousness manifests itself in the knowing and acting of individual men. The science of this manifestation, a phenomenology, is psychology. The distinction is no longer concerned with man's being itself; it is a distinction of treatment, of ways of looking at the same material.[51]

His reference to "ways of looking at the same material," so it seems, is an attempt to clarify the subject matter of philosophic discourse. No doubt he thought of God as an "absolute self-consciousness," who entails all the "subjects" or the material of philosophical discussion.

Dewey gives us a clear illustration of what the word "material" means in his philosophic discourse by asking an illustrative question:

> If the material of philosophy be the absolute self-consciousness, and this absolute self-consciousness is the realization and manifestation of itself, and as material for philosophy exists only in so far as it has realized and manifested itself in man's conscious experience, and if psychology be the science of this realization in man, what else can philosophy in its fullness be but psychology, and psychology but philosophy?[52]

Dewey's question seems to indicate how he treated the "material" of philosophy as the subject matter of his philosophical discussions. As we can see, he argued that the material of philosophy is made known via an absolute self-consciousness and therefore becomes a tangible substance for philosophic debate. So a good comprehension of his reference to the term "material" is needed indeed for a clear understanding of his maturing notion of truth.

Yet young Dewey divulges his view of truth quite clearly. For example, regarding truth about philosophy's subject matter, he says,

> The whole course of philosophic thought . . . has consisted in showing that any distinction between the form and the matter of philosophic truth, between the content and the method, is fatal to the reaching of truth.

> Self-consciousness is the final truth, and in self-consciousness the form as organic system and the content as organized system are exactly equal to each other. It is a process which, as form, has produced itself as matter. Psychology as the account of this self-consciousness must necessarily fulfill all the conditions of true method.[53]

During this early period, to be sure, Dewey argued that to make any distinction between "the form and the matter" of philosophic truth, or either between "the content and the method" of inquiry, is fatal to philosophers in their effort to grasp truth. But on the other hand, for those sincere philosophers who willingly admit that the origin of consciousness or sensations *can not* be accounted for in experience, they are able to reach truth. Indeed, young Dewey held that each individual philosopher has the capacity to experience truth; each one can come to know God as the proper subject matter of philosophy.

Dewey's conviction that we all can acquire truth and knowledge of God seems to be sustained by his contention that

> If man, as a matter of fact, does not realize the nature of the eternal and the universal *within* himself, as the essence of his own being; if he does not at one stage of his experience consciously, and in all stages implicitly, lay hold of this universal and eternal, then it is a mere matter of words to say that he can give no account of things as they universally and eternally are. To deny, therefore, that self-consciousness is a matter of psychological experience is to deny the possibility of any philosophy.[54]

This statement seems to clearly show the direction in which Dewey thought that philosophers should conduct their inquiries about truth.

When philosophers make erroneous distinctions between what they take to be "the form and the matter" of truth, as Dewey puts it, or make errant distinctions between "the content and the method" of inquiry, then how can inquiring philosophers obtain truth? As an answer, young Dewey stresses the importance of understanding what the subject matter of philosophy is primarily all about; for he says,

The conclusion of the whole matter is that a 'being like man,' since self-conscious, is an individualized universe, . . . his nature is the proper material of philosophy, and in its wholeness the only material. Psychology is the science of this nature, and no dualism in it. . . .[55]

During this this youthful stage of Dewey's philosophic development, we see that he championed Psychology as a method of philosophy. Moreover, with respect to the proper "material" or subject matter of philosophy, his article "Psychology as Philosophic Method" (1886), discloses a central and consistent strain in his argument about what may be regarded as legitimately scientific in philosophic discourse.

Dewey's employment of the term "God," and his continuous references to God, seem to provide a guiding thread that discloses his enduring belief that the word "God" is a legitimate scientific term. It is perhaps unfortunate, though, for those philosophers who refuse to open their mind to the possibility of God's actual existence. That is, if we omit God as Creator from our notion of truth, young Dewey says,

It would be fatal to the existence of philosophy as well as psychology to make any distinction here. Were not the universe realized in the individual, it would be impossible for the individual to rise to a universal point of view, and hence to philosophize. . . . In no way can the individual philosophize about a universe which has not been realized in his conscious experience. The universe, except as realized in an individual, has no existence. In man it is partially realized, and man has a partial science; in the absolute it is completely realized, and God has a complete science.[56]

The foregoing argument, so it seems, clearly shows that during this period he thought of God as an immanent Being, a being who, as he puts it, "always deals with what is located in time and place."

Explaining his notion of God's relation to "time and place," Dewey points out that

Time is not something that is outside the process of consciousness; it is a form within it, one of the functions by which it organically constitutes its own being. . . . If philosophy will deal with the absolute consciousness conceived as purely eternal, out of relation to time, then the existence of that which constitutes the actual content of man's experience is utterly inexplicable; it is not only a mystery, but a mystery which contradicts the very nature of that which is, *ex hypothesi*, the absolute. If philosophy does deal with the eternal absolute consciousness as forever realized, yet as forever having time as one of its organic functions, it is not open to anyone to bring charges against psychology as philosophy. . . .[57]

While extolling the merits of "psychology as philosophy," to use his terminology, it is evident that he endeavored to show how and why philosophers, as psychologists, should consider the subject matter of philosophy in its proper temporal context. For in those early years, Dewey held that "the very essence of psychology is that it treats experience in its absolute totality, not setting up some one aspect of it to account for the whole, as, for example, our physical evolutionist do, nor yet attempting to determine its nature from something outside of and beyond itself, as, for example, our so-called empirical psychologists have done."[58]

So apparently, then, the young Dewey must have thought that philosophers, as psychologists, should include or treat the term "God" as a legitimate scientific term. For instead of omitting references to God in philosophic discourse, we find the young Dewey specifically employing the word "God." Moreover, we see that his discussion of God is not about a Being who is completely independent of concerns and occupations that are distinctively human. With respect to his notion of God and the references that he uses, however, note that during this early stage of his development he adamantly argued that Psychology, and not Logic, is the "method of philosophy."[59]

A scrutiny of young Dewey's argument against Logic as the principle method of philosophy tends to sustain White's, Kuklick's, and Hook's contention that Peirce's teachings did not influence Dewey while they were colleagues at Johns Hopkins. On the other hand, it does raise a question of doubt about Eames' claim that Dewey had studied logic at Johns Hopkins with Peirce; but remember, though, Eames does qualify his interpretation by pointing out that Peirce's influence on Dewey was "perhaps unconscious." At any rate, let us keep in mind the questionable impact that Peirce might have had on him, and especially his ideas about employing the term "God."

As the following statement of Dewey seems to show, even if he did study logic with Peirce, apparently there was a great deal of difference in their views regarding truth and philosophic method. For in Dewey's early writings, he contends that

Logic cannot reach, however much it may point to, an actual individual. The gathering up of the universe into the one self-conscious individuality it may assert as necessary, it cannot give it as reality.[60]

Dewey goes on to explain what he takes to be the deficiency of Logic as the principle method of philosophy. He says, "Logic, while it is . . . only one moment of spirit, is still used to determine the nature of the whole."[61] Hence he argues that Logic alone cannot disclose the form and content of ultimate reality. It is deficient because, as he puts it, "The logical movement, considered by itself, is always balancing in unstable equilibrium between dualism and pantheism."[62] Thus, the conclusion he draws is that "Logic set up as absolute method reveals its self-contradiction by destroying itself."[63]

Now in light of the preceding distinction between Dewey's choice of Psychology over Logic as a principle method of Philosophy, it is hoped that we are in a better position to observe the shifts that slowly take place in his view of truth, and his use of the term "God." Moreover, as we further scrutinize the way he employs this term throughout his philosophic career, perhaps we shall see how his belief(s) about God determined his philosophical stance. As for his references to God and truth in his early writings, however, we have seen how he wished to get the subject matter of philosophy straight.

One of Dewey's clearest statements expressing his desire for philosophers to get the subject matter of philosophy straight may be found in "The Psychological Standpoint" (1886), where he reflects on the "future of philosophy," and says,

> It is a good omen for the future of philosophy that there is now a disposition to avoid discussion of particular cases in dispute, and to examine instead the fundamental presuppositions and method. This is the sole condition of discussion which shall be fruitful, and not wordbandying. It is the sole way of discovering whatever of fundamental agreement there is between different tendencies of thought, as well as showing on what grounds the radical differences are based. . . . It is the *psychological* standpoint which is the root of all the difference. . . . Yet I hope to be able to suggest, if not show, that after all the psychological standpoint is what both sides have in common.[64]

With regard to the psychological standpoint, the most important factor to bear in mind is that Dewey wanted philosophers to avoid discussion of "consciousness" or sensations as the subject matter of the "particular cases" that were in dispute. Instead of continuing to debate about such unprofitable issues in philosophic discourse, he held that the nature of "all objects of philosophical inquiry" should be fixed by finding out what experience has to say about them. Hence, even during that time, no doubt, Dewey's references to "consciousness" was an attempt to clarify the subject matter of philosophic discourse. In his concern about the future of philosophy and scientific progress, he argued that "the psychological standpoint is this: nothing shall be admitted into philosophy which does not show itself in experience, and its nature, that is, its place in experience shall be fixed by an account of the process of knowledge—by Psychology."[65] So indeed, he was convinced that "if psychology as method of philosophy means anything, it means that nothing shall be assumed except just conscious experience itself, and that the nature of all shall be ascertained from and within this."[66]

Let us keep the latter point in mind as we bring our survey of John Dewey's early years towards a close. In summarizing, let us note that we have considered his youthful conception of philosophy and its subject matter. Also, we have examined his notion of truth, as well as his views on Psychology and Logic. In concluding, though, let us bear in mind how Dewey fixed his religious belief(s) about the nature of human being(s). Remember, he says that "The life of the spirit [of humans] does not exist in a realm of things scientifically investigated and mathematically demonstrated. . . . The soul that religion has to do with always is, and needs no rediscovery [nor any] patronizing revival."[67] This last statement, so it seems, tends to clearly disclose his early religious convictions about the human soul; it also discloses a basic and consistent feature of the shifts in Dewey's thinking about philosophy and truth in his middle and later years.

For instance, undoubtedly because of his deep concern for humans, in an article entitled "The Church and Society" (1885) we find him contending that

> All society is based on the development of the universal side of the
> individual, and has as its function the realization of this universal
> element. The church lays this subordination of the individual to the
> ultimate universal, God, upon each as an obligation, and thus merely
> consciously proclaims what is unconsciously involved in the very
> substance of all society. For the church to become individualistic is
> precisely to see that men are bound together by truly universal or

social relations. This is the establishment of the kingdom of God. For the church not to interest itself actively in such questions as the industrial one, means not only loss to society, but death to religion.[68]

Clearly, then, as we've seen already from Hook's observation, Dewey was quite concerned about human beings, as individuals, who hoped to find some truth and meaning in their lives. Moreover, the young Dewey thought that humans needed, as he puts it, "a philosophical interpretation of religious truth as will show its thorough rationality," and yet he found that "the church has fallen short of its duty in this matter, and is so far responsible for some at least of the intellectual skepticism of the time."[69]

The youthful Dewey, however, had taken the position that "The scriptures are uniform in their treatment of scepticism."[70] Moreover, says young Dewey, "There is an obligation to know God, and to fail to meet this obligation is not err intellectually, but sin morally." [71] As he saw things from his ontological perspective, he was convinced that "Belief is not a privelege, but a duty."[72] However, with respect to the exponents of scepticism, we should "treat sceptics not as those who failed to meet a duty, but as unfortunates whose peculiar mental constitution is depriving them of the blessings of God's presence."[73] It is unfortunate, says Dewey, that they can't see it, and can't see that

> All knowledge is one. It is all of God, the universe, say rather, of God; and if any set of facts are regarded as something in themselves, out of relation to God and God's creatures, it is no knowledge. The whole of nature and history is worthless except as it is brought into relation with man's nature and activities; and that science or philosophy is worthless which does not ultimately bring every fact into guiding relation with . . . God.[74]

Yes, young Dewey apparently was convinced that "we must seek in order to find, and we find that for which we seek. If the desires and will of man are for God, he will find God in all his knowledge."[75] As young Dewey puts it, we can be sure that "God is everlastingly about us, and to fail to know Him is to show that we do not wish to know Him."[76]

Dewey's article "Science and the Idea of God" (1886) also shows how he fixed his religious beliefs in his early years. When criticizing John Fiske, for instance, Dewey points out that

> To say that God is, in part, unknown, is simply to say that God (so far as philosophy is concerned) *is* completed knowledge or truth, and that the mind of man must ceasely press on to grasp more of knowledge. To say that God is unknowable means that he is out of all relation to intelligence and knowledge, and consequently out of all relation to the known universe. It is an entire and complete shutting out of God from the known world of science . . . .[77]

In his debate with Fiske about whether men and God have an infinite personality, Dewey argued that "the truth of the case is that if we could only find out what the real 'ways of Man' are, we should know the ways of God, and that *all* personality is infinite, since it is at once the means and the end, the process and the result, the evolution and the goal of the universe."[78] Dewey concludes the article by saying, "why not recognize that the thorough working out of the idea of anthropomorphism will complete the idea of God? For the evil is only in the partial or inadequate ideas of man . . . ."[79]

By now it ought to be clear to the reader that John Dewey had fixed his religious beliefs firmly during his early years. If this is not clear, then in concluding Chapter 4, perhaps it will help to consider Dewey's article entitled "The Value of Historical Christianity" (1889), which the present writer deems worthy of an elongated citation.

In defense of his radical beliefs as a Christian philosopher, Dewey says,

> The unity that was to unite man to God [the Church] has somehow grown into an institution which with its dogmas, rites, sacred events, and sacred books keeps man from coming nearest to his God. [Yet] man seeks for that final peace, which only reconciliation with God can give in his own heart. . . .

> Christianity makes religion a social as well as an historical force, for it has its value in the power it has been to raise men out of their isolated individuality, and bind them into families and nations, and make them capable of higher social attainment in language, art and culture. . . .

> God is no remote Being away from the world. . . . God is neither a far-away Being, nor a mere philosophic conception by which to explain the world. He is the reality of our ordinary relations with one another in life. He is the bond of the family, the bond of society. He is love. . . .

The Spirit of God has entered into history, and . . . the Spirit is not a mystery working only in miracles, in revivals, etc., but is the intelligence present in all man's science, in his inspiration for whatever is better than himself. Such is the value of historical Christianity. . . .

The individual has but to surrender himself to the common interests of humanity in order to be freed from the claim upon him as an individual. He stands no longer isolated, but a member of that humanity whose living spirit is God Himself. . . .

The healthy religious life knows no separation of the religious from the secular. . . . He who finds in every true and pure relationship in life a bond of union with God, has his life built upon a rock which cannot be shaken by the storms of life, nor undermined by the subtleties of temptation.[80]

Judging from the preceding publication, isn't his "values" clear? To be sure, as we noted earlier, Dewey believed that "Jesus overcame the dualism of spirit and matter." Thanks to the life and teachings of Christ, no longer must we be isolated individuals. Now we can enjoy a "true and pure relationship" that forms a bond of "union with God." Dewey seemed very assured about this belief.

Dewey's final remarks in the latter article seem to also display a close affinity with a position that Plato adumbrates in the *Republic*. For instance, when presenting his utopian notion of humans living in an ideal society, Plato describes the individual philosopher who is waging a personal battle against evil; and he points out that

The philosopher remains quiet, minds his own affair, and as it were, standing aside under shelter of a wall in a storm and blast of dust and sleet and seeing others filled full of lawlessness, is content if in any way he may keep himself free from iniquity and unholy deeds throughout this life and take his departure with fair hope, serene and well content when the end comes (*Republic* VI: 496d6-e2).

Very much like Plato, no doubt, Dewey wished to increase the status of philosophy by providing answers and solutions to the ills of society. With respect to the "uncorrupted remnant of philosophers who bear the stigma of uselessness," as Plato puts it, we see young Dewey trying to exonerate them, and inspire a "genuine passion for true philosophy" (*Republic* VI: 499c). In his effort to do so, no doubt, he had tried to build his life "upon a rock which cannot be shaken by the storms of life, nor undermined by the subtleties of temptation."

Did John Dewey follow Plato's ethical ideal of a perfect society, where *education* is regarded as the key to success and survival? Or, did Dewey retain his notion of an immanent God who manifests truth in the "knowing and acting of individual men"? After Kuklick had finished researching Dewey's early years, he concluded that

> It is not clear that Dewey by the 1890s still intended to provide a respectable basis for the theology of immanence.[81]

As we have seen, Dewey strongly upheld his idea of an immanent God in "The Value of Historical Christianity" (1889). Is it probable that Dewey would have abandoned his bold stance for God, and for Christ, in such a short period of time? By the 1890s, was Dewey's religious life no longer "built upon a rock," even though he probably had not been converted to pragmatism yet? With respect to the position taken by the present author, and based upon his research, John Dewey evidently still believed in God's immanence by 1890, and even at his death in 1952.

Of course the key to understanding the shifts that take place in the evolution of Dewey's conceptions of philosophy, truth, and God, so it seems, requires a good grasp of his notion of "education." A superb example of the direction that young Dewey's educational pusuits had began taking may be found in "Poetry and Philosophy" (1890). Not only does this writing disclose his views on education, philosophy, truth, religion, and art, but he affirms his belief in an immanent God. For instance, he concludes the article by asserting that

> The same movement of the spirit, bringing man and man, man and nature into wider and closer unity, which has found expression by anticipation in poetry, must find expression by retrospection in philosophy. Thus will be hastened the day in which our sons and our daughters shall prophesy, our young men shall see visions, and our old men dream dreams.[82]

In the last sentence of this quote, we can see that Dewey once again paraphrases biblical scriptures in his writing.[83]

Nevertheless, with regard to our educational task as philosophers, Dewey does explicitly discuss the "separation of science and art," and he tells us,

We must bridge this gap of poetry from science. We must heal this unnatural wound. We must, in the cold, reflective way of critical system, justify and organize the truth which poetry, with its quick, naive contacts, has already felt and reported.[84]

In light of Dewey's assertions, it is hoped that the reader can see the path that he wished to chart for his beloved discipline of philosophy. In any case, surely the value that he saw in education should be clear. For Dewey reminiscently says,

> The opening of Johns Hopkins University marked a new epoch in higher education in the United States. We are probably not in a condition as yet to estimate the extent to which its foundation and the development of graduate schools in our universities, following its example, mark a turn in our American culture.[85]

Let us keep this background material in mind, then, as we survey his middle years, and scrutinize some of the views that influenced his thoughts about philosophy and truth.

# Notes

1.  John J. McDermott, *The Philosophy of John Dewey* (Chicago: University of Chicago Press, 1981). p. xxxv.
2.  John Dewey, "From Absolutism to Experimentalism" (1930). Reprinted in *Later Works,* Vol. 5, p. 149-50.
3.  *Ibid.,* p. 147.
4.  *Ibid.,* p. 149.
5.  Dewey, "From Absolutism to Experimentalism" (1930). Reprinted Reprinted in *Later Works,* Vol. 5, p. 153. With regard to the "special set of convictions" that Dewey refers to, at least one implication seems clear. That is, most philosophers during his era must have been convinced (or would have agreed) that St. Bonaventure was correct in arguing that: ". . . faith itself, is the first root of theology. Thus it is evident that the order followed by theology is the reverse of that followed by philosophy: philosophy ends at the point where theology begins . . . philosophy starts from reason and sense experience . . . " (see Etienne Gilson's *The Philosophy of St. Bonaventure*, p. 91f). Moreover, drawing from the writings of Hugh of St. Victor, Bonaventure had concluded that "Christian theology is the end of philosophy." See Emma T. Healey's *Works of Saint Bonaventure*, p. 12). It is along this line of thought that most early American philosophers were convicted, or so it seems; for as Dewey's statement indicates, the "requirements of religion, or theology," played an integral part in their American experience. Our study tries to show, however, why Dewey came to reject the "special set of convictions" that "Christian theology is the end of philosophy."
6.  Bruce Kuklick, *Churchmen and Philosophers* (New Haven: Yale University Press, 1985). p. 231.
7.  Kuklick, *Churchmen and Philosophers* (New Haven: Yale University Press, 1985). p. 241.
8.  Neil Coughlan, *Young John Dewey* (Chicago: University of Chicago Press, 1975). p. 5.
9.  George Dykhuizen, *The Life and Mind of John Dewey* (Carbondale, Illinois: Southern Illinois University Press, 1973). p. 6.
10. John Dewey, "The Place of Religious Emotion," reprinted in *Early Works*, Vol. 1, p. 91.
11. Dewey, "From Absolutism to Experialism," reprinted in *Later Works*, Vol. 5, pp. 147-48.
12. Dewey, "From Absolutism to Experialism," reprinted in reprinted in *Later Works*, Vol. 5, p. 148.
13. *Ibid.,* pp. 148-49.
14. *Ibid.,* p. 150.
15. *Ibid.*
16. *Ibid.,* p. 151.

17. Dewey, "From Absolutism to Experialism," reprinted in *Later Works*, Vol. 5, p. 151.
18. *Ibid.*, p. 148.
19. Lewis S. Feur, "H. A. P. Torrey and John Dewey: Teacher and Pupil," *American Quarterly* 10 (1958). p. 41.
20. Coughlan, *Young John Dewey*, p. 11.
21. Dewey, "From Absolutism to Experimentalism," reprinted in *Later Works*, Vol. 5, p. 152.
22. *Ibid.*, p. 152. It should be noted here that Morris' *Philosophy and Christianity* (1883) provides plenty of evidence to support the correctness of Dewey's criticism of Morris' thinking concerning "things to be proved by philosophy."
23. *Ibid.*, p. 152.
24. Dewey, "From Absolutism to Experimentalism," reprinted in *Later Works*, Vol. 5, p. 153.
25. *Ibid.*, p. 154.
26. Coughlan, *Young John Dewey,* p. 83.
27. Dewey, "From Absolutism to Experimentalism," reprinted in *Later Works*, Vol. 5, p. 154.
28. Dewey, "From Absolutism to Experimentalism," reprinted in *Later Works,* Vol. 5, p. 154.
29. Morris Eames, "Introduction," in *Early Works*, Vol. 3, p. x.
30. Eames, "Introduction" in *Early Works*, Vol. 3, p. xi.
31. Morton G. White, *The Origin of Dewey's Instrumentalism* (New York: Octagon Books, Inc., 1964). p. 6.
32. *Ibid.*, p. 7.
33. *Ibid.*
34. Morton G. White, *The Origin of Dewey's Instrumentalism* (New York: Octagon Books, Inc., 1964). p. 8.
35. Kuklick, *Churchmen and Philosophers*, pp. 234-35, Notes. As we shall see later, it is quite questionable whether Kuklick is correct in holding that Dewey's "conception of logic still differed dramatically from Peirce's" in 1938. For instance, in his 1936 article "What Are Universals?" Dewey says, "It is my conviction that Peirce has laid the basis for a valid logical theory of universals." See *Later Works,* Vol. 11, p. 108. So just how dramatic was the difference, if any, between Peirce's and Dewey's concept of logic?
36. See *Later Works*, Vol. 17, p. xxxiv.
37. Hook, *John Dewey: An Intellectual Portrait* (Westport, Connecticut: Greenwood Press, Publishers, 1939). p. 12. Perhaps it will be helpful here to note the importance that Dewey placed upon personal encounters with people, apart from the academic world of books. That is, Dewey contends that most of his learning came from listening to people and observing their actions; book-learning was secondary on his view of philosophy. When he writes "From Absolutism to Experimentalism"

(1930), for example, he reflects back on his youthful years, and tells us, "Upon the whole, the forces that have influenced me have come from persons and situations more than from books—not that I have not, I hope, learned a great deal from philosophical writings, but what I have learned from them has been technical in comparison with what I have been forced to think upon and about because of some experience in which I found myself entangled. (Reprinted in McDermott's *The Philosophy of John Dewey*, p. 9.) It is also interesting to note that Dewey goes on to name William James as, "the great exception to what was said about no very fundamental influence issuing from books." For James, says Dewey, was "one specifiable philosophical factor which entered into my thinking so as to give it a new direction and quality" (p. 10).

38. Charles S. Peirce, in *The Collected Papers of Charles Sanders Peirce,* 6 vols., Charles Hartshorne and Paul Weiss eds. (Cambridge: Harvard University Press, 1931-35). Paragraphs 2.227 - 2.232.
39. Charles S. Peirce, in *The Collected Papers of Charles Sanders Peirce,* 6 vols., Charles Hartshorne and Paul Weiss eds. (Cambridge: Harvard University Press, 1931-35). Paragraphs 2.227 - 2.232.
40. Dewey, "What Is the Demonstration of Man's Spiritual Nature?" (1886), reprinted in *Later Works,* Vol. 17, p. 15.
41. *Ibid.,* p. 17.
42. Dewey, "The Psychological Standpoint" (1886), in *Early Works,* Vol. 1, p. 128.
43. *Ibid.*
44. *Ibid.,* p. 9.
45. Dewey, "The Psychological Standpoint"(1886), in *Early Works,* Vol. 1, pp. 130-31.
46. *St. Luke* 11: 9, 10 (King James Version).
47. Dewey, "What Is the Demonstration of Man's Spiritual Nature?" (1886), *Later Works,* Vol. 17, p. 14.
48. *Romans* 1:17 (King James Version).
49. Dewey, "The Revival of the Soul" (1885), in *Later Works*, Vol. 17, p. 13.
50. *Ibid.*
51. Dewey, "Psychology as Philosophic Method" (1886), in *Early Works,* Vol. 1, p. 156.
52. Dewey, "Psychology as Philosophic Method" (1886), in *Early Works,* Vol. 1, p. 157.
53. Dewey, "Psychology as Philosophic Method," *Early Works,* Vol. 1, p. 163.
54. Dewey, "Psychology as Philosophic Method" (1886), in *Early Works,* Vol. 1, p. 152.
55. Dewey, "Psychology as Philosophic Method" (1886), in *Early Works,* Vol. 1, pp. 166-7.

56. Dewey, "Psychology as  Philosophic Method" (1886), in *Early Works,* Vol. 1, pp. 148-49.
57. Dewey, "Psychology as a Philosophic Method" (1886), in *Early Works,* Vol. 1, pp. 160-61.
58. Dewey, "Psychology as a Philosophic Method" (1886), in *Early Works,* Vol. 1, pp. 160-61.
59. Dewey, "Psychology as a Philosophic Method" (1886), in *Early Works,* Vol. 1, p. 163.
60. Dewey, "Psychology as a Philosophic Method" (1886), in *Early Works,* Vol. 1, p. 166.
61. *Ibid.*
62. Dewey, "Psychology as a Philosophic Method" (1886), in *Early Works*, Vol. 1, p. 166.
63. *Ibid.*
64. Dewey, "The Psychological Standpoint," in *Early Works,*   Vol. 1, p. 122.
65. Dewey, "The Psychological Standpoint," in *Early Works,*   Vol. 1, p. 124.
66. Dewey, "Psychology as Philosophic Method" (1886), *Ibid.*, p. 145.
67. Dewey, "The Revival of the Soul" (1885), in *Later Works*, Vol. 17, p. 14.
68. Dewey, "The Church and Society" (1885), in *Later Works,*  Vol. 17, pp. 19-20.
69. Dewey, "What is the Demonstration of Man's Spiritual Nature? " (1886), in *Later Works*, Vol 17, p. 17.
70. Dewey, "The Obligation to Knowledge of God" (1884), in *Early Works,* Vol. 1, p. 61.
71. *Ibid.*
72. Ibid.
73. *Ibid.*
74. *Ibid.*, p. 62.
75. Dewey, "The Obligation to Knowledge of God" (1884), in *Later Works,* Vol. 1, pp. 62-63.
76. Dewey, "The Obligation to Knowledge of God" (1884), in *Later Works,* Vol. 1, p. 63.
77. Dewey, "Science and the Idea of God" (1886), in *Later Works,* Vol. 17, p. 95.
78. *Ibid.*, p. 96.
79. *Ibid.*, p. 97.
80. John Dewey, "The Value of Historical Christianity," in *Later Works,* Vol. 17,  pp. 529-533.
81. Bruce Kuklick, *Churchmen and philosophers*  (Yale University Press, 1985). p. 238.
82. Dewey, "Poetry and Philosophy" (1890), in *Early Works,* Vol. 3, pp. 123-24.

83. This statement seems to be echoing the poetic message of the prophet Joel, who informs us that God says, "I will pour out my spirit upon all flesh; and your sons and daughters shall prophesy, your old men shall dream dreams, your young men shall see visions" (*Joel* 2: 28, King James Version).

84. Dewey, "Poetry and Philosophy" (1890), in *Early Works,* Vol. 3, p. 123.

85. Dewey, "From Absolutism to Experimentalism," reprinted in *Later Works,* Vol. 5, p. 151.

# Chapter 5

ಐಂ

# *Dewey's Shifting Conceptions of Philosophy and Truth: His Middle Years, 1890-1921*

This fourth chapter endeavors to show how John Dewey starts to mold his own distinct philosophy of truth. That is, in 1890, around age thirty-one, Dewey was no longer a rookie philosopher searching for truth. His amateur days were behind him. He had been under Morris's Hegelian influence for more than five years. And as a result, he now had much more knowledge about truth.

In other words, with regard to John Dewey's effort to make sense of things—the formal and the material—no longer did he have to question his competency, or his "union of abilities." For indeed, as the subsequent list clearly indicates, Dewey became one of America's premiere philosophers during his middle years. McDermott outlines those years as follows.

    1890    Professor of philosophy, University of Michigan, 1889-94

1894     Professor of philosophy and chairman of the Department
         of Philosophy, Psychology, and Education, University of
         Chicago, 1894-1904
1899     President of the American Psychological Association,
         1899-1900
1904     Professor of Philosophy, Columbus University, 1904-30
1905     President of the American Philosophical Association,
         1905-06
1915     A founder and first president of the American Association
         of University Professors
1919     Lectures in Japan
         Lectures in China, 1919-21[1]

The preceding outline indicates that Dewey's chief interest during his middle years was education. So let us suppose that his philosophy of truth was based upon his view of learning, schooling, and teaching.

As we noted earlier, it can hardly be denied that the philosophy of John Dewey has affected American society most directly and most broadly in the field of education—the field that equips us with the apparatus we need to search for truth. No doubt Dewey took the position that without properly educated people there could be no fruitful discussion of truth. Thus, in hope of getting a clearer understanding of his conceptions of philosophy and truth, we shall try to clarify his view of education in this chapter.

Due to the longevity of Dewey's life-work, however, there is one crucial problem that needs explaining before we undertake our investigation. The problem concerns the many different writings that Dewey produced during his long life span. Perhaps the problem is best stated by Jo Ann Boydston, one of the premeire authorities on the work of John Dewey. Explaining some of the initial difficulties that were encountered when trying to put together the 37 volumes of *The Collected Works of John Dewey, 1882-1953,* she says,

> This venture began in 1961 at Southern Illinois University as a small
> project entitled "Cooperative Research on Dewey Publications," with
> the goal of preparing a concordance of the terms in John Dewey's
> writings. In 1961, many of Dewey's writings were scattered, hard
> to find, and difficult of access; . . . . Locating and collecting copies
> of everything Dewey produced throughout his highly productive
> seventy-year publishing career was the obvious first step in such a
> project. However, even our preliminary investigation of the corpus

revealed its size and inaccessibility, and it soon became clear that developing a concordance would not be possible in the absence of a uniform collected edition of Dewey's works. Further, it was apparent early on that a collected edition of Dewey's writings was urgently needed to preserve the rapidly disappearing copies of materials published in pamphlets, newspapers, and nineteenth-century journals.[2]

From the present writer's perspective, it appears that Dewey's "highly productive seventy-year publishing career" is the problem or reason why some of his critics and commentators have failed to fully understand his philosophy of truth. The problem especially applies to his contemporaries, since they did not have the advantage of a retrospective look at his works. But it applies to more recent critics and commentators too, those who reviewed his writings before *The Collected Works* were published.

However, thanks to the efficiency of Boydston and those who contributed to the publication of his work, there is now available a very well coordinated collection of his many writings, a collection that has been "done well," as Boydston puts it, and "done before the end of this century."[3] Therefore, for the benefit of those who have not had the luxury, or the availability, of *The Collected Works,* this survey endeavors to share the fruit of their labor by using various volumes of the publication to demonstrate the consistency of Dewey's conceptions of philosophy and truth. So in our examination of his voluminous works, let us proceed by considering the words of John Dewey himself, as he alerts us to the problem of "specialization." He cites a problem that researchers may meet if studying in different areas of specialization besides their own, and he says,

> It is a matter of common notice that men who are expert thinkers in their own special fields adopt views on other matters without doing the inquiring they know to be necessary for substantiating simpler facts that fall within their own specialities.[4]

What Dewey seems to be saying is that even "expert thinkers" do not always have the time to do *all* the research that is required to defend *all* of their beliefs and claims. Therefore, instead of presuming that the reader is familiar with the many writings of Dewey's highly productive seventy-year publishing career, the procedure employed here is to point out some important factors that may be unknown about the man and his work.

Tracing the evolution of Dewey's thoughts about truth during his middle years would be much less complicated if he had focused his writings solely on the problems of religion, or metaphysics. But after receiving his doctorate from Johns Hopkins in 1884, and joining G. S. Morris in a teaching career at the University of Michigan, Dewey started to grow more and more dissatisfied with the pure speculation that his mentor's form of Hegelian idealism had proposed for solving the problems of religion. Consequently, we find that he had started to shift his attention away from religious problems by 1894, when he became professor of philosophy and chairman of the Department of Philosophy, Psychology, and Education, at the University of Chicago.

Apparently the latter appointment provided Dewey with an excellent opportunity to consolidate his diverse interests; for it was during this time that his concerns about education became the main focus of his writings, instead of his concerns about religion. Evidence of the shift in Dewey's thinking can be seen in one of his earliest and most important books on education, *The School and Society* (1899). Afterwards, Dewey published *The Child and the Curriculum* (1902). These writings show a shift taking place in his interests at that time.

One of his most vexatious critics, Bertrand Russell, seems to have recognized the importance that Dewey attached to education, and in his historical survey of Western philosophy reports that

> When Dewey became professor of philosophy at Chicago in 1894, pedagogy was included among his subjects. He founded a progressive school, and wrote much about education. What he wrote at this time was summed up in his book *The School and Society* (1899), which is considered the most influential of all his writings. He. . . continued to write on education throughout his life, almost as much as on philosophy.[5]

In light of Dewey's strong emphasis on education, our scrutiny of his middle years tries to shed some light on one of his chief concerns, as he puts it, "the importance that the practice and theory of education have had for me; especially the education of the young."[6] Why was Dewey so concerned about the "education of the young"?

He sheds some light on his concern for the practice and theory of education, and especially the education of the young, in his commitment to the famous Laboratory School. According to Dewey's description of it,

The school . . . was animated by a desire to discover in administration, selection of subject matter, methods of learning, teaching, and discipline, how a school could become a cooperative community while developing in individuals their own capacities and satisfy their own needs.[7]

While in Chicago, Dewey had helped found the school in 1896, and it was not terminated until 1903. It was initiated by his efforts to assemble a group of sympathetic colleagues working close together. A fruitful result of that endeavor is that their research findings were published in *Studies in Logical Theory* (1903).

During that period, though, his political, economic, and social views had become increasingly radical. His disenchantment with pure speculation, and his diligent attempt to make philosophy relevant to the practical affairs of human beings, apparently had caused trouble at the University of Chicago. Richard Berstein tells us that "Dewey left Chicago for Columbia in 1904 because of increasing friction with the university administration concerning the laboratory school."[8] Yet it was fortunate for Dewey that his appointment at Columbia—where he remained until he retired— gave him the opportunity to further express his radical views. While at Columbia, thanks to F. J. E. Woodbridge's founding of *The Journal of Philosophy,* a public forum was provided in which Dewey could discuss and defend his ideas.

Of course when Dewey moved to Columbia he already had earned a national reputation for his philosophical ideas and his educational theories. Thanks to Woodbridge's journalistic forum, though, the maturing Dewey finally had more freedom to express himself on pressing political and social issues. As a result, once those doors of opportunity were opened, Dewey gained international prominence.

Indeed, during his middle years, Dewey was heading toward the apex of his philosophic career. It was during this time that he published *Democracy and Education* (1916), one of his most powerful books, the book in which he claims his philosophy was "most fully expounded," as he puts it. Yet because of his emphasis upon the education of the young, so it seems, his major mark was *not* made in the field of philosophy itself. Instead, we find that Dewey's most impressive accomplishments have been noted in the field of American education. Of course Dewey recognized and explained the primary reason for this turn of events. Reflecting upon his contributions to both disciplines, he informs us that

I have never been able to feel much optimism regarding the possibilities of "higher" education when it is built upon warped and weak foundations. . . . [Furthermore] I can recall but one critic who has suggested that my thinking has been too permeated by interest in education. Although a book called *Democracy and Education* was for many years that in which my philosophy, such as it is, was most fully expounded, I do not know that philosophic critics, as distinct from teachers, have ever had recourse to it. I have wondered whether such facts signified that philosophers in general, although they are themselves usually teachers, have not taken education with seriousness . . . .[9]

Now judging from the preceding remarks, Dewey was undoubtedly well aware of the reason why some of his critics had misunderstood his views on the connection between philosophy and education. For as he points up, some of them criticized him without actually reading or scrutinizing his work. Consequently, they failed to see that on his view "philosophizing should focus about education as the supreme human interest in which, moreover, other problems, cosmological, moral, logical, come to a head."[10]

If Dewey's critics had understood *Democracy and Education*, perhaps they would have recognized that on his view "education is not a means to living, but is identical with the operation of living."[11] Moreover, they would have recognized that as Dewey saw things, education inevitably leads to philosophy. That is to say, as he puts it, "if we are willing to conceive education as the process of forming fundamental dispositions, intellectual and emotional, toward nature and fellow men, philosophy may even be defined as the general theory of education."[12] Yet it seems that some of his critics didn't see how the problems of education come to a head under the umbrella of philosophy.

In any event, as we examine the way Dewey's conceptions of philosophy and truth evolved during his middle years, we find that his instrumental method of experimentalism was continuing to have more and more of an impact, not only in America, but also in other countries. In 1919-21, for example, Dewey was invited to lecture in China and Japan. By that time, however, his international reputation had been increased already. That is, in 1915, he became a founder and first president of the American Association of University Professors. Moreover, his repute had been increased by his appointment at the Columbia Teachers College, which was a training center for teachers from various countries. Apparently this helped make possible the spread of his educational philosophy throughout the world.   Dewey's *Reconstruction in Philosophy* (1920), one of his most popular books, is one of the happy results of his invitations from other countries.   He based it on the lectures that he delivered at the Imperial University of Japan.   However, the radical ideas constituting his lectures in Tokyo, Peking, and Nanking, were elaborations of his 1917 article, "The Need for a Recovery of Philosophy."[13]

To clarify his ideas about the "recovery" and "reconstruction" of philosophy, let us pause here.  Let's investigate some of the shifts in his thinking about philosophy and truth during this period.

Perhaps one of the best ways to elucidate Dewey's ideas about philosophy and truth as he conceived them during his middle years, is for us to re-survey the trail marked by his writings.  Let us look back at the period of Dewey's graduate work at Johns Hopkins, the time when "thinking and writing" became "hard work," as he puts it, because of the "effects of philosophical teaching."[14]   By examining the early formulation of his ideas in written form, perhaps it will help clarify the gradual shifts in his thinking about these subjects.   A chronological examination of his work, for the most part, indicates his desire to recover and reconstruct philosophy through education.   In order to illustrate and sustain this position, let's try to make clear some of the difficulties that he encountered with his writing style.

On beginning our re-assessment, let's get clear on the historical context that led to his initial philosophic writings.  Horace M. Kallen, one of Dewey's colleagues, provides a succinct recapitulation of the historical context.  Judging from Kallen's description of the American environment in 1859, we can see that Dewey was born into a climate of intense democratic transformation.  Kallen informs us that

> A poetic fancy might make something of the coincidence that . . . the year of John Dewey's birth should be the year that Darwin's *Origin of Species* was given the world.  That year, it was half a century since Thomas Paine had been laid in his friendless grave, thirty-three years since Thomas Jefferson had been laid in his public one. . . .

> To the people of the United States an inexorable option was then coming to its term.  It had been in the making [no doubt] from the day that the Declaration of Independence affirmed that all men were created equal, . . . and that governments were but tools and devices instituted solely to secure these rights. [However] in actuality "all

men" meant only white males with a certain property. It did not denote black men, nor women, nor very poor men, nor men of dissent in religion.[15]

Now as we consider the environment that Dewey was born into, let us bear in mind that only six years after his birth, he experienced the start of wartime reconstruction, and consequently,

> Restoring the seceded states to the Union was the central issue in American politics from 1865 to 1869.  . . .  Behind the rhetoric of state's rights and federal supremacy the core elements in the reconstruction problem were the status and rights of the former Confederates, on the one hand, and the status and rights of the emancipated slaves, on the other.[16]

As we proceed with our re-survey, bear in mind that Dewey carried memories of this reconstruction problem with him when he entered the evangelical atmosphere at the University of Vermont and Johns Hopkins. Therefore, whatever appraisal that is made regarding his writings— whether early, middle, or later years—the milieu of this historical context should not be neglected or underestimated, if one wishes to clearly grasp the changes in his conception of philosophy, his notion of truth, and his view of education.

A scrutiny of John Dewey's writing style seems to disclose his technical treatment of diverse subject matters, and it also seems to help us understand the strategy of his creative style.  Apparently Dewey devised his technical strategy to separate the problematic subject matters in his writings.  As we've seen from his comments on the Laboratory School, he had started to stress the selection of subject matter even then.  Hence his emphasis upon the proper treatment of subject matter (as we noted in the preceding chapter), remained a major theme throughout his life-career.

A survey of his early psychological writings indicate that he was incorporating a new language into his discussion of philosophic problems, the language of James's *Principles of Psychology* (1890). For example, from the mature Dewey's reflections on his middle years, we can see how James's *Psychology* was employed to criticize, as he puts it, "the atomism of Locke and Hume as well as the *a-priorism* of the synthesis of rational principles by Kant and his successors, among whom should be mentioned in England, Thomas Hill Green, who was then at the height of his influence."[17]

Following the lead of James's criticism, what Dewey tried to do in "The Reflex Arc Concept in Psychology" (1896) was demonstrate the inadequacy of the reflex arc idea as a principle of behavioral unity with regard to sensory stimulus and motor responses. That is, Dewey wanted to use James's language to address the philosophic problem of dualisms. Instead of considering individual human beings as mere spectators, set apart from the environmental forces of daily living, Dewey tried to show why there are no splits, or breaks, between a person and his or her environment. When he explained where the reflex arc concept had gone wrong, Dewey argued that

> The older dualism between sensation and idea is repeated in the current dualism of peripheral and central structures and functions; the older dualism of body and soul finds a distinct echo in the current dualism of stimulus and response. Instead of interpreting the character of sensation, idea and action from their place and function in the sensorimotor circuit, we still incline to interpret the latter from our preconceived and preformulated ideas of rigid distinctions between sensations, thoughts and acts. . . . As a result, the reflex arch is not a comprehensive, or organic, unity, but a patchwork of disjointed parts. What is needed is that the principle underlying the idea of the reflex arch as the fundamental psychical unity shall react into and determine the values of its constitutive factors. More specifically, what is wanted is that sensory stimulus, central connections and motor responses shall be viewed, not as separate entities in themselves, but as divisions of labor, functioning factors, within the concrete whole, now designated the reflex arch.[18]

At the time that he raised the above criticism regarding the reflex arc concept, Dewey was trying to resolve the terminological problem posed by the external world. For instance, when reflecting back on his middle years, he tells us about his concern for philosophy during that stage of his growth, and clearly acknowledging James's influence on his thinking and writing about the problem, Dewey says,

> As my study and thinking progressed, I became more and more troubled by the intellectual scandal that seemed to me involved in the current (and traditional) dualism in logical standpoint and method between something called "science" on the one hand and something called "morals" on the other. I have long felt that the construction of a logic, that is, a method of effective inquiry, which would apply without abrupt breach of continuity to the fields designated by both

of these words, is at once our needed theoretical solvent and the supply of our greatest practical want.[19]

As Dewey continues the statement above, he additionally tells us that

This belief has had much more to do with the development of what I termed, for lack of a better word, 'instrumentalism,' than most of the reasons that have been assigned.[20]

As we can see, Dewey desired to unite the theoretical and practical aspects of philosophy. Moreover, he had hoped to accomplish this goal and resolve the problem of the external world by using the language of James's *Psychology* . Therefore, let it suffice here to point out that on Dewey's view, "this dualism should not be made . . . between an inner, subjective, mentalistic realm of ideas and an outer, objective realm of facts, with logic considered as a third thing intermediate between the two."[21] What we should also bear in mind, however, is that "the problem of overcoming the dualism which had developed between logic and science," as Eames has observed, "set a problem for Dewey on which he worked until the end of his life."[22]

With regard to Dewey's middle years, when he tries to find the basis for "unity of science, religion, poetry, and ethics," as Eames further points out,

[Dewey's] solution is to ground them in the continuity of an individual life; . . . There remains the difficulty, however, of how an individual human intelligence can relate the various activities of his life to one another; such a harmony requires not only a common source but a functioning interaction of the activities themselves. For instance, the relations of scientific endeavors and moral practices in a single individual life posed a problem on which Dewey worked for many years.[23]

As we can see from Eames' interpretation, Dewey must have really encountered great difficulty trying to illustrate "the continuity of an individual life." So, it is in light of this difficulty that the present writer suggests looking at the middle years of Dewey's life-work on the analogy of an "arch," or bridge, between his early and later years.

Perhaps the significance of proceeding in this manner shall become even clearer if we briefly consider Richard J. Bernstein's criticism of Dewey. With regard to Dewey's self-realization theory, Bernstein claims that "the weakest part of Dewey's entire philosophy is his analysis of the self—the focal point of the existentialist and phenomenological movement."[24] What is more important, though, Bernstein also says,

> Dewey was a half-hearted metaphysician. . . . The consequences of this uncertainty are serious for Dewey's entire philosophy. Many of his most basic categories are left in 'limbo.' Such key concepts as quality and continuity, which play such a fundamental role throughout his philosophy, suffer from ambiguity and lack of clarity.[25]

With regard to the criticism Bernstein advances, it is hoped that the reader sees the need to elucidate Dewey's theory of self-realization, continuity, and quality. But there is no intention here to try to defend his theory of self-realization against Bernstein's criticism.

However, it should be understood that Dewey readily admits on several occasions that he does not pretend to provide a finished account of his personal development, or let us say his "theory of self-realization." For example, one of those occasions occurred when Dewey was around seventy-one years old. In 1930, as he looked back over his life and tried to explain from whence he had come, Dewey candidly tells us that

> The story of my intellectual development I am unable to record without more faking than I care to indulgence in. . . . The philosopher, if I may apply that word to myself, that I have become as I moved away from German idealism, is too much the self that I still am and is still too much in process of change to lend itself to record. . . . I cannot write an account of intellectual development without giving it a semblance of a continuity that it does not in fact own . . . .[26]

Dewey already had reached full maturity, of course, when he made the above statement; and he saw himself as a dynamically changing individual, not a mere static being, or person. Why did John Dewey never provide a completely elaborated theory of self-realization, or a full account of his own personal development?

With respect to Dewey's theory of self-realization, and his concept of continuity, let us keep in mind a very important point concerning his beliefs about "personality," or personal development. That is, as we noted in "Science and the Idea of God" (1886), when Dewey refers to the "ways of Man" and the "ways of God," he explicitly states his conviction that "*all* personality is infinite." Let us suppose, then, that Dewey retained this belief in his middle years; if this is so, it seems safe to say that some of his critics have failed to recognize his practical approach to the problem of personality.

For example, consider Bernstein's criticism. Although he seems to be right about the weakness of Dewey's self-realization theory, his conclusion that "Dewey was a half-hearted metaphysician" appears to be mistaken. As an attempt to clarify this, let's raise a few questions: Is Bernstein interpreting the sensorimotor circuit from "preconceived and preformulated ideas of rigid distinctions between sensations, thoughts and acts"? Why does he hold that such key concepts as quality and continuity, which play a fundamental role throughout Dewey's philosophy, "suffer from ambiguity and lack of clarity"? Could it be that Dewey's use of some key concepts is not clear to Bernstein because he does not see how Dewey's self-realization theory is sustained by his notion of "infinite personality"? The latter questions, of course, are not intended to cast aspersion on Bernstein's scholarship; for as Fred Dallmayr clearly points out regarding the "resurgence of pragmatist (or neo-pragmatist) discourse,"

> Among American philosophers today, no one has kept his finger more attentively and probingly on the pulse of these developments than Richard Bernstein. . . . More importantly, his writings provide a kind of logbook of the contemporary shift from epistemology to pragmatics, a shift inaugurating a potential rejuvenation of social and political thought.[27]

Now considering Bernstein's prominence as an American philosopher, perhaps it is unwise to criticize or question his views on Dewey. Yet it seems only fair for us to ask ourselves: Is it possibly the case that Bernstein has misunderstood how John Dewey's "basic categories" are employed, and this is why they seem to be "left in 'limbo,'" to him? From the present writer's perspective, the answer to this latter question is: Maybe so!

Although there will be no attempt here to criticize Berstein's criticism of Dewey's theory of personality, this study does try to show that Dewey was *not* a "half-hearted metaphysician." Dewey's article "The Subject-Matter of Metaphysical Inquiry" (1915) seems to free him from the charge of being a "half-hearted metaphysician." When Dewey concludes that article, for instance, he plainly tells us,

> I am not concerned to develop a metaphysics; but simply to indicate
> one way of conceiving the problem of metaphysical inquiry as distinct
> from that of the special sciences, a way which settles upon the more
> ultimate traits of the world as defining its subject-matter, but which
> frees these traits from confusion with ultimate origins and ultimate
> ends—that is, from questions of creation and eschatology.[28]

So following Dewey's lead, our task is not to defend his metaphysics,
but to help clarify his conceptions of philosophy and truth. In this
respect, as the statement above seems to make clear, during Dewey's
middle years he was still deeply concerned about the dogmatism of the
"evangelical atmosphere." Therefore, let it suffice here to note that
he was trying to get beyond one truism, which is: "theology used to
have the idea of ultimate origin in connection with creation, and that at
a certain juncture it was natural to regard the theory of evolution as a
substitute or rival of the theological idea of creation."[29]

With regard to Dewey's endeavors to get beyond this truism, let
us suppose that Bernstein wishes to raise objections against his efforts
to direct metaphysical inquiry (or philosophical inquiry) away from
the "theological idea of creation." More than likely, so it seems, if
Bernstein did raise objections, then Dewey undoubtedly would hold
that criticism of Bernstein is justifiable. For as we have seen already,
Dewey held that constructive criticism can be fruitful in philosophy, as
"Poetry and Philosophy" (1890) bears witness.

Let us remember that when Dewey explains the difference between
the role of the poets (who primarily express emotion) and the
philosophers (who mainly seek scientific verification), he says, "We
must, in the cold, reflective way of critical system, justify and organize
the truth which poetry, with its quick, naive contacts, has already felt
and reported."[30] What is more important, though, we can see that he
displayed this predilection toward criticism by the end of his early
years, and at the beginning of his middle years. So, it seems that his
open-minded notion of criticism tends to shed some light on his treatment
of metaphysical issues.

For instance, a scrutiny of the trail marked by Dewey's writings
clearly indicate that the technical strategy of his style required that he
employ criticism *in his own* literary art to help clarify the subject matter
of metaphysics, and the other branches of philosophy as well. Perhaps
one of the most important influences on Dewey's artistic use of literary
criticism, apart from Plato, was Ralph Waldo Emmerson. An article
bearing the title "Ralph Waldo Emerson" (1903) provides plently

evidence of his impact on Dewey's thinking.  In this writing he vehemently launched his criticism against those who dare say: "Emerson is not a philosopher."[31]   Moreover, it is also interesting to note that Emerson might have influenced the literary criticism that Dewey employed in "The Reflex Arc Concept in Psychology" (1896). Seemingly, in this article, Dewey's reference to the "principle underlying the idea of the reflex arc as the fundamental psychical unity" may be an echo of Emerson's "The American Scholar" (1837).

Remember, now, Dewey says "the fundamental psychical unity shall react into and determine the values of its constitutive factors." This statement seems to be clearly in line with Emerson's discussion of the American Scholar, where he reminds us of the old fable that

> There is One Man, —present to all particular men only partially, or through one faculty; and that you must take the whole society to find the whole man.  Man is not a farmer, or a professor, or an engineer, but he is all.  . . .  The fable implies that the individual, to posess himself, must sometimes return from his own labor to embrace all the other laborers.[32]

Now doesn't it seem highly plausible that Emerson's formulation is what Dewey had in mind, and the reason why the latter believed that "sensory stimulus, central connections and motor responses [should] be viewed, not as separate entities in themselves, but as divisions of labor, functioning factors, within the concrete whole"?  Isn't it plausible that Dewey reformulated the prose of Emerson into the language of philosophy?  The present writer sure thinks so; and furthermore, Lewis Feur informs us that "Dewey always remained in the New England tradition of Ralph Waldo Emerson, the preacher turned lecturer, who, feeling the call to educate the citizenry in democratic virtues, journeyed the far length of the land to do so."[33]

In any case, regardless to whether Dewey's critics pay close attention to Emerson's influences on his treatment of metaphysics, we can rest assured that Dewey did mostly take his lead from the language employed James.  Consequently, it seems that Dewey's new discourse was intended to provide a conception of philosophy that includes not just a critical component, but a transformational  thrust as well.  In other words, what we find is that Dewey was attempting to construct a philosophy that would reflect and respond to its cultural context, to the processes of change taking place all around it.  Dewey sought to develop a conception of philosophy that would enable philosophers to participate in a shared conversation.

By using his new language, no doubt, Dewey was convinced that philosophers would be able to share in a discussion that could help determine a course of action to better the human condition. Some of the amenities of his new language can be seen in two of his 1910 publications, *How We Think* and *The Influence of Darwin and Other Essays on Contemporary Thought.* Both books indicate Dewey's pragmatic turn. The language that constitutes these writings shifts our attention towards the genetic traits of human existence.

With regard to Darwin's *On the Origin of Species,* for example, Dewey tries to clarify the controversial issues that the book creates. In an attempt to clarify his position, we find him saying,

> The vivid and popular features of the anti-Darwinian row tended to leave the impression that the issue was between science on the one hand and theology on the other. Such was not the case—the issue lay primarily within science itself, as Darwin himself early recognized.[34]

Apparently, though, some of Dewey's contemporaries had not yet understood this simple point. So regarding the ideas of those who opposed Darwinism, Dewey informs his readers that "their origin and meaning are to be sought in science and philosophy, not in religion."[35]

The latter statement seems indicative of the direction that Dewey's thinking and writing was headed; for it clearly expresses his desire for a genre of discourse that would be free of religious dogma. His article "The Experimental Theory of Knowledge" (1906), no doubt, was a result of his desire; and his main theme seems to correspond with James' "radical empiricism." Dewey sketches his metaphysics of experience in this paper and he emphasizes the meaning of relations in the knowing process; he stresses the "intending" character of knowing, and the relational character of truth.

For example, consider the term "species." Its meaning and relation to science also needs explaining, he thinks; and without inculcating religious dogma. Thus, he claimed that his method could help procure a sufficient explanation; but before we can effectively define terms such as "species," he thought that we must first make clear the meaning of "science" itself. Therefore, he maintains that his pragmatic language can help elucidate scientific terminology.

Dewey tells us that, "The experimental or pragmatic theory of knowledge explains the dominating importance of science; it does not depreciate it or explain it away."[36] One of the clearest expressions of his position, perhaps, is made in the following statement.

> What the pragmatic theory has in mind is precisely the fact that all
> the affairs of life which need regulation—*all values of all types* —
> depend upon utilizations of meanings.[37]

There seems to be at least one pertinent implication of his position.
His method requires "knowers" who *must* be able to recognize terms,
and define their utilizations of meanings.  As for scientific progress,
then, we can see that the conative and denotative truth of the terms
employed *must* depend on their relations to the "users," who *must*
have "values."

So it appears that he thought science could be advanced by utilizing
his method because its "users" would reflect the quality that defines
the purpose of their thought.  In other words, their discourses would
disclose the way they think.  Those individuals, to be sure, could not
go outside of their own experiences to find truth, or meanings.  As
Dewey reminds us, "truth is an experienced relation of things, and it
has no meaning outside of such relations."[38] Thus, truth is not a property
of any thing, in and of itself; instead, truth is the property of "things
where the problem of assurance conciously enters in."[39]

Hence Dewey's method of experimentalism, or instrumentalism,
was designed to give "truth" a scientific meaning; it was to be based on
the public features of human communication, and not the private ideas
of human beings.  That is why his discourse became more and more
scientific after his pragmatic turn.  Dewey came to see "truth" as simply
a generic term; he viewed it as a species, a member of the Word family.[40]

By classifying "truth" under the genus Word, he felt that we could
make more rigid denotations in scientific terminology.  Dewey states
his nominal conception of truth in the following way.

> That truth denotes *truths* , that is, specific verifications, combinations
> of meanings and outcomes reflectively viewed, is, one may say, the
> central point of the experimental theory.  Truth, in general or in
> abstract, is a just name for an experienced relation among the things
> of experience.[41]

So we can see that Dewey does indeed espouse a form of nominalism.
Moreover, it is apparent that this is why he emphasizes his genetic
method of reference as a way to make some fruitful scientific progress.
By following his method of experimentalism, Dewey thought that we
could make some great strides in science.  During his middle years, he
had come to believe that "the experimentalist, rather than the absolutist,
is he who has the right to proclaim the supremacy of Truth, and the

superiority of life devoted to Truth for its own sake over that of 'mere' activity."[42]

Although Dewey had drifted away from Absolutism at this point, and repudiated the absolutists, we should bear in mind that he never completely left Hegel. Remember, Sleeper reminds us that "Hegel's refusal to draw a hard and fast line between 'theory' and 'fact' was the one feature of Hegelian logic that Dewey wanted to save."[43] Yet it seems that some of Dewey's commentators and critics have failed to see the direction his genetic method of reference was taking him.

Nevertheless, an examination of the trailed marked by his writings clearly show that Dewey was trying to explain his genetic method of referring in *How We Think*. This book exhibits his earnest desire to get his readers to consider "words" in their generic sense of meaning. Dewey explicitly tells us that

> This book represents the conviction that the needed steadying and centralizing factor is found in adopting as the end of endeavor that attitude of mind, that habit of thought, which we call scientific.[44]

In other words, John Dewey was convinced that unless a peron posessed the "attitude of mind" or "habit of thought" reflected by scientists, one can hardly comprehend the generic sense of how words mean. Therefore, his aim in this particular work is to provide the "needed steadying and centralizing factor" which is requisite for thinking about words in a scientific manner.

Bear in mind, however, at this stage of Dewey's growth, he had "never been able to feel much optimism regarding the possibilities of 'higher' education." And apparently that is why *How We Think* is mainly concerned with the teaching of children; for Dewey believed that their training is essential for the future of scientific progress. No doubt he recognized that they tend to be naturally inclined to think scientifically. That is apparently why Dewey informs us that the kind of "scientific attitude of mind" that he advocates is manifested in "the native and unspoiled attitude of childhood, marked by ardent curiosity, fertile imagination, and love of experimental inquiry."[45] Moreover, he plainly tells us that

> If these pages assist any to appreciate this kinship and consider seriously how its recognition in educational practice would make for individual happiness and the reduction of social waste, the book will amply have served its purpose.[46]

With this latter statement in mind, let us begin to bring Chapter 5 to a close. Thus far our study has tried to show how John Dewey began moving in the direction of "educational practice," and focusing more and more on his philosophy of education. We have noted that he received national and international recognition because of his great success in the educational field. Moreover, we have seen that recovering and reconstructing philosophy took top priority in his educational endeavors. In other words, Dewey felt that too little progress was being made in philosophy because of the failure to move beyond "metaphysical disputes," to use James's terminology. (Disputes that might be interminable without the pragmatic method).

As Dewey explained in *Reconstruction in Philosophy* (1920), he wanted to go beyond the theory of "fixed ends," which inevitably "leads thought into the bog of disputes that cannot be settled."[47] Undoubtely this is why he tried to direct philosophers who concern themselves with metaphysical inquiry to turn away from the theological idea of creation. Rather than focusing on the usual questions of metaphysics, Dewey wished to focus moreso on the social order of his surrounding environment, which had resulted from New England's evangelical atmosphere. However, even though he desired to do so, it should be understood that Dewey was not rejecting the idea of God as creator.

*Essays in Experimental Logic* (1916) seems to clearly show that during his middle years, he retained his earlier ideas about God as a subject matter of philosophy. That is, instead of omitting references to God during this period, we find him saying,

> God only knows how many of the sufferings of life are due to a belief that the natural scene and operations of our life are lacking in ideal import, and to the consequent tendency to flee for the lacking ideal factors to some other world inhabited exclusively by ideals. That such a cut-off, ideal world is impotent for direction and control and change of the natural world follows as a matter of course.[48]

Moreover, says Dewey,

> If philosophers could aid in making it clear to a troubled humanity that ideals are continous with natural events, that they but represent their possibilities, and that recognized possibilities form methods for a conduct which may realize them in fact, philosophers would enforce the sense of a social calling and responsibility.[49]

Not only does Dewey indicate his beliefs about God in the *Essays*, but he even tries to elucidate the question of God's existence. For instance, in Essay XII, entitled "What Pragmatism Means By Practical," he provides an excellent exegesis of James's approach to the problems of philosophy. From his elucidation of the standpoint held by James, we get a clue to the manner in which Dewey wished to direct the attention of philosophers away from the theological idea of creation. That is to say, in explicating James' s position, Dewey infoms us that

> The briefest and at the same time the most comprehensive formula for the method is: "The attitude of looking away from first things, principles, 'categories,' supposed necessities; and of looking towards last things, fruits, consequences, facts."[50]

Furthermore, with respect to James's notion of truth, we are informed that in the wider sense of pragmatism's meaning, James's theory is "a genetic theory of what is meant by truth." Truth for pragmatists is "a matter of course, agreement, correspondence, of idea and fact."[51] Thus, it was James's "genetic theory" of what truth means that led to Dewey's emergence into the problem of his genetic method of reference.[52] However, perhaps we can see where Dewey's method of experimentalism, or Instrumentalism tends to diverge from James's pragmatism if we consider the former's critique of the latter's treatment of metapysical questions that pertain to God.

With respect to the philosophical argument from design, for example, we find that Dewey was critical of James's starting point because he began by "accepting a ready-made notion, to which he then applie[d] the criterion."[53] Somewhat unfortunately for James's position, as Dewey points out, when James discussed "spiritualistic theism *versus* materialism," the propositions that he employed to support his genetic theory of what truth means had failed to clarify the meaning or conception of God; because his method proceeded from "a prior definition of God."[54] As a result, says Dewey, James's propositions "cannot prove, or render more probable, the existence of such a being." Yet on the other hand, "if the pragmatic method is not applied simply to tell the value of a belief or a controversy, but to fix the meaning of the terms involved in the belief, resulting consequences would serve to constitute the entire meaning."[55] Therefore, embracing this latter aspect of James's pragmatic method, Dewey formulated his Instrumentalism to "abolish the meaning of an antecedent power which will perpetuate eternally some existence. For that consequence flows not from the belief or idea, but from the existence, the power. It is not pragmatic at all."[56]  So in hope of avoiding confusion regarding any such form of "antecedent power," Dewey advocated his method of experimentalism, and abandoned James's starting point of a fixed meaning or conception of God.

Of course one unfortunate consequence for his readers and his critics, so it seems, is that his writings do not always clearly exhibit his own personal conceptions of God, philosophy, and truth.  However, it may be rather fortunate for us that Kuklick's research sheds some light on this problem.  For example, in *Churchmen and Philosophers* (as we noted at the end of Chapter 4), after Kuklick had examined the period of Dewey's early years, he tells us, "It is not clear that Dewey by the 1890s still intended to provide a respectable basis for the theology of immanence."[57]  In his effort to clear up Dewey's position, and to make amends for an "uninformed statement" made about John Dewey in an earlier study, says Kuklick, he furnishes an additional interpretation of Dewey that is "more adequate."[58]  Accordingly, as he explains his new way of interpreting Dewey's position, Kuklick says,

> Although religious liberalism contributed to the intellectual traditions studied in this book, the ideas of liberals have been placed within the Trinitarian dialogue.  In this way, I outline the framework from which Dewey emerged.  In the 1880s and 1890s, he was drawn to the issues of Congregational philosophy of religion.  Yet the accepted view of Dewey as an experimental secularist ignores his interest in these issues.  His great achievement was incorporating what were recognized at the time as religious values into a scientific conception of man and nature.[59]

Moreover, concerning Dewey's religious affiliation with the Andover liberals, Kuklick also tells us that

> Three themes of the new theology structured Dewey's thought throughout his life.  Like Andover, Dewey heralded science as the method of philosophy.  With the new theologians he also controverted the dichotomies between God and man and between the natural and the supernatural.  For him God was incorporated in humanity, and spirit in nature.  An emphasis on science and a concern to deny these two distinctions essentially characterized Dewey's thought through the eighties and early nineties.  He wanted a more genuine philosophy of immanence, and, . . . a speculative spine for Progressive Orthodoxy.[60]

Now apparently the key to understanding Kuklick's report turns on his assertion that throughout the eighties and early nineties Dewey wanted a more genuine "philosophy of immanence."

Why does Kuklick assert that Dewey wanted a more genuine philosophy of immanence during the eighties and early nineties, then on the other hand allege that by the 1890s it is not clear that Dewey intended to provide a respectable basis for a "theology of immanence"? As an adequate answer to this question, it seems safe to conclude that Dewey advocated a philosophy of immanence instead of theology of immanence in hope of directing philosophers away from the theological idea of creation. In other words, Dewey wanted to go forward with a broader form of philosophical inquiry —in James's "wider sense" of what truth means—unhampered by interminable disputes about metaphysics.

In summarizing Chapter 5, it is hoped that this survey of Dewey's middle years has shown that a shift took place in his anxiety about problems of religion. It seems evident that he had been quite disturbed by a lack of consensus regarding metaphysical issues. Yet as we also have seen, during his middle years he was no longer as adamant about religious concerns as he had been during his early years. Consequently, Dewey's treatment of such subjects as matters of philosophic discussion had shifted; and this was mostly because of James's influence on him.

With respect to James's influences, however, it is important to remember how "misleading" it can be to lump Dewey in all together with the pragmatists as a single school. For as we have seen, in some ways Dewey's instrumental method departs from them. Stephen Toulmin's interpretation seems to sustain this point when he suggests that Dewey's readers may increase their understanding of his methods, arguments, and purposes, if they compare his work with that of his younger contemporaries, Ludwig Wittgenstein and Martin Heidegger.[61]

As the present writer has suggested, however, he thinks that one of the best ways to understand the shifts in Dewey's thinking about philosophy and truth during his middle years is to see him working in the tradition of Emerson; for as Feur has reminded us, "Dewey always remained in the New England tradition of Ralph Waldo Emerson, the preacher turned lecturer." Of course as we have seen, not only did Dewey, like Emerson, feel the call to educate America's citizery in democratic virtues, but he even felt the call to leave the western hemisphere and carrry his message as far east as China and Japan. To be sure, John Dewey, like Emerson, was very deeply concerned about education; and in Dewey's case, especially the education of the young. Hence, it seems undeniable that Emerson greatly influenced Dewey's view of education. For indeed, Dewey regarded him as not merely an educator and philosopher, because "he is more than a philosopher. He would work, he says, by art, not by metaphysics, finding truth 'in the sonnet and the play."[62]

As we conclude our summary and prepare to examine Dewey's later years, perhaps one of the best ways to picture him emerging from his middle years is to see him fulfilling the role of a virtuous "thinker," as depicted by Emerson. Consider, for instance, how Dewey takes care to reiterate Emerson's admonition, which says,

> Beware when the great God lets loose a thinker on this planet. Then all things are at risk. The very hopes of man, the thoughts of his heart, the religion of nations, the manner and morals of mankind are all at the mercy of a new  generalization.[63]

How well does Emerson's admonishment depict the virtue of Dewey as a "great thinker"? From the present writer's perspective, the answer is: Quite well!

For present purposes, moreover, this  view of Dewey seems to shed some light on Eames's queries about Dewey's attempt to ground the "unity of science, religion, poetry, and ethics" in "the continuity of an individual life." As we noted earlier, Eames was puzzled by the difficulty of how an individual human intelligence can relate the various activities of his or her life to one another; because such a harmony requires not only a common source but a functioning interaction of the activities themselves. Now judging from Dewey's praise of Emerson, so it seems, we may safely answer Eames's query in just a few words. That is to say, the "common source" which harmoniously grounded Dewey's intelligence was, no doubt, the "great God" that Emerson refers to.

However, in order to get a better grasp of the way Dewey related the various activites to his own personality development, it is suggested in closing that the reader consider G. H. Mead's influences on Dewey's middle years. For example, we are informed by Sidney Ratner that "Mead ranks with William James as a major influence in Dewey's transition from Hegelianism to experimental naturalism."[64] So apparently, then, Mead must have had a major impact on Dewey's personality development as well as his conceptions of philsosophy and truth.  At any rate, no doubt, Dewey obviously labored in the field of education with the same kind of vigor that he attributes to Mead.  For rather similar to Russell's observations regarding Dewey's passion for education, Ratner also tells us that "The philosophy of education was for Dewey a lifetime concern."[65]  Let us therefore bear this  in mind while we are examining his later years.

In our examination of his conceptions of philosopy and truth in Chapter 6 we shall find that Dewey was moving more and more towards a common sense notion of what philosophy and truth means, or should mean.  For instance, we observed in Chapter 4 that during his early years Dewey made a very important common sense distinction between philosophy and science; he explained that the former deals with "love," whereas the latter does not, and cannot.  Now as we get ready to survey his later years, let us consider this feature in conjunction with another important distinction that he notes about education during his middle years.  That is to say, in *How We Think* (1910) Dewey explains why the study of information does not necessarily develop "wisdom," which is what philosophers should love.  As he puts it,

> The distinction between information and wisdom is old, and yet requires constantly to be redrawn.  Information is knowledge that is merely acquired and stored up; wisdom is knowledge operating in the direction of powers to the better living of life.[66]

This notable distinction, as we shall see, guides the thinking of John Dewey throughout his mature years.  He loved learning and he loved helping others learn.  Yet he believed that far too many individuals fail to recognize the "value" of learning and thinking wisely.

No doubt he realized that thinking wisely is important because "it emancipates us from merely impulsive and merely routine activity."  Stated in his more positive terms,

> Thinking enables us to direct our activities with foresight and to plan according to ends-in-view, or purposes of which we are aware.  It enables us to act in deliberate and intentional fashion to attain future objects or to come into command of what is now distant and lacking.  By putting the consequences of different ways and lines of action before the mind, it enables us to *know what we are about* when we act.  *It converts action  that is merely appetitive, blind, and impulsive into intelligent action.*[67]

In considering this description of what thinking enables us to do, the reader should notice that Dewey's view is clearly in line with Peirce's notion of "abstract observation," which was pointed up in Chapter 4. Anyway, with regard to Dewey's notion of logic during his middle years, it should be understood that he retained the same view advocated in his early years. For example, in his *Essays* (1916) he makes the following assertion.

> The abstract logician may tell us that sensations or impressions, or associated ideas, or bare physical things, or conventional symbols, are antecedent conditions [of thought]. But such statements cannot be verified by reference to a single instance of thought in connection with actual practice or actual scientific research.[68]

Of course the reader should not get the impression that Dewey denies the value of logic for judicious thinking; rather, he simply believed that

> General logic cannot become an instrument in the immediate direction of the activities of science or art or industry; but it is of value in criticizing and organizing tools of immediate research. It also has direct significance in the valuation or life-purposes . . . . [And] value of reasearch for social progress . . . the adjustment of religious aspirations to scientific statements; the justification of a refined culture for a few in face of economic insufficiency for the mass . . . . —such are a few of the many social questions whose answer depends upon the possession and use of a general logic of experience as a method of inquiry and interpretation.[69]

So as we can see, Dewey definitely attributes a great deal of value to logic. But does his notion of logic change during his later years? As we turn to Chapter 6 and ponder the latter question, let's consider the evolution of Dewey's conceptions of philosophy and truth with the kind of "open-minded" approach that he would doubtless desire.

Thus far in this chapter we have attempted to point up some factors about Dewey and his work that might have been unknown to some of his readers, and in keeping with this procedure, let us note here that Dewey entered his later years emphasizing the need to get more men to "think" open-mindedly. "Open-mindedness," as he conceived of it, "may be defined as freedom from prejudice, partianship, and such other habits as close the mind and make it unwilling to consider new problems and entertain new ideas."[70] Moreover, says Dewey, "It includes an active desire to listen to more sides than one; and to give full attention to alternative possibilities; to recognize the possibility of error even in the beliefs that are dearest to us."[71]  Unfortunately, a major problem for some men is that, as Dewey puts it, "Self-conceit often regards it as a sign of weakness to admit that a belief to which we have once committed ourselves is wrong."[72]  Therefore, in light of Dewey's conception of an open-minded philosophical approach, it is suggested that we take heed to his message, and read his work as he would undoubtedly want us to do.  Like him, we should face the fact that "No one can think about everything, to be sure; [but] no one can think about anything without experience and information about it."[73] Chapter 5, it is hoped, has shown that John Dewey shared the information of his learning experience through the medium of education, and specially in his philosophic lectures and literature.  Is the wisdom of John Dewey to be found in his method of applying knowledge to public as well as personal problems?[74]  Let us turn to Chapter 6 and ponder his wisdom.  Let's look further and see why his unique conception of philosophy is a "perspective that brings coherence to the whole, an *elenchus* that distinguishes it most sharply from the systems of his predecessors from Plato to Peirce," as Sleeper has reminded us.  What is more important, let us be mindful of the consistent and persistent guiding thread that runs throughout his entire philosophic career; that is, the way he employs the term "God."

# Notes

1. McDermott, *The Philosohy of John Dewey,* p. xxxv.
2. Jo Ann Boydston, "Forward," in *Later Works,* Vol. 17, pp. xi, xii.
3. Jo Ann Boydston, "Forward," in *Later Works,* Vol. 17, p. xv.
4. Dewey, *How We Think* (1910). Reprinted in *Later Works,* Vol. 8, p. 135.
5. Bertrand Russell, "Dewey's New Logic," in *The Basic Writings of Bertrand Russell,* R. E. Egner and L. E. Denonn, eds. (New York: Simon and Schuster, 1961). p. 207.
6. Dewey, "From Absolutism to Experimentalism" (1930), reprinted in *Later Works,* Vol. 5, p. 156.
7. Dewey, "The Dewey School: Introduction," in *Later Works,* Vol. 11, p. 192.
8. See Richard Bernstein's summary of John Dewey's life-work in *The Encyclopedia of Philosophy,* (New York: The MacMillan Company & The Free Press, 1967). Vol. 2, p. 380.
9. Dewey, "From Absolutism to Experimentalism" (1930), reprinted in *Later Works,* Vol. 5, p. 156.
10. *Ibid.*
11. Dewey, *Democracy and Education* (New York: MacMillan Co., 1916). p. 281.
12. Dewey, *Democracy and Education* (New York: MacMillan Co., 1916). p. 383.
13. First published in *Creative Intelligence, Essays in the Pragmatic Attitude* (New York: Henry Holt and Co., pp. 3-69. The Essays that constitute the book represent an attempt at intellectual cooperation. Though there is no unanimity of belief among the authors, there is a basic consensus in their outlook and conviction of what would most likely be a fruitful method of approach in philosophy. The contributing authors are: B. H. Bode, H. C. Brown, John Dewey, H. M. Kallen, G. H. Meade, A. D. Moore, H. W. Stuart, and J. H. Tufts.
14. Dewey, "From Absolutism to Experimentalism," reprinted in *Later Works,* Vol. 5, pp. 150-51.
15. Horace M. Kallen, "Freedom and Education" (1940), in *The Philosopher of the Common Man: Essays in Honor of John Dewey* (New York: Greenwood Publishers, 1968). p. 20.
16. Herman Beltz, Winfred A. Harbison, Alfred H. Kelly, *The American Constitution* (New York: W. W. Norton & Company, Inc., 1983). p. 328.
17. Dewey, "The Development of American Pragmatism" (1925), reprinted in *Later Works,* Vol. 2, p. 15.
18. Dewey, "The Reflex Arc Concept in Psychology" (1896), reprinted in McDermott's *The Philosophy of John Dewey,* p. 137.

19. Dewey, "From Absolutism to Experimentalism" (1930), reprinted in *Later Works*, Vol. 5, p. 156.

20. Dewey, "From Absolutism to Experimentalism" (1930), reprinted in in *Later Works,* Vol. 5, pp. 156-57. As for the development of "instrumentalism" during Dewey's later years, perhaps it should be mentioned here that Dewey says of James' influence: "I take it for granted that the *Principles of Psychology* is the greatest among the great works of James. . . . the *Principles* contain an exposition of the nature of experience which renders both sensationalistic empiricism and rationalistic criticisms of empiricism wholly out of date. The work of James replaces a dialectic analysis of experience with one based upon scientific knowledge that is now available, but was not formerly accessible. . . . James has provided those who would use empirical and experimental method with a new equipment of intellectual weapons and instrumentalities. See Dewey's "William James as Empiricist" (1942), reprinted in *Later Works,* Vol. 15, p. 11. About sixteen years earlier, in "The Development of American Pragmatism" (1925), Dewey had acknowledged that "the instrumentalists recognized how much they owed to William James for having forged the instruments which they used . . . . But it is curious to note that the 'instruments' to which allusion is made, are not the considerations which were of the greatest service to James. They precede his pragmatism and it is among some of the pages of his *Principles of Psychology* that one must look for them" (see *Later Works,* Vol. 2, p. 15). Also, perhaps we should mention here that, "The term 'instrumentalism' is ambiguous," on Morris Eames' view, "and toward the end of Dewey's career he abandoned its use." For Eames' observation, see "Introduction" to *Early Works*, Vol. 3, p. x.

21. Morris Eames, "Introduction," *Early Works*, Vol. 3, p. xii.

22. *Ibid.*, p. xi

23. Morris Eames, "Introduction," *Early Works,* Vol. 3, p. xvii.

24. Richard J. Bernstein, *John Dewey* (New York: Washington Square Press, Inc., 1966). p. 176.

25. *Ibid.*, p. 179.

26. Dewey, "From Absolutism to Experimentalism" (1930), reprinted in *Later Works,* Vol. 5, p. 155. McDermott's research efforts may help the reader see why it is so difficult to trace Dewey's intellectual development; for McDermott says: "Aside from Dewey's brief autobiographical piece, 'From Absolutism to Experimentalism,' published in 1930, and some isolated reminences of colleagues and friends, Jane Dewey, who edited a brief biography written by herself and her two sisters, Evelyn and Lucy, from material provided by their father. Virtually all of the biographical material written by subsequent commentators thus far is a reduction of portions of this material." See McDermott's *The Philosophy of John Dewey*, (p. xv).

27. Fred R. Dallmayr, *Critical Encounters: Between Philosophy and Politics* (Indiana: University of Notre Dame Press, 1987). p. 165.

28. Dewey, "The Subject-Matter of Metaphysical Inquiry," in *The Journal of Philosophy , Psychology, and Scientific Methods,* Vol. xii, no. 13, June 24, 1915. p. 345. For a more elaborate discussion of Dewey's metaphysical argument, see Paul Welsh's critique, "Some Metaphysical Assumptions in Dewey's Philosophy," in *The Journal of Philosophy,* Vol. li, no. 26, December 23, 1954. In the same Journal, also see Elizabeth R. Eames' article, "Quality and Relation as Metaphysical Assumptions in The Philosophy of John Dewey" (pp. 166-69); her keen analysis tends to defend Dewey against Welsh's criticism.

29. Dewey, "The Subject-Matter of Metaphysical Inquiry," in *The Journal of Philosophy , Psychology, and Scientific Methods,* Vol. xii, no. 13, June 24, 1915. p. 339.

30. Dewey, "Poetry and Philosophy" (1890), in *Early Works,* Vol. 3, p. 123. With regard to Dewey's attitude towards criticism, perhaps it will be helpful here to note that directly in line with this train of thought that extends from his early years to his middle years, we find Dewey displaying the same persistent and consistent attitude towards criticism during his later years. As we shall see in the next chapter, his *Experience and Nature* (1925) provides us with some very important insight concerning the way we should interpret his view of criticism, especially in light of those who may criticize his theory of personality. For example, in briefly considering what the mature Dewey concluded about the relation of philosophic criticism to metaphysics, we find him explaining that: "Metaphysics, as a statement of the generic traits manifested by existences of all kinds without regard to their differentiation into physical and mental, seems to have nothing to do with criticism and choice, with an effective love of wisdom" (p. 412). In other words, then, the wise metaphysician, on Dewey's view, "begins and ends with analysis and definition." By using this approach, as he sees it, criticism may either result from a person's wisdom, or lead someone to wisdom.

31. Dewey, "Ralph Waldo Emmerson" (1903), reprinted in McDermott's *The Philosophy of John Dewey,* p. 24. With respect to this particular writing of Dewey's, we are informed by McDermott that "the readers of the later John Dewey will be struck by the anticipation here of Deweyan themes: the affection for the ordinary, a logic of inquiry, and the close relationship of philosophy and poetry."

32. Ralph Waldo Emerson, "The American Scholar" (1837), reprinted in *Factual Prose,* Walter Blair and John Gerber, eds. (Chicago: Scott, Foresman and Co., 1959). p. 282.

33. Lewis S. Feuer, "Introduction" to *Later Works,* Vol. 15, p. xxxiii.

34. Dewey, "The Influence of Darwinism on Philosophy," in *The Influence of Darwin on Philosophy* (New York: Henry Holt and Company, 1910). p. 2. Apparently Dewey believed that some of Darwin's critics had

misconstrued his biological conception of evolution as an attempt to "satisfy the needs of daily life." For Dewey informs us that "Malthus was still sufficiently imbued with deistic piety to wish to justify the scantiness of the board which nature set for her children on the ground that this niggardliness was a needed providential spur to work and to invention—the sources of human progress. It is all the more pertinent because Darwin has recorded his personal indebtedness to this doctrine of political economy for his conceptions of struggle for existence, selection and survival, as keys to understanding the origin of species." See "Some Connexions of Science and Philosophy" (1911), in *Later Works,* Vol. 17, p. 411.

35. *Ibid.*, p. 3. It may be helpful to note here that during this stage of Dewey's development, he was already attempting to make his readers aware of the dualism between philosophy and science; more than four decades later, however, his article "Modern Philosophy" was published, and we find him still trying to get philosophers to see the need to overcome this dualism. For he informs us that, "the dualism which is probably the most fundamental of all the dualisms with which modern philosophy deals is one that is rarely mentioned. It is the split between philosophy and science." When Dewey explains the "ideas" that originated the problem, historically speaking, he says, "In the basic dualism of scientific and philosophic subjectmatters, philosophy became the owner, guardian, and defender of the interests, activities, and values that had been violently expelled from science. . . . And as the prestige of the supernatural declined philosophy took over the office of rational justification of those higher values that were no longer taken care of by science . . . ." An unfortunate result of this dualism is that some philosophers have become overly concerned about "questions said to be those of form and form only; that is, not forms of *any* subjectmatter." But what is worst, says Dewey, "This course leads to philosophy's becoming a form of Busy-work for a few professionals." (See *Later Works*, Vol. 16, pp. 410-11).

36. Dewey, "The Experimental Theory of Knowledge" (1906), in *The Influence of Darwin on Philosophy* (New York: Henry Holt and Company, 1910). p. 109.

37. *Ibid.* Perhaps it should also be noted here that on Dewey's view of value, "We *employ* meanings in all intentional constructions of experience—in all anticipations, whether artistic, utilitarian, or technological, social or moral" (*Ibid.*, p. 108). See Dewey's *Theory of Valuation* (1939) for more elaboration.

38. Dewey, "The Experimental Theory of Knowledge" (1906), in *The Influence of Darwin on Philosophy* (New York: Henry Holt and Company, 1910). p. 95.

39. *Ibid.*

40. Perhaps one of the best ways to comprehend Dewey's genetic method of referring to terms such as "truth" as a species, or as a members of what the present writer calls "Word family," is to compare Dewey's treatment

of word meanings to the later Wittgenstein's notion of language-games and family resemblances. That is, in his posthumously published *Philosophical Investigations,* Wittgenstein points out the need for philosophers to "bring words back from their metaphysical to their everyday use" (116). Thus, in his own endeavor to do so, he discusses "all sorts of language-games," though he never actually says "what the essence of a language-game, and hence of language, is" (65). Nevertheless, as a result of Wittgenstein's attempt to determine the essence of words and their meanings, he drew the following conclusion: " I can think of no better expression to characterize these similarities [between the *general form of propositions* and of language] than 'family resemblances'; for the various resemblances between members . . . I shall say: 'games' form a family. . . " (65-67). See G. E. M. Anscombe's translation (New York: Macmillan Publishing Co., Inc., 1953). When comparing Wittgenstein's treatment of word meanings with Dewey's method, however, it is urged that the reader bear in mind Sidney Hook's contention that, "Long before Wittgenstein, Dewey had established, by linguistic analysis of the way in which the question was posed, that the so-called problem of the external world was not a genuine problem and that the very use of mental or sensory predicates, without which the question could not be asked, already presupposed the world of physics and the environment of everyday things." See Hook's "The Relevance of John Dewey's Thought," in Introduction to *Later Works,* Vol. 17, pp. xxx-xxxi.

41. Dewey, "The Experimental Theory of Knowledge" (1906), in *The Influence of Darwin on Philosophy* (New York: Henry Holt and Company, 1910). p. 109. Perhaps it should be pointed out here that Dewey provides us with an example of his early efforts to define "truth" generically when he asserts that "It would be a great gain for logic and epistemology, if we were always to translate the noun 'truth' back into the adjective 'true,' and this back into the adverb 'truly'; at least, if we were to do so until we have familiarized ourselves thoroughly with the fact that 'truth' is an abstract noun, summarizing a quality presented by specific affairs in their own specific contents." *Ibid.*, pp. 95-96.

42. Dewey, "The Experimental Theory of Knowledge" (1906), in *The Influence of Darwin on Philosophy* (New York: Henry Holt and Company, 1910). p. 110.

43. Ralph W. Sleeper, "Introduction" to *Later Works,* Vol. 14, p. xi.

44. Dewey, *How We Think* (1910), reprinted in *Later Works*, Vol. 8, p. 109.

45. Dewey, *How We Think* (1910), reprinted in *Later Works,* Vol. 8, p. 109.

46. *Ibid.*

47. Dewey, *Reconstruction in Philosophy* (1920), p. 166.

48. Dewey, *Essays in Experimental Logic* (1916), p. 72

49. Dewey, *Essays in Experimental Logic* (1916), p. 72.

50. Dewey, *Essays in Experimental Logic* (1916), p. 303.

51. *Ibid.*, pp. 303-4.

52. With regard to Dewey's problem of presenting a "genetic theory" of what truth means, perhaps it should be noted here that in his "Introduction" to his *Essays in Experimental Logic* (1916), Dewey admits that, "One of the points which gave much offense in the essays was the reference to genetic method—to a natural history of knowledge. I hope what has now been said makes clearer the nature of that reference. I was to blame for not making the point more explicit. . . . It had not occurred to me that anyone would think that the history by which human ignorance, error, dogma, and superstition had been transformed, into knowledge was something that goes on exclusively inside of men's heads, or in an inner consciousness. I thought of it as something going on in the world. . . " (p. 66).

53. Dewey, *Essays in Experimental Logic* (1916), p. 313.

54. *Ibid.*, p. 315.

55. Dewey, *Essays in Experimental Logic* (1916), p. 315

56. *Ibid.*

57. *Ibid.*, p. 238.

58. Bruce Kuklick, *Churchmen and Philosophers* (New Haven: Yale University Press, 1985). p. xiv.

59. Bruce Kuklick, *Churchmen and Philosophers* (New Haven: Yale University Press, 1985). p. xx.

60. *Ibid.*, p. 233.

61. See Stephen Toulmin's "Introduction" to *The Quest for Certainty* in *Later Works,* Vol. 4, p. ix. Toulmin maintains that by making this comparative analysis, the reader can see that Dewey's notable point of departure is his creative use of language. In close agreement with Toulmin's interpretation, Sidney Hook holds that, "There is a haunting similarity between some pages of Wittgenstein and some pages of Dewey." See Hook's "The Relevance of John Dewey's Thought," in Introduction to *Later Works,* Vol. 17, pp. xxx-xxxi).

62. Dewey, "Ralph Waldo Emerson" (1903), reprinted in McDermott's *The Philosophy of John Dewey,* p. 25. With respect to Emerson's view of education, it is interesting to note the analytic interpretation that Frederick Mayer furnishes in *A History of Educational Thought*. Mayer informs us that: "Real education , Emerson held, would be like a religious conversion; it would challenge man's total loyalty and it woul be a lifelong process. . . . The scholar would of necessity be a rebel. . . . The wise man, Emerson felt, is his own court and creates his own party, and he seeks a direct contact with God" (Columbus, Ohio: Charles E. Merrill Publishing Company, 1973). pp. 352-53.

63. Quoted by Dewey in "Ralph Waldo Emerson" (1903), reprinted in McDermott's *The Philosophy of John Dewey,* p. 27.

64. Sidney Ratner, "Introduction" to *Later Works,* Vol. 6, p. xii. In conjunction with Ratner's assessment of Mead's influence on Dewey, it is interesting to note Dewey's article "George Herbert Mead as I Knew

Him" (1931), reprinted in *Later Works*, Vol. 6. Clearly in line with Ratner's interpretation, we find Dewey saying: "As I look back over the years of George Mead's life, and try to sum up the impression which his personality left upon me, I seem to find running through everything a sense of energy, of vigor, of vigor unified, outgoing and outgiving (p. 22). . . . He was not one to rush about breathless with the conviction that he must somehow convince others of his activity. . . . For his vigor was unified from within, by and from the fullness of his own being. More, I think, than any man I have ever known, his original nature and what he acquired and learned, were one and the same thing. It is the tendency of philosophic study to create a separation between what is native, spontaneous and unconscious and the results of reading and reflection. That split never existed in George Mead (p. 23). . . . For him philosophy was less acquired from without, a more genuine development from within, than in the case of any thinker I have known. . . . his mind was deeply original,—in my contacts and judgments the most original mind in philosophy in America of the last generations (p. 24). . . . More than any one I have known he maintained a continuity of ideas with constant development. . . . I attribute to him the chief force in this country in turning psychology away from mere introspection and aligning it with biological and social facts and conceptions (p. 25). . . . Every one who knew him philosophically at all is aware of his interest in the immediate aspect of human experience—an interest not new in literature but new in the form which it took in his philosophy (p. 27). . . . Would that he might have lived longer with his family, his friends, his students, his books and his studies. But no added length of years could have added to the completeness of his personal being . . . (p. 28).

65. Ratner, "Introduction" to *Later Works*, Vol. 6, p. xxi.
66. Dewey, *How We Think* (1910), reprinted in *Later Works*, Vol. 8, p. 163.
67. *Ibid.,* p. 125.
68. Dewey, *Essays in Experimental Logic* (1916), p. 124.
69. Dewey, *Essays in Experimental Logic* (1916), pp. 98-99.
70. Dewey, *How We Think* (1910), in *Later Works*, Vol 8, p. 136.
71. Dewey, *How We Think* (1910), in *Later Works*, Vol 8, p. 136.
72. *Ibid.*
73. Dewey, *How We Think* (1910), in *Later Works*, Vol 8, p. 139.
74. With respect to this dichotomy of interest, perhaps we should note that it creates, as Richard Rorty interprets it, "a certain inevitable tension which runs through Dewey's relation to his various audiences, and also through his own presentation of his work: the tension between the image of the philosopher as social activist . . . and the philosopher as politically neutral theoretician.—a specialist in, and authority upon, such peculiarly philosophical topics as the rules of logic, the nature of science, or the nature of thought." Thus, in Rorty's appraisal of Dewey's attempt to

resolve this dichotomy of interest, he reminds us that "a theoretical resolution of a theoretical tension cannot, by itself, resolve the tension between these two public images. The tension between the image of philosopher as activist and as sage is between rhetorical tropes rather than between contradictory doctrines." See Rorty's "Introduction" to *Later Works,* Vol. 8, p. x.

# Chapter 6

ဢၢ

# *Dewey's Common Sense View of Philosophy and Truth: His Later Years, 1921-1952*

In this chapter we shall investigate the common sense view of Dewey's mature conceptions of philosophy and truth. As an endeavor to sufficiently do so, we shall try to disclose and focus on the wisdom of John Dewey. What we hope to show is that not only did Dewey retain his passionate concern for the problems of education, but there was a resurgence in his concern about religion as well; not merely for his own sake, of course, but in his effort to help other individuals understand the human predicament.

In proceeding, let us note McDermott's chronological outline of his later years; it sheds some light on Dewey's deep concern about education, though it sheds none on his religious aspirations.

| | |
|---|---|
| 1921 | Lectures in China, 1919-21 |
| 1924 | Visits Schools in Turkey |
| 1926 | Visits schools in Mexico |
| 1927 | Death of Alice Chipman Dewey |

| 1928 | Visits Schools in Soviet Russia |
| 1930 | Professor Emeritus, Columbia |
| 1946 | Married to Roberta (Lowitz) Grant |
| 1952 | Dies on June 1, in New York City[1] |

As illustrated by the outline above, Dewey continued to demonstrate his passion for the field of education throughout the first decade of his later years. What is more important, though, it should be clear to the reader that Dewey's incredibly high level of global consciousnes indicates his open-minded outlook. To be sure, John Dewey had no narrow-minded view of man's place in the universe.

While traveling around in other countries visiting various schools, Dewey was convinced that we should be willing to "learn from every quarter." Thus he apparently had traveled abroad to enhance his own personal information, and to share with others. Dewey's endeavors, in other words, were based upon his belief that

> The unity of all the sciences is found in geography. The significance of geography is that it presents the earth as the enduring home of the occupations of man. The world without its relationship to human activity is less than a world. . . . The earth is the final source of all man's food. It is his continual shelter and protection, the raw material of all his activities, and the home to whose humanizing and idealizing all his achievements returns."[2]

So with regard to Dewey's concern for educational activities abroad, it seems quite evident that he was attempting to increase his knowledge about mankind's global affairs.

Of course it is rather unfortunate, perhaps , that after returning to America from visiting schools in other countries, Dewey later summarized his findings and reports that

> From the standpoint of any European country, except Great Britain, the American public school system is a chaos rather than a system. [But] the British system, from the Continental standpoint is even more chaotic than ours, because public education there is superimposed upon schools carried on by religious bodies.[3]

Dewey, however, recognized the apparent reasons for the variances. From his viewpoint, "The historical causes for our peculiar difference are fairly evident." What apparently happenned is that "Regions developed in the country before the nation, and localities before regions.

Settlers had no choice save to go without schools or themselves to form a school for their own locality, the latter not being even a village but a collection of farm-homesteads scattered over a considerable territory."[4] Hence the formation of America's national system of education differed fundamentally from the nationalistic systems that he had visited abroad.

As Dewey defines a "nationalistic system," to use his terms, it is "one in which the school system is controlled by the Government in power in the interest of what it takes to be the welfare of its own particular national state, and the social-economic system of Government is concerned to maintain. [For example], the school systems of Japan, Italy, the U.S.S.R., and [also] Germany, define better what is meant by 'nationalistic' education than will any abstract descriptions."[5] How do they compare with America's schools?

When describing the public form of America's national system, in contrast to their nationalistic systems, Dewey held that "Roughly speaking, [America's] is an educational system that corresponds to the spirit, the temper, the dominant habits and purposes that hold the people of a country together, so far as they are held together in a working unity of life."[6] But unfortunately, as Dewey reminds us, in America he witnessed masses of individuals being denied the right to freely develop their capacities. From his viewpoint, so it seems, a major problem of schooling in America must turn on the earlier educational policies of Jefferson, which must be considered in light of the ensuing political liberalism of Lincoln; for these events had created an environment of intense democratic change that required some new adjusments.

As we noted earlier (in Chapter 3), the mature Dewey had candidly faced the fact that "Our anti-democratic heritage of Negro slavery has left us with habits of intolerance toward the colored race—habits which belie profession of democratic loyalty." Moreover, he plainly admitted that "The very tenets of religion have been employed to foster antisemitism." Indeed, Dewey faced up to the fact that "There are still many, too many, persons who feel free to cultivate and express racial prejudices as if they were within their personal rights."[7] Yet he warns us about the consequences of such thoughts/actions.

As we listen to accounts of the repression of cultural freedom in countries which have been swept by totalitarian terror, let us bear in mind that our chief problems are those within our own culture. In the modern world, every country under some circumstances becomes fertile for seeds out of which grow conflict, intolerance, racial oppression. The attitude which prevails in some parts of our country towards Negroes, Catholics, and Jews is spiritually akin to the excesses that have made a shambles of democracy in other countries of the world. . . .

We cannot sit back in complacent optimism. History will not do our work for us. Neither is there any call for panic or pessimism. We, members and friends of the Committee for Cultural Freedom, must dedicate ourselves to the task of securing and widening cultural freedom with our eyes open and minds alert to every danger which threatens it. . . . [But let us] be on guard against those who paint a rosy future which has no date in order to cover up their theft of our existing liberties. Only thus can we be sure that we face our problems in details one by one as they arise, and with all the resources provided by collective intelligence operating in cooperative action.[8]

Now in light of Dewey's admonishment regarding the realization of democratic ideals, let us note here that in the previous chapters we have tried to duly consider how some philosophers—Plato, Hegel, Emerson, Peirce, James, and Mead—have impacted Dewey's thinking about philosophy and truth, but we have not duly considered the strong influence of Jefferson upon his views. From the present writer's perspective, however, it would be a significant mistake for Dewey's readers to neglect or underestimate Jefferson's impact upon his philosophical approach in the field of education. Therefore, it is deemed worthwhile to pause and briefly note how Jefferson helped Dewey's common sense view of philosophy and truth develop into full bloom.

For instance, in "Presenting Thomas Jefferson" (1940), Dewey explains why he opted to work in the tradition of Jefferson's educational and political philosophy. First, says Dewey, "[Jefferson's] deep-seated faith in the people and their responsiveness to enlighment properly presented was a most important factor enabling him to effect, against great odds, 'the revolution of 1800.' It is the cardinal element bequeathed by Jefferson to the American tradition."[9] Moreover, for the benefit of those who may not be familiar with Jefferson's open-minded approach to discovering truth, Dewey points out that

He was also skeptical about theories not backed by evidence gained through observation, and thought the French *philosophes*, whose acquaintance he made, indulged in altogether too much unverifiable speculation. He says in one letter: 'I am myself an empiric in natural philosophy, suffering my faith to go no further than my facts. I am pleased, however, to see the efforts of hypothetical speculation, because by the collisions of different hypotheses, truth may be elicited and science advanced.[10]

As we can see, Dewey was very impressed by Jefferson's ideas about truth, which were quite conducive to his own notion of truth. To be sure, the emphasis that Jefferson placed upon the need for a method of publicly verifying truth claims was well in line with Dewey's pragmatic instrumentalism, or experimentalism.

On the other hand, concerning the brilliance of Jefferson's educational theories, Dewey provides a vivid appraisal. As he also reminds us, though, we have not yet taken full advantage of Jefferson's ideas about education. For instance, Dewey informs us that

> The balanced relation in Jefferson's ideas between the well-being of the masses and the higher cultivation of the arts and science is best expressed in his educational project. Elementary popular schooling educated the many. But it also served a selective purpose. It enabled the abler students to be picked out and to continiue instruction in the middle grade. Through the agency of the latter the 'natural aristocracy' of intellect and character would be selected who would go on to university education. State universities have carried forward Jefferson's idea of a continuous ladder. . . . But in some respects, the plan is still in advance of what has been accomplished.[11]

What Dewey apparently wants us to see is that some educators and philosophers have not recognized and exploited Jefferson's idea of a "continuous ladder" in education. A major hindrance to fully exploiting the practical aspects of Jefferson's ideas, as Dewey seems to interpret the obstruction, stem from the evangelical atmosphere that has been created by the New England environment.[12]

Scrutinizing the Colonial period, Dewey goes to the core of the problem and shows that human communication through language is at the center of the issue. In his effort to clarify Jefferson's position, Dewey says,

> The essentially moral nature of Jefferson's political philosophy is concealed from us at the present time because of the change that has taken place in the language in which moral ideas are expressed. The 'self-evident truths' about the equality of all men by creation and the existence of 'inherent and inalienable rights,' appear today to have a

legal rather than a moral meaning; and in addition, the intellectual
basis of the legal theory of natural law and natural rights has been
undermined by historical and philosophical criticism. In Jefferson's
own mind, the words had a definitely ethical import, intimately and
vitally connected with his view of God and Nature.[13]

What Dewey wishes to make clear, no doubt, is that Jefferson's
conception of God, truth, and the purpose of education had been
misunderstood by his more narrow-minded, or narrowly focused
contemporaries. Then too, since some of Dewey's own contemporaries
had misinterpreted his conception and treatment of subject matters such
as philosophy, God, truth, and education, no doubt he could easily
relate to Jefferson's experience(s). For as Dewey also points up,
"Jefferson was a sincere theist. Although his rejection of
supernaturalism and of the authority of the churches and their creeds
caused him to be denounced as an atheist, he was convinced . . . on
*natural* and rational grounds of the existence of a divine righteous
Creator who manifested his purposes in the structure of the world,
especially in that of society and the human conscience."[14]  So beyond
any reasonable doubt, on Dewey's interpretation of Jefferson's position,
"The connection of justice—or equity—with equality of rights and duties
was a commonplace of the moral tradition of Christendom. Jefferson
took the tradition seriously."[15]

It is hoped that by now the reader can see that Dewey himself took
the tradition of Jefferson seriously. Moreover, quite similar to the
communicative difficulties that Jefferson encountered, it should be clear
that Dewey was also confronted by the problem. In any event, Dewey's
"Statement on Jefferson" (1943) definitely furnishes further proof of
his debt to the insights of Jefferson's philosophy. In this article Dewey
says rather emphatically,

> Even those persons who are akin to the men who abused and vilified
> him while he was alive have given lip service to his memory. In
> sober fact, only those who are continuing to fight for the freedoms
> for which he strove so valiantly have a right to appeal to his name.

> Since Jefferson held that free inquiry and a free education that would
> put in possession of the truths it revealed was the sole ultimate guar-
> antor of a free government and a free society, it is fitting, it is
> necessary at this particular time to reaffirm the faith, and to re-state
> the reasons upon which this faith is grounded. For everywhere
> around us we find evidences of the growth of recourse to

authoritarianism. . . . They are found in philosophy, education, in morals, in religion, where they take the form of insidious attacks upon scientific method, and assertion of a necessity to returm to unquestioning acceptance of 'first principles' as they are laid down by authority [or Bilble] that can be investigated or criticized, so we are repeatedly told, at the cost of social confusion and interminable moral conflict.

For this fundamental reason, I welcome with all my heart and conscience the Conference that will discuss on a constructive basis the intrinsic and inalienable connection of the Scientific Spirit with Democratic Faith in a Free Society.[16]

The statement above concludes our brief pause to note the influences of Jefferson upon Dewey's thinking about philosophy and its subject matters: such as God, truth, morals, education, politics, and economics.[17] An apparent misfortune, of course, is that much like Jefferson, Dewey's treatment of philosophy's various subject matters has resulted in a misconstrual of his message by some of his critics. Nonetheless, except Dewey's readers can conceive of him working in the tradition of Jefferson, then it seems unlikely that one will be able to grasp his mature conceptions of philosophy and truth.

What the reader needs to understand, no doubt, is that his espousal of Jefferson's notion of a "continuous ladder" of education should be seen as a way of attaining truth through "free inquiry." For as we noted earlier, the mature Dewey was well convinced that "the intercourse of free minds will always bring to light an increasing measure of truth."[18] Thus, if the reader does not (or doesn't try to) conceptualize him working in this vein of thought, then the wisdom of Dewey may be overlooked, and especially his conception of the way Jefferson's "continuous ladder" of educational should be employed.

One of the best ways to consider Dewey's view of its employment, perhaps, is to think about him in his capacity at Columbia, after having served for a year (1905-06) as President of the American Philosophical Association (APA).[19] Of course the accomplishments that he achieved while serving in this office shall not be our main concern to us here; rather the pertinent point for our present purpose is the insight that he gained from his services. For example, his "Introduction" to *Problems of Men* (1946) informs us of a report issued by a Committee of members who were concerned with teaching and writing philosophy, The American Philosophical Association.[20] The Committee had been invited to undertake an examination of the state of philosophy and the role it might play in the postwar period. "The invitation came from and was financed," says Dewey, "by a nonprofessional body, The Rockefeller Foundation. This fact is an indication that the theme is considered to be of public, not merely professional concern."[21]   Their task was to inquire into the "function of philosophy in the development of a free and reflective life in the community," and it was asked to disscuss the "function of philosophy in liberal education." As a result, *Philosophy and American Education* was published; however, because of "internal division," to use Dewey's terms, this "kept the Committee from dealing with the more important of the two tasks entrusted to it."[22]   Therefore, taking the task upon himself, Dewey addresses the problem, and says, "I propose, then, to discuss the present state of philosophy in its human bearings."[23]

Quite explicit in his discussion of the problem, Dewey points out the need to face the fact that "scientific methods take effect in determining the concrete economic conditions under which the mass of men live," while simultaneously "the more important things are left to decision by custom, prejudice, class interests, and traditions."[24]   Yet in regard to earlier decisions resulting from economic conditions, Dewey tells us plainly that

> Separation of mind and matter, the elevation of what was called ideal and spiritual to the very summit of Being and the degradation of everything called material and worldly to the lowest position, developed in philosophy as a reflection of economic and political division of classes. Slaves and artisans (who had no more political freedom than did outright slaves) were occupied with the "material," and hence with mere means to the good life in which they had no share.[25]

Of course, as Dewey also points out, "We have moved away from downright slavery and from feudal serfdom. But the conditions of present life still perpetuate a division between activities which are relatively base and menial and those which are free and ideal."[26]

Concerning the establishment of such economic practices and class divisions, bear in mind that approximately three years later we find Dewey explicitly saying,

> I would not assert that the absolutist morality that was embodied for untold generations in social institutions was a slave morality. But it

did hold in effect if not always in words that in the great mass of people the mind is too weak and character too corrupt to be trusted with freedom, so that social order depends upon the possession of moral authority by a few who have power to impose obedience to moral principles upon the mass.[27]

But educators and philosphers who insists upon seeing the masses of humans in this light, on Dewey's view of things, are missing the point of Jefferson's notion of a continuous ladder of education. Instead of taking advantage of the educational foundation that he helped lay, such professionals tend to divert potentially productive students away from Graduate and public schools.

It is no wonder, then, that Dewey was disturbed by the condition of America's educational institutions when he returned from visiting schools in other countries. He was highly disturbed; and as he reminds us in "Politics and Culture" (1932),

> We pride ourselves, and with some good reason, on a free universal system of education. But, leaving out even all questions of quality, our accomplishment is rather elementary from the standpoint of the population that it reaches. Of course, there are a great many more colleges now than there existed forty years ago. But still over half the school population leaves school at twelve, fourteen, fifteen years old.[28]

Undoubtedly Dewey was disturbed because he believed that the misfortunate individuals who find school repulsive, instead of attractive, should be climbing the continuous ladder of education. For as he also points out, "the period from, say, fourteen to twenty-two is a comparatively short portion of a normal life time. The best that education can do during these years is to arouse intellectual interests which carry over and onwards."[29] Thus, as philosophers and educators, what we should recognize is that "If a student does not take into subsequent life an enduring concern for some field of knowledge and art, lying outside his [or her] immediate profession preoccupations, schooling for him [or her] has been a failure, no matter how good a 'student' he [or she] was."[30]

John Dewey, of course, wished to help put an end to the ridiculous waste of so many young brains, brains that possibly could be aiding us in bringing to light more and more measures of truth. However, Dewey did not desire to assist them simply because of their individual needs, but he wanted to stamp out ignorance, and help keep the crime rate down. In other words, he reminds that

> Racketeering is a profession. . . . Human beings, especially the young, have a greater and greater difficulty in detecting where business leaves off and racketeering begins. Is not profit the measure of both according to our economic system?[31]

In response to the latter question, Dewey's argument is that "The full development of democracy will not be secured in a day. [Rather] We must enlist for life, for our own lives and for the sake of the lives of our children." "It is [our] task," says Dewey, "to educate the American public to fundamental economic realities and the necessity of a new political order [if needed] so that the spirit of democracy may have a re-birth."[32]

Further exposing some of the problems confronting us and our misguided youth, Dewey also takes care to remind us that "countless thousands believe that the real satisfaction and enjoyments of life are to be found in 'leisure' which is thought of as a period of amusement and idle relaxation if not dissipation. It is but a short step from this attitude to the psychology of the racketeer and gangster whose motto is 'get by the shortest possible course, the one which involves the minimum work and the maximum excitement.'"[33] Yet Dewey doesn't find this confused conception of "leisure" surprising; for as he points out, "It is a matter of common notice that as a nation we are laggards in interest in ideas as ideas."[34] Why? It seems that Dewey puts his finger directly on the problem when he says,

> Much recent indoctrination from highly placed sources has identified the doctrine of American individualism with strictly economic activity of a competitive kind, and has taught that success in obtaining wealth is the natural measure and criterion of moral qualities. . . .

> [Consequently] The development of machine industry necessarily brought about concentration. This tendency is reflected in the growth of cities, and within the cities in the congestion of population in crowded quarters, only the especially well-to-do living in habitations exclusively possessed by themselves. . . . [In this respect] There has followed in turn the concentration of great wealth in the hands of the few, with an accompanying concentration there of effective power in the direction of social affairs, the setting of standards, the moulding of public opinion.[35]

In his relentless efforts to reduce the ills of ignorant individuals, and expose the economic exploitations of the well-to-do, no doubt Dewey stood firm for truth. Without freedom of inquiry, how can we get or know truth? In response to this question, as the following statement makes clear, Dewey sharply criticizes a main source of the problem.

> The actual leaders rulers, of society, the people who are most influential (newspaper people, maybe, and members of Congress, cabinet and whatever other officers), certainly don't bother a great deal, in spite of the temporary brain trust, about ideas and ideologies and methods that are worked out intellectually.[36]

How can miguided youth make adequate moral decisions when their significant others (the leaders, or role models) are not doing so? Reminding us about the conditions of his social environment, Dewey informs us that, "Often the officials of the law are the worst offenders, acting as agents of some power that rules the economic life of a community."[37] However, if this problem is to be resolved by philosophy, one must come to grips with the fact that "The system that goes by the name capitalism is a systematic manifestation of desires and purposes built up in an age of ever threatening want and now carried over into a time of ever increasing potential plenty."[38] Judging from Dewey's view, then, an important job for American philosophy is making capitalism a viable system.

Unfortunately for Americans, though, as Dewey points out,

> In this counntry, . . . during the greater part of our history, resort to violence is especially recurrent on the part of those who are in power. In times of imminent change, our verbal and sentimental worship of the Constitution, with its guarantees of civil liberties of expression, publication and assemblage, readily goes overboard. . . .

> It is not pleasant to face the extent to which, as matter of fact, coercive and violent force is relied upon in the present social system as a means of social control. It is much more agreeable to evade the fact. But unless the fact is acknowledged as a fact in its full depth and breath, the meaning of dependence upon intelligence as the alternative method of social direction will not be grasped.[39]

Of course, for Americans who are willingly to work or fight for a better democractic way, Dewey's reminder is that "liberty of expression is tolerated and even lauded when social affairs seem to be going in a quiet fashion, and yet is so readily destroyed whenever matters grow critical."[40] Indeed, says Dewey, "liberty is tolerated as long as it does not seem to menace the *status quo* of society."[41] Who would dare disturb the *status quo*?

As for those individuals who are willing to take a stand for truth and freedom of inquiry, Dewey would have them remember that, "As long as freedom of thought and speech is claimed as a merely individual right, it will give way, as do other merely personal claims, when it is, or is successfully represented to be, in opposition to the general welfare."[42] Illustrative of this point, he cites an American minority member who exemplifies the democratic cause; for Dewey admirably says,

> No more eloquent words have ever come from any one than those of Justice Brandeis in the case of a legislative act that in fact restrained freedom of political expression. He said: 'Those who won our independence believed that the final end of the State was to make men free to develop their faculties. . . . They believed that freedom to think as you will and to speak as you think are means indispensable to the discovery and spread of political truth; that without free speech and assembly discussion would be futile.[43]

Although the American Constitution does indeed guarantee individual rights, as Dewey obviouslyly recognized, there remains the big problem of getting people to realize their rights and take advantage of them. Attempts to inform massive numbers about their rights, no doubt, implies a need to talk about education. Talking about education on a large scale, of course, implies a need to talk about economics, which in turn, requires talking politics. This was one of the major difficulties confronting Dewey during his later years, as he endeavored to guide students up the continuous ladder of education.

He seems to helps us grasp the complexity of the problem when he explains that

> This [American] public is moved by love of money, and the higher learning responds to anything that promises to bring money to the college and university whether from donors, student-fees, or state legislatures. The result is that these institutions become public service-stations; and as there is no special tide in public opinion and sentiment, but only a criss-cross of currents, the kind of service that is to be rendered shifts with every change in public whim and interest. Love of money results in demand for large numbers of students, and

the presence of large numbers renders training even more indiscriminate in order to meet the demands of unselected heterogeneous groups.[44]

Dewey's statement seems to show why he was so weary with "higher" education. That is to say, as we observed in Chapter 5, when he wrote *Democracy and Education* (1916) Dewey asserted that he had "never been able to feel much optimism regarding the possibilities of 'higher' education when it is built upon warped and weak foundations."[45] What he wanted was to take advantage of the "unselected heterogeneous groups," and not raise funds to herd students through colleges and universities as if they were cattle.

As for Dewey's conception of the "unselected heterogeneous groups" and their potential value as an asset to the continuous ladder of higher education, he tells us that

> For many years I have consistently—and rather persistently—maintained that the key to a philosophic theory of experience must proceed from initially linking it with the processes and functions of life as the latter are disclosed in biological science. . . . I have held that experience is a matter of an "affair". . . of interaction of living creatures with their environments; *human* experience being what it is because human beings are subject to the influences of culture, including definite means of intercommunication, and are what in anthropological jargon are called *acculturated* organisms.[46]

Apparently, though, because so many people seem to have a foolish love of money, his hopes were hampered by having to defend his own views about pecuniary profits. Not only did he have to maintain the virtue of his position against his American critics, but Dewey had to defend his integrity against philosophers in other countries as well. It was noted in the Overview (see Chapter 3, note 29), for example, that he thought it necessary to uphold the doctrines of Peirce and James against the egregious misreadings of Russell and his obnoxious conception of American pragmatism.

As ironic as it may seem, though, it appears that Russell did recognize the value of Dewey's pragmatic stand, for he says himself that

> Dr. Dewey has an outlook which, where it is distinctive, is in harmony with the age of industrialism and collective enterprise. It is natural that his strongest appeal should be to Americans, and also that he

should be almost equally appreciated by the progressive elements in countries like China and Mexico. . . . Dr. Dewey's world, it seems to me, is one in which human beings occupy the imagination. . . . His philosophy is a power philosophy, though not, like Nietzsche's, a philosophy of individual power; it is the power of the community that is valuable. It is this element of social power that seems to me to make the philosophy of instrumentalism attractive to those who are more impressed by our new control over natural forces than by the limitations to which that control is still subject.[47]

Probably, however, one of the most important factors that prevented Russell from fully understanding Dewey's instrumentalism, and his ideas about pecuniary profits, was the fact that he was not American born and bred. For as noted in the Overview, Dewey's Americanism is a feature that apparently accounts for his highly evolved conceptions of philosophy and truth; that is, in contrast to his foreign born and bred contemporaries, such as Russell, Wittgenstein, and Heidegger.

On one occasion, for instance, Russell furnishes an excellent illustration of the way his perception of heterogeneous humans differs from Dewey's. In other words, Russell divulges his more narrow-minded view when he asserts that, "A negro can see the difference between one negro and another: one is his friend, another his enemy. But to us [Englishmen] such different responses are impossible: we can merely apply the word 'negro' indiscriminately."[48] Contrary to Russell's perception, however, which seems to stem from a lack of concrete experience, Dewey's conception of a negro was obviously much more highly evolved. In his "Dedication Address of the Barnes Foundation" (1925), for example, we find Dewey saying,

It is, I think, significant that you will find in this gallery one of the finest collections in the world of African art, . . . . For it suggests that members of the Negro race, of people of African culture, have also taken a large part in the building up of the activity which has culminated in this beautiful and significant enterprise. I know of no more significant, symbolic contribution than that which the work of the members of this institution have made to the solution of what sometimes seems to be not merely a perplexing but a hopeless problem—that of race relations. The demonstration that two races may work together successfully and [quite] cooperatively, that the work has the capacity to draw out from among our Negro friends something of that artistic interest and taste . . . is something to be dwelt upon . . . .

While it is always dangerous to attempt the role of the prophet, I feel confident we can open our eyes and look into the years ahead, to see radiating from this institution, from the work of this Foundation, influences which are going to effect education in the largest sense of that word: development of the thoughts and emotions of boys and girls, youths, men and women all over this country. . . .[49]

Now judging from the words of his dedication address, perhaps the reader can see that on Dewey's conception, unlike Russell's, we should regard them as "our Negro friends," and not mere indiscriminate beings. Plus, we ought not jump to the conclusion that Russell's conception diverges from Dewey's because of any racial prejudice. Why is this so?

Seemingly, Russell, like Dewey, was well aware of social conditions in the world; for he makes the following assertion, which seems to be demonstrative of his view.

In the matter of race, there are different beliefs in different societies. . . . Among white men, it is held that white men are by nature superior to men of other colours, and especially to black men. . . .

All this is, of course, pure nonsense, known to be such by everyone who has studied the subject. In schools in America, children of the most diverse origins are subjected to the same educational system, and those whose business it is to measure intelligence quotients and otherwise estimate the native ability of students are unable to make any such racial distinctions as are postulated by the theorists of race. In every national or racial group there are clever children and stupid children. It is not likely that in the United States, coloured children will develop as successfully as white children, because of the stigma of social inferiority; but in so far as congenital ability can be detached from environmental influence, there is no clear distinction between different groups. The whole conception of superior races is merely a myth generated by the overweening self-esteem of the holders of power. It may be that, some day, better evidence will be forthcoming; perhaps, in time, educators will be able to prove (say) that Jews are on the average more intelligent than Gentiles. But as yet no such evidence exists, and all talk of superior races must [or should] be dismissed as nonsense.[50]

Clearly in accord with Russell's assertion, we find Dewey taking a similar stand, as he asserts that "No systematic effort has ever been made as yet to find out what the real capacities of human nature in the mass are. The idea that in spite of our public school system, the intelligence quotient of a large part of the population ranges low, has no force as evidence of this point."[51] Moreover, "Before it could have any weight as positive evidence, we should have to know all of the conditions out of schools as well as in schools, the social, economic, political, indirect influences of all kinds that played on those persons who do not show up well in tests."[52] Thus, for those American educators and philosphers who are concerned about the problem, Dewey's reminder is that

> We never have tried the experiment of producing a widespread culture throughout the whole society. Culture instead, has been the private possession of a small number of individuals. In order to try the experiment we shall have to modify the economic system so as to provide a secure basis for the free operation of mind, imagination and emotion. We shall have to remove all of the barriers that now prevent the free circulation of knowledge and ideas. We shall have to change the motivation of human energy so that it shall not be diverted and deflected into channels of getting power over others . . . . [However] the greatest part of mental ability, acuteness of thought, ingenuity, etc., in this country has gone into business.[53]

As we can see from Dewey's assertion, it appears that he and Russell held very similar views regarding the potential intellectual capacity of all humans. What is more pertinent for our present purpose, though, is the need to understand the reason for their different experiences with blacks, or Negroes. That is to say, Russell's aristocratic birthright as an Englishman may have prevented him from receiving any firsthand encounters with them; but in Dewey's case, it obviously was quite the contrary.

Let us bear in mind that Dewey's place of birth, the state of Vermont, "became the first to abolish slavery in 1777."[54] Therefore, it seems safe to say that he lived among white folk who were willing, able, and did try to help bring an end to the inhumane treatment of Negroes. Much different from the atmosphere that Russell experienced in Wales, no doubt, the American environment of Dewey's later years was one where blacks and whites worked together and sometimes became friends; but on the other hand, in different parts of the country, ignorance, racism, and even sexism was rampant. Yet Dewey, observant of the latter environmental conditions, drew the following conclusion.

I do not see how any very high popular artistic standard can exist where a great many of the people are living in slums. Such persons cannot get artistic culture simply by going to free concerts or the Metropolitan Musuem to look at pictures, or the public library to read books, as long as their immediate surroundings, or what they come into direct contact with, unconsciously habituates them to ugly, sordid things. A small number of people may come through with genuine aesthetic appreciation even under these circumstances. Even those who have, economically speaking, the most opportunities for higher culture, become insensitive to the ugliness that exist in our human environment.[55]

Dewey, of course, being brought up in the tradtion of the Andover Liberals, employed his philosophic literature to help enable those people living in slums get away from "ugly, sordid things," and instead get "artistic culture." He used his writing and speaking skills to help get rid of the ugly sexist and racist practices in the American environment. However, Dewey recognized that "our chief problems are those within our own culture." Therefore, for the most part, this is where he directs his messages.

As we observed in the Overview, the mature Dewey obviously was convinced that "philosophy occupies a peculiar position with respect to literature."[56] Thus, following the lead of Plato's notion of employing literary art, instead of using it merely as a means of gaining pecuniary profits, Dewey believed that "The function of literature is to use a language which potentially is capable of being understood, and of being conveyed to great masses."[57] It is in this respect, no doubt, that Russell was correct in thinking that "Dewey's world," as he puts it, "is one in which human beings occupy the imagination." For indeed, the world that Dewey wrote and talked about was the one he experienced with his own imagination; yet as we can see from his work, the world of his imagination is the one in which we human beings live. It is no wonder, then, that Dewey produced philosophic writings that should appeal to and occupy the human imagination.

In this sense of looking at his philosophic literature, it is quite important to note that *Human Nature and Conduct* (1922) was one of Dewey's first publications after returning from visiting schools in other countries. Perhaps a good way of understanding the literary strategy that he employs in this particular writing is to picture him trying to help clear up some of the mistakes committed by Descartes. The latter, as the generally acclaimed "Father" of modern philosophy, had attended, so he says, "one of the most famous schools in Europe," and he had concluded that "theology instructs us how to reach heaven," while "philosophy gives us the means of speaking plausiby about any subject and of winning the admiration of the less learned."[58] Of course Dewey would doubtless agree with Descartes's assessment of philosophy, but undoubtedly he would oppose Descartes's view of theology; and instead argue that philosophy instructs us how to "reach heaven," if it can be reached.   From Dewey's perspective, where Descartes and his successive followers had erred, so it seemed, was in their initial acceptance of the classic Greek notion of "two orders of existence."   In hopes of countering this problem, Dewey designed *Human Nature and Conduct* to attract the attention of philosophers and educators in order to direct their thoughts towards *one* order of existence.

To help illustrate this point, let us consider Dewey's "Problems of Contemporary Philosophy: The Problem of Experience" (1933).   In this article Dewey reflects upon the course of philosophic history and reminds us that

> The mass of people through the whole of recorded history have not accepted actually in their conduct a philosophy of experience. They have accepted standards which cling to, claim to have, an authority and a sanction beyond experience.   . . .they have put their chief attention and attached their importance to things that cling to, belong to, realms that were beyond our actual experience here on earth.[59]

Further reflecting upon the origin of this inadequate notion of experience, with respect to the history of philosophy, Dewey's reminder is that "notions about experience comes to us from the great philosophies of ancient Greece, of ancient Athens: great philosophers of the fifth century before the Christian era, Plato, and his pupil, but not exactly disciple, Aristotle."[60] But, as he also points out, "We must remember that the philosophy which was dominant in Europe for centuries and still influences that of the Catholic church was based, as far as possible, upon the teachings of Aristotle."[61]

With respect to the early Greek view of the universe, Dewey additionally explains that based on their concept of experience,

> They had two levels:  the higher level of rational science which gave us eternal universal necessary truths which were found in science and which ought to govern man's moral behavior, ought to control human institutions; and the lower level of the experience of the

average man, of carpenter and the shoemaker and even the physician and all the other people who just did the best they could, utilizing the customs and ideas, beliefs, that had been handed down to them from the past.[62]

Apparently *Human Nature and Conduct* was Dewey's attempt to channel philosophic thought away from this primitive notion of experiencing the universe. That is, regarding the dualisms which have resulted from the classic Greek doctrines, and especially the subsequent dichotomy of the human body (mind vs. matter). For indeed, Dewey argued that, "It has always been a bit of a mystery as to just how the commonplace 'soul' of the Middle Ages, which possessed many of the Aristotelian virtues as well as defects, came to blossom out into the overstrained, tense, and morbid 'psychic' of the last century or two. To Descartes, whether rightly or wrongly, has fallen much of the blame."[63]

In Dewey's effort to re-direct the focus of philosophic thought, and get it away from the controversial debates about the dualisms attributed to Descartes, it is apparent that *Human Nature and Conduct* proved to be rather successful. For Sidney Ratner renders an excellent appraisal of it; he thinks that it "indicates how much thought Dewey gave to the study of history and anthropology."[64] Also, says Ratner, "His friendship and interchange with the historians James Harvey Robinson and Charles Beard and the anthropologist Franz Boas undoubtedly enriched his approach to social philosophy."[65] Moreover, we are informed by Ratner that "Dewey's insights influenced these and other historians and anthropologists. Ruth Benedict, for example, once said that one of the sources of her inspiration for her *Patterns of Culture* (1934) was Dewey's *Human Nature and Conduct*."[66]

As we can see from Ratner's appraisal of Dewey's work, the latter had started to reach a much wider audience with his literature. Just as he had inspired Ruth Benedict, however, Dewey likewise desired to get his fellow philosophers to see the value of investigating patterns of human culture. Instead of continuing with fruitless debates about the dualisms that epistemological and metaphysical questions pose, Dewey wanted philosophers to recognize the value of the unselected heterogeneous groups that were entering American colleges and universities; for this is where inquiry needs employing most. No doubt, Dewey would have been elated if only he could have gotten his critics to consider the potential in those students who wished to contribute to making this world a better place to live. Anyway, a scrutiny of his mature writings seems to clearly show that not only did he wish to disclose his thoughts about philosophy and truth by employing his literary style, but he hoped that others would see the need for proceeding in this manner.

During the first stage of his later years, for instance, after the publication of *Human Nature and Conduct,* Dewey published "The Art of Thought" (1926), and asked: "Is there a legitimate possibility of an art of social thought which is one with increase of control, or is the idea a dream? If it is a legitimate possibility, how is it to be realized?"[67] Dewey's answer to the former question appears to be a resounding "Yes," and his answer to the latter, no doubt, is that philosophic literature is the means to realizing the dream. For as we have seen already, Dewey follows Plato's and Emerson's lead in this respect.

With regard to Dewey's notion of conveying ideas through literary works of art, consider the narration that he provides in "Affective Thought" (1926). He explains that "There has long been vague talk about the unity of experience and mental life, to the effect that knowledge, feeling and volition are manifestations of the same energies, etc.; but there has now been put in our hands the means by which this talk may be made definite and significant."[68] In order to do so, however, educators and philosophers must recognize that "works of art of a new style have to create their own audience."[69]

As for the individual doing the creating, Dewey tells us that at first the person experiences largely the jar of dissonance with the superficial habits most readily called into play. Yet changes in the environment involve changes in the organism, which means that one's eyes and ears gradually adapt to the surroundings. Then, says Dewey, "what was first condemned as *outre* falls into its serial place in the history of artistic achievement."[70] But unfortunately, as he also points out, "the variety of physiological details involved has not yet been adequately organized nor has there been time to digest them and get there results."[71] Nonetheless, he was convinced that "reasoning is a phase of the generic function of bringing about a new relationship between organisms and the conditions of life, and like other phases of the function is controlled by need, desire and progressive satisfaction."[72] Therefore, granting this view of reasoning, "The 'stuff' from which thinking draws its material," according to Dewey, "may be termed habits."[73] It is in this sense that "the material of thought all comes from the past; but its purpose and direction is future, the development of a new environment as the condition of sustaining a new and more fully integrated self."[74]

As Dewey further explains, though, "the great gap which is traditionally made between the lower physiological functions and the higher cultural ones, is due first to isolating the organism from the environment, failing to see the necessity of its integration with environment, and secondly, to neglect of the function of needs in creating ends, or consequences to be attained."[75]    Unless educators and philosophers can comprehend this explanation of the way human organisms may create and apply art, from Dewey's view, one shall hardly be able to take advantage of the heterogeneous groups in America's institutions of higher learning.    How can one help others climb the continuous ladder without even trying to understand the students, or without a desire to help them?    In any event, as indicated by Dewey, when one does pose questions for the inquisitive minds of the heteregeneous students, while helping them put their brains to work, one should remember that

> In the past we have had to depend mostly upon phrases to explain the production of artistic structures.   They have been referred to genius or inspiration or the creative imagination.   Contemporary appeal to the Unconscious and the Racial Unconscious are the same thing under a new name.   Writing the word with a capital letter and putting "the" before it, as if it were a distinct force, gives us no more light than we had before.[76]

Approximately twelve years later, in "Time and Individuality" (1938), we find Dewey again trying to clarify the importance of conveying thoughts through literature; but this article points up some significant distinctions between art, thought, and science.   He argues, for example, that "art is the compliment of science," and he also maintains that

> Science as I have said is concerned wholly with relations, not with individuals.   Art, on the other hand, is not only the disclosure of the individuality of the artist but the manifestation of individuality as creative of the future, in an unprecedented response to conditions as they were in the past. . . .   [Thus] Discontent with things as they are, is normally the expression of vision of what may be and is not, art in being the manifestation of individuality is this prophetic vision. . . .   [In other words] The artist in realizing his own individuality reveals potentialities hitherto unrealized.   This revelation

is the inspiration of other individuals to make the potentialities real, for it is not sheer revolt against things which stirs human endeavor to its depths, but vision of what might be and is not.[77]

As indicated by the statement above, Dewey retained the same notion of art and science as he did when "Poetry and Philosophy" (1890) was published. However, as we can see, the view that he advocates during his later years focuses more on individual initiative. Hence, he explains that, "Freedom of thought and of expression are not mere rights to be claimed. They have their roots deep in the existence of individuals as developing careers in time."[78] For this reason, then, Dewey tries to make clear the significance of seeing that "The ground of democratic ideas and practices is faith in the potentialities of individuals, faith in the capacity for positive developments if proper conditions are provided."[79]

Dewey's faith in the "potentialities of individuals," and his deep commitment to "democratic ideas," apparently marks only a portion of the widom that he displayed in his later years. Yet it seems to be quite a momentous portion. In other words, from Dewey's perspective, if people practice a true form of democracy, it means treating other persons as they wish to be treated themselves; and it gives the best assurance of reaching heaven.* So indeed, Dewey's devotion to true democracy appears to demonstrate a resurgence in his concern for religion. This interpretation seems to be sustained by Lewis Hahn, one of the foremost Dewey interpreters in America, and perhaps the whole wide world. He says,

> [Dewey's] final publication during the years 1882-88 was an essay on "The Ethics of Democracy," which was an expression of the current social liberalism of the objective idealists. Drawing upon the organicism of Plato's *Republic* and that of Hegel, he gave an ethical interpretation of democracy. This essay is noteworthy in that, first, though mainly a statement of principles, its author touched upon a current controversial social issue in insisting that to make democracy a reality, it had to be industrial as well as civil and political,

---

\*    According to Dewey, "It is said, and said truly, that for the world's peace it is necessary that we understand the peoples of foreign lands. How well do we understand, I wonder, our next door neighbors? It has been said that if a man love not his fellow man whom he has seen, he cannot love the God whom he has not seen." See Dewey's "The Problem of Method," in *The Public and Its Problems* (1927), reprinted in *Later Works,* Vol. 2, p. 368.

and secondly, in that it was his first major treatment of the democratic theme which in somewhat altered form was shortly to replace his religious emphasis.[80]

Dewey's article "The 'Socratic Dialogues' of Plato" (1925) is clearly in line with Hahn's observations. This later writing further elaborates the democratic theme that Dewey defended during his early years. He reflects on Plato's role as statesman, employing his literature to deal with problems emanating from the intercommunication of the various cultures in and around the Mediterranean Basin.

The purpose of the dialogues, as Dewey interprets them, "is not just to ridicule Plato's rivals in philosophy. It is also to bring out the nature of certain problems and to define them in such a way as to prepare for a constructive treatment."[81] As for those "certain problems" that needed constructive treatment, Dewey informs us that "the main theme of these earlier dialogues is the relation of knowledge, virtue and good."[82] Then, moreover, Dewey attempts to show that the problems of government that existed during Plato's era are not much different than those of the twentieth-century; for as he puts it,

> We are struggling with the ethical problems of Plato's time. . . .
> We project our mental muddiness and one-sidedness upon the Sophists, and laying our sins upon them fail to recognize that, comparatively speaking, the Sophists were direct and honest and that it is we who are sophisticated. If we cannot get instruction by recurring to the Platonic scene, we may at least discover the charm of free and direct mental play directed to the fundamental themes of life.[83]

Seemingly, Dewey's message in this article is primarily designed to emphasize the point that diverse cultures may indeed assimilate in a friendly manner.[84] However, in order for philosophers to "discover the charm of free and direct mental play," they must have open minds; they must open up to others, as well as among themselves.

At any rate, in light of the foregoing interpretation by Hahn, it is hoped that the reader can see that the mature Dewey had been developing his ideas about democracy for a number of years. Of course not only did Dewey disclose his religious views through his defense of democracy, but he did so in other ways too. For example, consider his article "Religion and Morality in a Free Society" (1942), where he says,

> In this country we thought that free institutions would combine with
> the advantages of our geographical location to enable it to be a leader
> in promotion of all the means by which the reign of international
> peace would be forwarded. . . . We were aware that the question of
> the relation to one another of different races and religions was still a
> thorny one, since here too the past had left an evil heritage. But
> here too we believed that the kindly office of time, with growth of
> mutual respect and sympathetic understanding, would gradually heal
> the wounds that lower stages of civilization had created in the social
> body.[85]

It seems that the preceding statement provides clear evidence of his
open-mindedness towards cultural diversity. No doubt this is why
Dewey was not only willing to embrace blacks or Negroes as friends,
but he also had enough love in his heart to try befriending an atheist, or
agnostic, such as Russell.[86]

Apparently, though, Russell failed to see that Dewey longed for a
world where theists and atheists would love each other. Dewey seems
to assert this as his genuine ground when he notes that the second of the
freedoms of the so-called Atlantic charter reads "the freedom of every
person to worship God in his own way everywhere in the world."[87]
Then, as he responds to this view of what "freedom" means, Dewey
asks: "Does this freedom include a right *not* to worship any God in any
way? Does it include the right to be an atheist?" [88]  What Dewey
apparently is trying to make clear is the need to create an environment
where individuals can feel comfortable with their  inalienable right to
believe or disbelieve in God's existence. Of course an unfortunate
problem in America (as in other countries, so it seems) is that the
subject of God has frequently created the most debates and divisions
among individuals.[89]

Evidently, if this is the case, then Dewey's theory of human
communication must contain the key to understanding his logic, as
pointed up in the conclusion of Chapter 2. From the following statement
we can see just how essential communication is to Dewey's entire
philosophy.

> As a matter of general social philosophy and of scientific sociological
> doctrine, there is much to be said for the proposition that the essence
> and life blood of human society, that which makes our connections
> with one another genuinely social, not just physical, is the existence
> of *communication*—the fact that by means of language the net outcome
> of every experience, the meaning of every discovery, the occurence

of every fresh insight and stimulating outlook can be communicated to others, thereby becoming a common possession. And the entire process of education has for its foundation and the fact that mind and character develop through contact and intercourse.[90]

Apparently, then, Dewey's theory of human communication played a fundamental part in his mature conception of philosophy. At this point of our survey, however, it would take us too far afield to digress into a discussion of this topic. In the next chapter, though, we shall reflect on the way Dewey's theory of communication relates to his logic and the way he employs the word "God."

In the meantime, as we prepare to bring Chapter 6 to a close, the present writer hopes that the wisdom of Dewey's view of education is clear. We have seen how he wished to use Jefferson's notion of a continuous ladder in education, and we have seen how much emphasis he placed upon communicating ideas through philosophic literature. Moreover, we've seen that during Dewey's later years, he maintained the same important distinction between science and art that we observed in Chapter 4. In Chapter 6, though, we have reflected on his efforts to employ his literature to direct philosophic thought away from debates about Cartesian dualisms, and the classic Greek notion of two orders of existence. So it is hoped that the reader recognizes the wisdom Dewey displays in his mature writings, as they focus upon this world in which we live.

The wisdom of Dewey's common sense view of philosophy and truth, to be sure, is manifested in his thoughts about science and its relation to problems in our world, such as racism, sexism, and just downright ignorance. Hence, it should be clear that Dewey was dissatisfied with the progress of science during his later years because he believed that "Habits of thought and desire remain[ed] in substance what they were before the rise of science, while the conditions under which they take effect [had] been radically altered by science."[91] Dewey, however, reveals his own wisdom when he says,

In truth science is strictly impersonal; a method and a body of knowledge. It owes its operation and its consequences to the human beings who use it. The beginning of wisdom is, I repeat, the realization that science itself is an instrument which is indifferent to the external uses to which it is put. Here lies the heart of our present social problems. Science has hardly been used to modify men's fundamental acts and attitudes in social matters. . . . The fact that motor cars kill and maim more persons yearly than all factories, shops, and farms is a fair symbol of how backward we are in that province where we have done most.[92]

Judging from Dewey's own words, apparently his cultivated view of science is the main reason he was able to work so wisely in the field of education.   Therefore, in Chapter 7  we shall give some further consideration to his view of science, as we attempt to elucidate some of the implications of his mature conceptions of philosophy and truth.

As we conclude Chapter 6, however, let us get clear on one last point about Dewey's scientific attitude.  That is, thus far we have tried to indicate the impact that Jefferson's democratic ideals and his notion of education, truth, and science had upon Dewey.  But we should bear in mind that Jefferson's influences were limited, no doubt, by his having philosophized decades before Lincoln and his constituents amended the Constitution.  Nevertheless, it should be clear that Jefferson had provided Dewey with some common sense principles that would probably hold true for all of America's scientists as long as the earth continues to last.  Dewey shares those valuable principles with us when he says,

It is instructive, if not especially important, to note [Jefferson's] attitude on the growth of the English language, his idea on this special point being completely consistent with his general philosophy.  After saying he is a foe of purisms and a friend of neologisms, since language grows by their introduction and testing, he says: "Dictionaries are but the depositories of words already legitimated by usage. Society is the workshop in which new ones are elaborated. When an individual uses a new word, if ill formed it is rejected in society; if well formed, adopted, and after due time laid up in the depository of dictionaries.  And if, in this process of sound neologisation, our trans-Atlantic brethren shall not choose to accompany us, we may furnish, after the Ionians, a second example of a colonial dialect improving on its primitive."  The principles here expressed are now generally accepted, but I doubt if a half-dozen men in this country were bold enough to assert them when Jefferson gave expression to them.[93]

Now in light of the principles adumbrated by Jefferson, let us remember that it was John Dewey's elder contemporaries, Peirce and James, who primarily helped him see how to apply them not only in a scientific manner, but with good common sense.  For instance, with respect to Peirce's view of science, Dewey says,

Peirce will always remain a philosopher's philosopher. . . . Peirce, more than any other philosopher of modern times, insisted that philosophy should begin with the common-sense world and its conclusions and terminate in application to the common-sense world. . . . [For Peirce] the universal or common subject matter of philosophy consists "of those observations which every person can make in every hour of his [or her] waking life." Although Peirce was above all a scientist and had what he called the laboratory mind as distinct from the "seminary mind," he had no sympathy with those who hold that philosophy must be based upon the conclusions of science.[94]

Also, quite impressed with James's scientific mind, Dewey tells us that,

James had achieved himself, along with an acute and penetrating insight into intellectual sham and pretense when they are elaborately formulated, the kind of spiritual innocence which his father thought the ultimate goal, in connection with his feeling for the rights of others.[95]

In concluding, then, let us remember that the works of these thinkers played a big part in the development of Dewey's common sense view of philosophy and truth.

# Notes

1. McDermott, The *Philosophy of John Dewey,* p. xxxv.
2. Dewey, *The School and Society* (1902). p. 13.
3. Dewey, "Towards a National System of Education" (1935), in *Later Works,* Vol. 11, p. 356.
4. *Ibid.*
5. Dewey, "Towards a National System of Education" (1935), in *Later Works,* Vol. 11, p. 357.
6. *Ibid*
7. Dewey, "The Basic Values and Loyalties of Democracy" (1941), in *Later Works,* Vol. 14, p. 277.
8. Dewey, "Democratic Ends Need Democratic Methods for Their Realization" (1939), in *Later Works,* Vol. 14, pp. 367-68.
9. Dewey, "Presenting Thomas Jefferson" (1940), in *Later Works,* Vol. 14, p. 214.
10. Dewey, "Presenting Thomas Jefferson" (1940), in *Later Works,* Vol. 14, p. 205.
11. *Ibid.,* pp. 210-11. With regard to Jefferson's accomplishments in helping to lay the foundations of American educational theory, it is interesting to note Frederick Mayer's brief summary. Mayers says, "Thomas Jefferson (1734-1826) , especially, was influential in the development of the development of the American public school system. While serving in the Virginia legislature, Jefferson introduced a measure which would have established free public education for that state. This bill, however, was defeated, for most members of the legislature regarded this as a radical measure. [Nevertheless] Jefferson played a great role in the establishment of the University of Virginia, which tried to combine the classics and humanities with scientific instruction. Throughout his career he agitated for the separation of state and church, and for freedom of expression on the part of teachers." See *A History of Educational Thought* (Columbus, Ohio: Charles E. Merill Publishing Company, 1973). p. 345.
12. With respect to the germinal forces behind the evangelical atmosphere, it is interesting to consider Frederick Mayer's account; he tells us, "Religious ideals were fundamental in the founding of the American universities. Thus, the Congregationalists founded Harvard, the Episcopalians helped to establish William and Mary and Columbia University, the Presbyterians founded Princeton, while Brown University was established by the Baptist. The oldest and best known university is Harvard, founded in 1636. Its establishment is described in the following document: 'After God carried us safe to New England, and wee had builded our houses, provided necessaries for our liveli-hood, rear'd convenient places for God's worship, and settled the civill government; One of the next things we longed for and looked after was to advance learning and perpetuate it to prosperity;

dreading to leave an illeterate ministery to the churches, when our present ministers shall lie in the dust. And as wee were thinking and consulting how to effect this great work; it pleased God to stir up the heart of one Mr. Harvard (a godly gentleman, and a lover of learning amongst us) to give the one half of his estate (it being in all about $1700) towards the erecting of a colledge, and all his Library; After him another gave $300, others after them cast in more, and the publique hand of the State added the rest; The colledge was by common consent, appointed to be at Cambridge . . . and it is called (according to the name of the first founder) Harvard . . . .' Most of the books in the Harvard library in the seventeenth century dealt with religion; the majority of the graduates became ministers. Chapel; was compulsory for students, who were warned against the deadly dangers of atheism, skepticism, and materialism." See *A History of Educational Thought* (Columbus, Ohio: Charles E. Merill Publishing Company, 1973). pp. 404-407.

13. *Ibid.*, p. 218. Perhaps it should be noted here that Dewey takes care to point out some of the tensions involved in the language disputes regarding the original Constitution; he tells us that "'Certain' was substituted for 'inherent' by the Congress. The first manuscript draft, later changed by Jefferson himself, read that 'All Men are created equal and independent; that from that equal Creation they derive rights.'" *Ibid.*, p. 218, see note 1.

14. Dewey, "Presenting Thomas Jefferson" (1940), in *Later Works,* Vol. 14, p. 218.

15. *Ibid.*, p. 219. With respect to the seriousness of Jefferson's beliefs about Christianity, his not-so-vocal Christian stand seems to raise some dubious questions. His book *The Life and Morals of Jesus,* for instance, provides a textial extraction from the Gospels , in about 25,000 words, the life and morals of Jesus. Yet as noted by Douglas Lurton, Jefferson's book was placed in the United States Museum at Washington (1895), and "Jefferson waived any intention of publishing his compilation with the words: 'I not only write nothing on religion, but rarely permit myself to speak on it.' However, the Fifty-seventh Congress provided for publication of a limited edition . . . to be given to members of the house and senate. It was printed in 1904, little more than a century after Jefferson first actively planned its compilation." Also, further disclosing the secretiveness or confidential nature of Jefferson's venture, Lurton cites a letter written to Benjamin Rush in 1803; it was "the syllabus of his comparison of the moral doctrines of Jesus with those of the other ancient philosophers." Jefferson said to Rush: "And in confiding it to you, I know it will not be exposed to the malignant perversions of those who make every word from me a new text for new misrepresentations and calumnies. I am, moreover, averse to the communication of my religious tenets to the public, because it would countenance the presumption of those who have endeavored to draw them before that tribunal, and to seduce public opinion

to erect itself into that inquest over the rights of conscience, which the laws have so justly proscribed." On the other hand, however, apparently quite proud of his work, we are informed by Lurton that Jefferson wrote a letter in 1813 to John Adams saying: "We must reduce our volume to the simple Evangelists; select, even from them, the very words only of Jesus, paring off the amphibologisms into which they have been led, forgetting often, or not understanding, what had fallen from Him, by giving their own misconceptions as his dicta, and expressing unintelligibly for others what they had not understood themselves." And finally, Lurton tells us that he wrote a letter to Charles Thompson in 1816, saying: "I, too, have made a wee little book from the same materials, which I call the philosophy of Jesus; it is a paradigma of his doctrines, made by cutting the texts out of the book, and arranging them on the pages of a blank book, in a certain order of time of subject. A more beautiful or precious morsel of ethics I have never seen; it is a document in proof that I am a real Christian, that is to say, a disciple of the doctrines of Jesus . . . ." See Lurton's "Foreword" in *The Life and Morals of Jesus* (Cleveland, Ohio: The World Publishing Company, 1940). pp. vii-ix.

16. Dewey, "Statement on Jefferson" (1943), in *Later Works*, Vol. 15, p. 366.

17. With respect to Dewey's interpretation of Jefferson's ideas about economics, he reminds us that "The social philosophy of Thomas Jefferson is regarded as outmoded by many persons . . . . This is a highly superficial view. Jefferson predicted what the effects of rise of the economics and politics of an industrial regime would be, unless the independence and liberty characteristic of the farmer, under conditions of virtually free land, were conserved." Nevertheless, says Dewey, "The democratic ideal that unites equality and liberty is . . . a recognition that actual and concrete liberty of opportunity and action is dependent upon equalization of the political and economic conditions under which individuals are alone free in *fact,* not in *some abstract metaphysical way.*" [But] "Above all, the Industrial Revolution gave scope to the abilities involved in acquiring property and to the employment of that wealth in further acquisitions. The employment of these specialized acquisitive abilities has resulted in the monopoly of power in the hands of the few to control the opportunities of the wide masses and to limit their free activities in realizing their natural capacities." Indeed, "The drift of nominal democracy from the conception of life which may  properly be characterized as democratic has come under the influence of a so-called rugged individualism that defines the liberty of individuals in terms of the inequality bred by existing economic-legal institutions." See Dewey's "Liberalism and Equality" (1936), in *Later Works,* Vol. 11, p. 368.

18. Dewey, "The Meaning of the Term: Liberalism" (1940), in *Later Works,* Vol. 14, p. 254.

19. See the McDermott's outline in Chapter 5.

20. Dewey, "Introduction" to *Problems of Men: The Problems of Men in the Present State of Philosophy* (1946), in *Later Works,* Vol. 15, p. 154.

21. *Ibid.*

22. Dewey, "Introduction" to *Problems of Men: The Problems of Men in the Present State of Philosophy* (1946), in *Later Works,* Vol. 15, p. 154.

23. *Ibid.*, p. 155

24. *Ibid.*, p. 158

25. *Ibid.*, pp. 163-64.

26. *Ibid.*

27. Dewey, "Religion and Morality in a Free Society" (1949), in *Later Works,* Vol. 15, p. 173.

28. Dewey, "Politics and Culture" (1932), in *Later Works,* Vol. 6, p. 46.

29. Dewey, "The Way Out of Educational Confusion" (1931), in *Later Works,* Vol. 6, p. 88. Perhaps it should be noted here that Dewey's assessment of the time-span in human life expectancy and productivity seems to be well in line with several other estimates. For example, Philip Wheelwright has observed that "Pythagoras died at the age of either eighty or ninety. The story of his dying at eighty fits in with his theory [of man's life as falling into four twenty-year periods]; but other accounts say that he lived to be ninety." See *The PreSocratics* (New York: The Odyssey Press, 1966). p. 222. Also it is interesting to note that this alleged theory of Pythagoras seems to be in keeping with King David's assertion that "The days of our years are threescore years and ten; and if by reason of strength they be fourscore years, yet is [humans] strength labor and sorrow; for it is soon cut off, and we fly away" (*Psalm* 90: 10, King James Version). Likewise, it seems that Confucius's assessment of the human life-span is in line with theirs; for he allegedly said, "At fifteen I had my mind bent on learning. At thirty I stood firm. At forty I had no doubts. At fifty I knew the decrees of Heaven. At sixty my ear was an obedient organ for the reception of truth. At seventy I could do what my heart desired without trangressing what was right . . . ." Reprinted in John B. Noss's *Man's Religions* (New York: MacMillan Publishing Company, Inc., 1969). p. 284.

30. Dewey, "The Way Out of Educational Confusion" (1931), in *Later Works,* Vol. 6, p. 88.

31. Dewey, "Democracy Joins the Unemployed" (1932), reprinted in *Later Works,* Vol. 6, p. 242.

32. *Ibid.,* p. 245.

33. Dewey, "The Social-Economic Situation and Education" (1933), in *Later Works*, Vol. 8, p. 62.

34. *Ibid.*

35. *Ibid.*, pp. 56-57.

36. Dewey, "Methods in Philosophy and the Sciences" (1937), in *Later Works,* Vol. 17, p. 447.

37. Dewey, "Renascent Liberalism" (1935), in *Later Works,* Vol. 11, p. 46.

38. *Ibid.*, p. 43.

39. *Ibid.*, p. 46.

40. *Ibid.*, p. 7.

41. *Ibid.*

42. Dewey, "Renascent Liberalism" (1935), in *Later Works,* Vol. 11, p. 7.

43. *Ibid.*

44. Dewey, "President Hutchins' Proposals to Remake Higher Education" (1937), in *Later Works,* Vol. 11, p. 397.

45. Dewey, "From Absolutism to Experimentalism" (1930), reprinted in *Later Works,* Vol. 5, p. 156.

46. Dewey, "Experience, Knowledge and Value: A Rejoinder" (1939), in *Later Works,* Vol. 14, p. 15.

47. Russell, "John Dewey," in *A History of Western Philosophy,* reprinted in *The Basic Writings of Bertrand Russell,* R. E. Egner and L. E. Dennon eds. (New York: Simon and Schuster, 1961). pp. 213-14. Perhaps it should be reiterated here that as Samuel Meyer interprets Russell's position, the latter made no "serious effort to grasp Dewey's theory of knowledge," but instead, "found in Dewey a handy foil for his fundamental dissatisfaction with the doctrines of pragmatism and instrumentalism." See Meyer's *Dewey and Russell: An Exchange* (New York: Philosophical Library, Inc., 1985). p. 12.

48. Bertrand Russell, *The Analysis of Mind* (New York: The MacMillan Company, 1921), p. 181. With respect to Russell's vague idea about the personal identity and communication of Negroes, perhaps the following historical account may help shed some light on his apparently distant perception of them. As for the environment that he grew up in, one English historian informs us that, "Blacks have a long history in Britain. Africans were here in the Third Century as soldiers in the Roman Army. Centuries later, some of the Africans sold into slavery ended up here. Black seamen and their families started communities in British ports in the 1800s and West Indians came during World War II. Nonetheless, Britain was virtually a homogeneous society until the 1950's. Its primary experience with nonwhites had been as their colonial master in the vast British empire. But in the 1950's, a postwar labor shortage, a damaged economy and a weakening grip on its territories forced Britain to encourage people from the Caribbeans, the Indian subcontinent and Africa to come here to fill manual jobs. About 125,000 West Indians came between 1948 and 1958, many of them to man buses and subways and to work in hospitals, hotels and restaurants." Also, we are informed that, "Under a 1948 law, people from the colonies were British citizens with the right to live here permanently. But historians and blacks who lived through the 1950's say that nonwhites were soon shunned as aliens. Amid an economic downturn, growing unemployment and strong winds of xenophobia, whites began to accuse nonwhites of stealing their jobs. The immigrants were also victims of Britain's class system, which labeled them second-class

citizens and stifled their social progress. Underpinning all of this was a sentimental longing for Britain's imperial past, some Btitons say." We are additionally told that it was "white American soldiers who brought their policies of racial discrimination and segregation to England with them in World War II. Blacks were barred from hotels, pubs and other public services." Finally, we are informed by Anthony Lester, a white lawyer who helped draft Britain's equal-opportunity law, that "White people in Britain don't have the legacy of guilt about the past as there is in America about the period of slavery, even though there is plenty to be guilty about. . . . Nor is the English dream like the American dream of equality. If you asked the average Briton what he was striving for, I don't think equality would be the first thing to come to mind." See *The New York Times International.* Sunday, March 31, 1991.

49. Dewey, "Dedication Address of the Barnes Foundation" (1925), in *Later Works,* Vol. 2, pp. 384-85.

50. Russell, "An Outline of Intellectual Rubbish," in *The Basic Writings of Bertrand Russell,* R. E. Egner and L. E. Dennon eds. (New York: Simon and Schuster, 1961). pp. 84-85.

51. Dewey, "Politics and Culture" (1932), in *Later Works,* Vol. 6, p. 46.

52. *Ibid.*

53. *Ibid.*, p. 47.

54. Raymond M. Corbin, *1999 Facts About Blacks* (Beckham House Publishers, Inc., 1986). pp. 4, 179. A survey of Dewey's formative years in Vermont seems to help explain his deep compassion for *all* humans, even the most debased. Consider, for instance, how Lemuel Haynes (1774-1833) possibly influenced Dewey's thinking indirectly. That is, Haynes was probably the most important black man in America before the emergence of Frederick Douglas. Haynes spent his life as the pastor of white churches in Granville, Massachusetts; Manchester, Vermont; Grandville, New York; and for thirty years in Rutland, Vermont. So Haynes, in other words, might have contributed to the creation of New England's evangelical atmosphere. See Richard Newman.'s *Black Preacher to White America: The Collected Writings of Lemuel Haynes, 1774-1883.* Also, quite indicative of Dewey's compassion for blacks, it is interesting to note the list of people who attended the NAACP's first conference. With respect to their main supporters, the astute historian John Hope Franklin, one of Dewey's younger contemporaries, plainly informs us that "It was a distinguished gathering of educators, professors, publicists, bishops, judges, and social workers. Among those who participated were Jane Addams, William Dean Howells, Ida B. Wells, John Dewey, John Millohand, [W. E. B.] Dubois, and [Garrison] Villard." See *From Slavery to Freedom* (New York: Alfred A. Knopf, Inc., 1947). p. 328. Above two decades later, we find Dewey yet demonstrating his compassion for blacks; for example, consider his "Address to the National Association for the Advancement of Colored People" (1932), where he

boldly says, "The paradise of folly in which we have been living has broken down. That is at least some gain. It is something to become aware of the need of new ideas, new measures, new policies, new leaders, to bring about a great social reconstruction. More specifically, I think our depression has compelled us to think more fundamentally on social matters, economic matters, political matters, than we have been for many years." Quite candid with his message, Dewey says, "Certainly, if any group of people should know that the economic, industrial issue is the dominant one in politics it is the colored people. Why were you kept in slavery except for economic reasons? . . . Fundamentally, the disadvantages, or the inequalities—civil, political, and cultural,—of the colored group, of every under-privileged group of this country, exist because we are living in a competitive order which, because it is competitive, has to set man against man, brother against brother, group against group." Therefore, in summarizing his Address, Dewey points out that "in a society which is economically and industrially organized as ours is, those who want the greatest profits and those who want the monopoly, power, influence, that money gives, can get it only by creating suspicion, dislike and division among the mass of the people. A cooperative economic and social order is the only kind of order in which there will be a genuine possibility for equality among human beings irrespective of race, color, and creed. . . ." See *Later Works*, Vol. 6, pp. 224-230.

55. Dewey, "Politics and Culture" (1934), in *Later Works*, Vol. 6, p.45.
56. Dewey, "Philosophy" (1934), in *Later Works*, Vol. 8, p. 26.
57. Dewey, "Politics and Culture" (1932), in *Later Works*, Vol. 6, p. 41.
58. Rene Descartes, *Discourse on the Method, in The Philosophical Writings of Descartes,* Translated by J. Cottingham, R, Stoothorff, and D. Murdoch (Cambridge: Cambridge University Press, 1985). Vol. 1, p. 113.
59. Dewey, "Problems of Contemporary Philosophy: The Problem of Experience" (1933), in *Later Works*, Vol. 17, p. 432.
60. *Ibid.*, p. 433. Perhaps we should note Descartes's assesment of Aristotle and early Greek thought. In his *Principles of Philosophy,* for example, we find Descartes telling us, "No soul, however base, is so strongly attached to the objects of the senses that it does not sometimes turn aside and desire some other, greater good, even though it may often not know what this good consists in. Those who are most favoured by fortune and possess health, honour and riches in abundance are no more exempt from this desire than anyone else. On the contrary, I am convinvced that it is just such people who long most ardently for another good—a higher good than all those that they already possess. Now this supreme good, considered by natural reason without the light of faith, is nothing other than the knowledge of the truth through its first causes, that is to say wisdom, of which philosophy is the study. . . . [There are] levels of wisdom that have so far been attained. . . . Now in all ages there have

been great men who have tried to find a fifth way of reaching wisdom—a way which is incomparably more elevated and more sure than the other four. This consists in the search for the first causes and the true principles which enable us to deduce the reasons for everything we are capable of knowing; and it is above all those who have laboured to this end who have been called philosophers. I am not sure, however, that there has been anyone up till now who has succeeded in this project. The first and most important of those whose writings have come down to us are Plato and Aristotle. The only difference between these two is that the former, following the footsteps of his master Socrates, ingenuously confessed that he had never yet been able to discover anything certain. He was content instead to write what seemed to him probable, and accordingly he used his imagination to devise various principles by means of which he tried to account for other things. Aristotle, by contrast, was less candid. Although he had been Plato's disciple for twenty years, and possessed no principles apart from those of Plato, he completely changed the method of stating them and put them forward as true and certain, though it seems unlikely that he in fact considered them to be so" (pp. 180-81).

61.  *Ibid*.
62.  Dewey, "Problems of Contemporary Philosophy: The Problem of Experience" (1933), in *Later Works*, Vol. 17, p. 435.
63.  Dewey, "Transactions of Known and Named" (1946), in *Knowing and the Known* (1949), co-authored with Arthur F. Bentley. Reprinted in *Later Works*, Vol. 16, pp. 123-24. On Dewey's interpretation of the problem, "When Descartes and others broke away from medieval interests, they retained as commonplaces its intellectual apparatus: Such as knowledge is exercised by a power that is extranatural and set over against the world to be known." See "The Need for a Recovery of Philosophy," in *Creative Intelligence* (1917), p. 31.
64.  Sidney Ratner, "Introduction," in *Later Works,* Vol. 6, p. xvi.
65.  *Ibid*.
66.  Sidney Ratner, "Introduction," in *Later Works*, Vol. 6, p. xvi.
67.  Dewey, "The Art of Thought" (1926), in *Later Works,* Vol. 2, p. 232.
68.  Dewey, "Affective Thought" (1926), in *Later Works,* Vol. 2, p. 105.
69.  *Ibid*. p. 108.
70.  *Ibid*.
71.  *Ibid*., p. 105.
72.  *Ibid*., pp. 105-06.
73.  *Ibid*., p. 106.
74.  *Ibid*.
75.  Dewey, "Affective Thought" (1926), in *Later Works,* Vol. 2, p. 10.
76.  *Ibid*., p. 107.
77.  Dewey, "Time and Individuality" (1938), in *Later Works*, Vol. 14, pp. 113-14.
78.  *Ibid*.

79. *Ibid.*

80. Lewis Hahn, "Introduction," in *Early Works,* Vol. 1, p. xvi.

81. Dewey, "The 'Socratic Dialogues' of Plato" (1925), in *Later Works,* Vol. 2, p. 125.

82. *Ibid.*, p. 127.

83. *Ibid.*, p. 140. With respect to the various interpretations of Plato's idealistic notion of the Forms, it is interesting to note Dewey's contention that: "The chief difficulty in more specific interpretation lies in the failure of Plato to make reference to atomism specific. This holds of his entire philosophy. His only serious intellectual rival, Democritus, his only rival in breadth and depth, Plato consistently ignores. Although Plato borrowed from him the concept of fixed forms, ideas or schemas, as the sole objects of true knowledge, and although the cleavage between the two systems is the deepest found in philosophy, Plato, so free in his references to the other philosophers, never gives hint of the existence of Democritus" (*Ibid.*, p. 140).

84. Perhaps a good illustration of Dewey's point may be seen in the subsequent activities of Plato's successors, the Epicureans. That is to say, with respect to governmental problems that gather around the issue of cultural diversity, we are reminded by Norman Melchert that: "The virtue of friendship [was] held in the highest esteem among the Epicureans. They are famous for it. Epicurus established in Athens a 'Garden' in which his followers lived, sharing work, study, and conversation. In this Garden and in similar communities across the ancient world, men—including at least some women and slaves—cultivated this virtue. Friendship, they believed, is the key to the higest blessings this life holds." See Melchert's *The Great Conversation: A Historical Introduction to Philosophy,* p. 189.

85. Dewey,"Religion and Morality in a Free Society" (1942), in *Later Works,* Vol. 15, p. 171.

86. Russell divulges his double-minded stance as follows. "Whenever I go into a foreign country or a prison or any similar place they always ask me what is my religion. I never quite know whether I should say 'Agnostic' or whether I should say 'Atheist.' It is a very difficult question. . . . As a philosopher, if I were speaking to a purely philosophical audience I should say that I ought to describe myself as an Agnostic, because I do not think that there is a conclusive argument by which one can prove that there is not a God. On the other hand, if I am to convey the right impression to the ordinary man in the street I think that I ought to say that I am an Atheist, because . . . . I cannot prove that either the Christian God or the Homeric gods do not exist. . . . It has been a very difficult problem, and sometimes I have said one and sometimes the other without any clear principle by which to go." See Russell's "Atheism: Collected Essays," in *The Atheist Viewpoint* (New York: Arno Press, 1972). p. 5.

87. Dewey,"Religion and Morality in a Free Society" (1942), in *Later Works,* Vol. 15, pp. 174-5.

88. *Ibid.*, p. 175.

89. With regard to the problem of human divisiveness due to religious disputes, Dewey reminds us that, "The cleavage of our one physical world is into two opposed worlds. Between them even the communication that is a condition of understanding and agreement is practically impossible. . . . [Thus] The fumdamental consideration, then, with respect to the forsaking of the 'scientific attitude of mind' would seem to be that the great mass of human beings has not deserted it for the simple reason that the mass never shared the attitude. . . . [At any rate] In view of the fact that religion in the degree in which they have depended upon the supernatural have been, as history demonstrates, the source of violent conflict, and . . . even now differences of religion divide the peoples of the earth . . . ." See Dewey's "Contribution to 'Religion and the Intellectuals'" (1950), in *Later Works*, Vol. 16, pp. 392-94.

90. Dewey,"Religion and Morality in a Free Society" (1942), in *Later Works*, Vol. 15, p. 179.

91. Dewey, "Science and Society" (1931), in *Later Works*, Vol. 6, p. 53. First published in *Philosophy and Civilization* (New York: Minton, Balch and Co., 1931).

92. Dewey, "Science and Society" (1931), in *Later Works*, Vol. 6, p. 53. First published in *Philosophy and Civilization* (New York: Minton, Balch and Co., 1931).

93. Dewey, "Presenting Thomas Jefferson" (1940), in *Later Works*, Vol. 14, pp. 207-08.

94. Dewey, "Charles Sanders Peirce" (1937), in *Later Works*, Vol. 11, pp. 480-81.

95. Dewey, "The Jameses" (1936), in *Later Works*, Vol. 11, pp. 444-45. Dewey also informs us that "James had scientific resources to draw upon that were not available to his predecessors. He used these resources to give support and body to ideas which had been not much more than hunches in the empirical strain of English thought." See Dewey's "William James as Empiricist" (1942), in *Later Works*, Vol. 15, p. 13. Dewey also says, "James was himself trained as a scientist more than other American philosophers of his day, save Peirce." Therefore, "To take the ground that the chief business of philosophy, its most distinctive function, is to show how desire and ideas, purpose and knowledge, emotion and science, can cooperate fruitfully in behalf of human good, is to take our stand where James stood a generation ago." See "William James and The World Today" (1942), in *Later Works*, Vol. 15, p. 7.

# Chapter 7

ഇൻരു

# Some Implications of Dewey's Mature Conception of Philosophy and His Notion of Truth

I n this final chapter we shall consider some of the implications of John Dewey's mature conceptions of philosophy and truth to see what bearings they may have upon philosophy's future. Apparently there are a number of conceivable implications we could deduce from the preceding chapters. Due to a delimited amount of space, however, our considerations shall be confined, for the most part, to the following:

(1) Dewey seems to be implying that he continued to maintain his belief in God.

(2) Dewey seems to be implying that he went to his grave with "that final peace, which only reconciliation with God can give."[1]

By reflecting on these two implications, it is hoped that Chapter 7 helps to shed some light on Dewey's theory of communication, which may provide some insight into his logic. Also, by proceeding in this manner, perhaps we shall see how he would *probably* suggest that we treat our own crucial philosophic problems here in this last decade of the twentieth-century.[2]

First, though, before we begin our reflections, let us briefly summarize the course that we have finished thus far. After the initial introduction in Chapter 1, we proceeded with Chapter 2 by focusing on Instrumentalism, one of John Dewey's most important doctrines. We tried to show that he formulated it after being attracted to pragmatism by James and Peirce. Moreover, we attempted to show how Dewey's endeavor to define pragmatism and instrumentalism was challenged by Russell, whose vexing criticisms intensified a difficult problem of communicating ideas through language. Nonetheless, Dewey kept insisting that philosophers need to get the subject matter of philosophy straight. Thus, we concluded that Dewey's theory of human communication must hold the key to understanding his logic.

Subsequently, an overview was rendered in chapter 3 to provide a general survey of Dewey's conceptions of philosophy and truth. The chapter tried to furnish sufficient background information to illustrate the direction in which Dewey developed his own philosophy of truth. In doing so, we considered the value of his mature philosophy in light of evaluations by some mainstream contemporary philosophers, such as Melchert, McDermott, Lavine and Sleeper. The latter, as we have seen, emphasized the importance of Dewey's holistic doctrine, and the value of his perspective. Thus, following Sleeper's interpretation, as an attempt to assess the value of Dewey's view, a triadic survey of his life-career works was suggested. And thanks to the efficient publication of his work by Boydston and her constituents, we were able to scrutinize the stages of his development during his early, middle, and later years. Also, of course, we tried to show that Dewey espoused Plato's notion of philosophic literature as a useful form of art.

In Chapter 4 we paid close attention to Dewey's early educational endeavors, and his initial religious activities as well. Consequently, we noted that Dewey had firmly fixed his beliefs about religion during his youth. However, we observed also that his religious concerns diminished after drifting away from Hegelianism. Nevertheless, as we have seen, Dewey continiued to pursue philosophy as a profession; and consequently, education became a major concern.

Chapter 5 enabled us to observe some of the shifts that occurred in his thinking about philosophy and truth as he came to be more and more impressed by the potentials of the pragmatic movement. As we noted, following the insights of Peirce and James, Dewey formulated his intrumentalism or experimentalism to determine the meaning of truth apart from dogmatic religious teachings. Thus, in his efforts to break away and become more scientific in his approach, he employed a genetic method of reference to define "truth." We observed in addition, however, that Dewey's procedure apparently led Bernstein to conclude that he was a half-hearted metaphysician. Of course our study has tried to show why Dewey, following the ideas of Emerson, Peirce, James, and Mead, should not be classified as a half-hearted metaphysician.

Chapter 6 disclosed some of the influence that Jefferson had upon John Dewey's conceptions of philosophy and truth. Thus, we observed the resurgence of his concern about religion, or let us say religious attitudes. And as we have seen, he manifested his thoughts through his defense of democratic ideals. Then too, of course, we've noted how Dewey tried to direct philosophic debates away from problems posed by the Cartesian dualisms and the Greek notion of two orders of existence. We have seen that he employed his philosophic literature to get educators and philosophers to direct their attention towards the study of patterns in human culture. For this is where he believed that philosophy may have a great work to do. Indeed, we've seen that Dewey desired to get the general public involved in philosophy. He wished to get more heterogeneous students to climb the continuous ladder of education, and help us bring to light more measures of truth. It is this unbiased scientific frame of mind, as we have tried to show, that truly reveals the wisdom of Dewey's common sense view of philosophy and truth.

Now after recollecting the chapters that brought us to this point, let us briefly consider the two implications listed above. Because no clear evidence has been detected to indicate that Dewey abandoned his initial belief in God, as an effort to make clear the implications, let us suppose that he retained his earlier ideas. Granting this supposition, and judging by the quality of his work as a philosopher, it seems safe to say that Dewey, very similar to Socrates, went to his grave believing "there is good hope that death is a blessing" or a "relocating for the soul from here to another place," a place where possibly "all who have died are there."[3] So, it is highly probable that he viewed death as a "wonderful way" for him to get the opportunity to meet with others who had preceded him; for he could then spend his time "testing and examining people there," as he had done here, to see "who among them is wise, and who thinks he is, but is not."[4]  Rather similar to Socrates, Dewey probably went to his grave believing that "It would be an extraordinary happiness to talk with them, to keep company with them and examine them."[5]  Therefore, if this interpretation of Dewey's ideas about his death and grave is conceivable, then it is possible that implications (1) and (2) could be valid.  Providing that implications (1) and (2) are valid propositions, it appears that we can draw some reliable conclusions about his theory of communication.  For instance, let's suppose that he held to his belief in an immanent God, and he looked forward to experiencing the unexamined life.  Such an attitude would apparently help explain why Dewey maintained that "*all* personality is infinite."  In other words, once we understand why he held the latter view, then we are able to adequately account for his anticipation of future communication in a deathless dimension of existence.

Dewey provides evidence that supports this interpretation in his "Introduction" to *Problems of Men* (1946), where he takes the position that "Present day philosophy cannot desire a better work than to engage in the act of midwifery that was assigned to it by Socrates twenty-five hundred years ago."[6]  Now  doesn't the latter statement indicate that Dewey patterned his method of inquiry, or communication after the method of Socrates?  Moreover, with regard to the problem of philosophic method during his own era, Dewey explicitly says, "The work that once gave its name to philosophy, Search for Wisdom, has progressively receded into the background.  For wisdom differs from knowledge in being the application of what is known to intelligent conduct of the affairs of human life."[7]  So, on his view, wise communication applies to the "affairs of human life."  For he tells us,

> Of all affairs, communication is the most wonderful. That things should be able to pass from the plane of external pushing and pulling to that of revealing themselves to man, and thereby to themselves; and that the fruit of communication should be participation, sharing, is a wonder by the side of which transubstantiation pales.[8]

Apparently, then, Dewey anticipated a life of communicating, participating, sharing in some great conversations.  In other words, after his diligent struggle to counter the classic Greek notion of two orders of existence, and after working to help provide a satisfactory moral theory for life in this world of error, terror, and confusion, Dewey could end his terrestrial pilgrimage with a peaceful disposition, as Socrates allegedly did.

We are reminded by Dewey that "Socrates, the initiator of Athenian reflection, deliberately strove to limit theoretical discussion to moral and political subjects."[9] And rather similar to Socrates, Dewey also endeavored to get clear on what the correct forms of holiness, justice, and virtue are, as the preceding chapters have tried to show. It is very important, however, that we get clear on a major distinction between their procedures; for Dewey diverges from the method of Socrates in a highly significant way.

He explains the reason for his divergence in "Has Philosophy a Future?" (1949). As we noted in Chapter 3, when Dewey tried to help philosophers see the need to get the subject matter of philosophy straight, he held that in the past "it has been looked for in the wrong direction," and therefore "it is worthwhile to try the experiment of turning around and about the direction in which what is comprehensive is to be looked for."[10] However, as Dewey continues to explain his procedure, he discloses his divergence from Socrates; and he tells us quite explicitly that

> This turn-*about* is . . . a *re*-turn to the view of philosophy put forward of old by Socrates. It constitutes the search for wisdom that shall be a guide of life. It makes a return to the original view of philosophy as a *moral* undertaking in the sense in which the moral and the deeply and widely human are identical. It diverges from the road which Socrates and subsequent philosophers pursued in their search. It diverges from their search for wisdom that will pilot Man over treacherous shoals and through panic-laden storms.[11]

Now let us ask ourselves: Why did Dewey diverge from "the road" which Socrates and subsequent philosophers pursued? Seemingly, a very probable answer is that Dewey, unlike Socrates, had the advantage of studying classic Greek philosophy after the alleged death, burial, and resurrection of Jesus Christ. That is to say, because of Dewey's Congregationalist or Christian upbringing, his ideas about communication in the eternal dimension of the unexamined life were probably much more refined than Socrates. Therefore, instead of concentrating on questions about immortality and what might happen in some possible transcendental world, or an underworld, Dewey directed his thoughts towards, as he puts it, "what is most comprehensive *within* human affairs and occupations, not towards that which is completely independent of concerns and occupations that are distinctively human."[12]

Dewey maintained that "only the open recognition that philosophical issues and problems are related to circumstances of time and place can avoid the gulf which [yet] exists between philosophy and science."[13] Therefore, since the question of immortality, for the most part, has nothing to do with "circumstances of time and place" in this world, it appears that Dewey gave little or no thought to the subject. For instance, consider what he says in his article "On Immortality" (1928), which was published in *New York Times*.

> I have no beliefs on the subject of personal immortality. It seems to be a subject, being one of continued existence, for science rather than philosophy or a matter of physical evidence. If it can be proved, it would have to be along the lines of the psychical researchers, and so far I haven't been much impressed with their results.[14]

Unlike Socrates, then, Dewey focused his attention upon the problematic subject matters of life here on earth. Rather than deliberating about questions pertaining to immortality, his thoughts were concerned with helping create better environmental conditions where physical human beings must live.

No doubt Dewey was more concerned about getting people to understand some basic facts and consequences regarding the problem of death. For example, in his article "Dewey Describes Child's New World" (1932), he bluntly says,

> It is the simplest and most familiar of all facts that all who have matured to adult life die. The fact is familiar, but its full import is often overlooked. Civilization is not transmitted by physical means, but by care, nurture and education. It would die out in two short generations if it were not renewed by the newly born.[15]

Instead of thinking about immortality and communication in some other world, it should be clear that Dewey directed his thoughts towards preserving and improving human lives. As he reminds us, "There must be a proper environment, including not merely protection against foul air, milk and water, bad and inadequate food," but we must also supply the "positive conditions of a proper home and facilities for recreation."[16] So indeed, it seems safe to say that the problem of communication in this world was Dewey's main concern. He was primarily concerned about understanding how human organisms survive in their earthly environment; his big concern was getting philosophers and educators to see that "The brain and nervous system are part of the body, but they develop properly only when an adequate mental and moral education is secured."[17] To be sure, it was the latter kinds of concerns that took precedence over Dewey's ideas about communicating after death. Undoubtedly, though, because of the dread or fear that the subject of death poses for some people, we find that occasionally he did express his opinion(s) about the topic.

In his article "Intimations of Mortality" (1935), for instance, Dewey tells us,

> Many persons and movements allied with historic religions have made immortality more important than the existence of God, and indeed have conceived God's existence to be important chiefly as a warrant for personal continuance. The insistent fact of death, moreover, has tended to give the problem of immortality a first place in human thinking.[18]

As we have seen, though, the problem of immortality apparently did not receive first place in Dewey's thinking. No doubt he viewed death from a common sense perspective; that is, Dewey regarded the terrestrial period of each human organism as a "transaction." According to him, "From birth to death every human being is a *Party,* so that neither he nor anything done or suffered can possibly be understood when it is separated from the fact of participation in an extensive body of transactions—to which a given human being may contribute and which he modifies, but only in virtue of being a partaker in them."[19]

Dewey's physical communication and all of his other earthly transactions expired, as noted by Lavine, "on June 1, 1952, in his ninety-third year."[20] At Dewey's expiration, however, it seems clear that due to the historical advantage of his post-Socratic position, he knew that a final Judgment Day might determine what kind of communications and transactions he would experience in the eternal dimension of the unexamined life. He was well aware of the possibility, no doubt, that at some point "all that are in the graves," so we are told, "shall come forth; they that have done good unto the resurrection of life; and they that have done evil, unto the resurrection of damnation."[21] Dewey, of course, probably was confident that in case a final day of judging does occur, he would escape the "everlasting fire, prepared for the devil and his angels."[22] As we have seen, though, Dewey apparently did not give much thought to questions about immortality; and most likely, the reason why he didn't is because he knew that his good works would help keep him from being cut-off from all communication. Indeed, he probably knew that he wouldn't be among those who are going to be "cast out into outer darkness."[23]

It has been pointed up by McDermott, however, that Dewey "had an undeveloped doctrine of evil, the demonic, and the capacity of human beings *en masse* to commit heinous crimes against other human beings."[24] With respect to McDermott's observation, let us try to get clear on the context of Dewey's thoughts about this matter. That is to say, it is very important for us to understand his position. For example, he explicitly tells us,

> It is not the part of philosophy, as past thinkers held, to solve the problem of evil and to justify the ways of God to man. The real problem of evil is not to account for evil but to show how to control and lessen it.

> Philosophy may be conceived as a process of devising methods and hypotheses for the improvement of human life. It will not stop with analyzing and classifying as science does, but must devise ends worth striving for, and must find what resources we have for accomplishing these ends.[25]

Now considering his ideas about the problem of evil and the ways of God, it seems that Dewey was confident with his stand. What is more important, we see that he surely was concerned about the "improvement of human life," as he puts it. Therefore, despite the claims of McDermott, it appears that Dewey obviously was ready for a final judgment day, if there should be one.

Correctly comprehending the proper context of Dewey's thoughts about this topic apparently makes a great difference in determining what view we should attribute to him.

For as Dewey reminds us, "the most pervasive fallacy of philosophic thinking goes back to neglect of context."[26] What we should recognize, according to him, is that

> We grasp the meaning of what is said in our own language not because appreciation of context is unnecessary but because context is so unescapably present. It is taken for granted; it is a matter of course, and accordingly is not explicitly specified. Habits of speech, including syntax and vocabulary, and modes of interpretation have been formed in face of inclusive and defining situations of context. The latter are accordingly implicit in most of what is said and heard. We are not explicitly aware of the role of context just because our every utterance

is so saturated with it that it forms the significance of what we may say and hear.[27]

In light of Dewey's argument regarding the proper context of thought, this study has tried to depict his thinking in the correct context. Of course, Dewey additionally tells us that, "In the face to face communications of everyday life, context may be safely ignored."[28] What he seems to mean is that when individuals talk face to face, instead of through philosophic literature, for instance, they may be able to clarify their plausibly different interpretations of a given topic.

If the present writer could speak face to face with McDermott, for example, then it might be possible that the two of us could come to an agreement about Dewey's view of evil as a problem for humans. At any rate, when individuals enter dialogues attempting to clarify the context of a person's thought, Dewey informs us to bear in mind that

> Philosophy is criticism; criticism of the influential beliefs that underlie culture; a criticism which traces the beliefs to their generating conditions. . . . Such an examination terminates, whether so intended or not, in a projection of them into a new perspective which leads to new surveys of possibilities.[29]

With regard to Dewey's notion of philosophy as a criticism of beliefs, consider the observation we made in Chapter 6, for instance, where we noted Descartes's belief that "theology instructs us how to reach heaven." Now we've seen already that Dewey would most likely criticize such thinking, and he even indicates that "ideas of heaven have been conditioned by the cultures in which they were entertained."[30] What is more important, though, Dewey explicitly states the context of his thoughts about the issue. For he tells us, "It may be argued, I think, that much of the current belief in immortality is not primary, but is the product of inculcation, from infancy throughout life, of the idea that persons are rewarded in heaven and punished in hell."[31] Suppose, however, that Dewey could have spoken face to face with Descartes, then perhaps they would have been able to reconcile their different views. Likwise, maybe the present writer could come to an agreement with McDermott's reading of Dewey's position, if we could engage in face to face dialogue.

In any case, for those who remain here in this world of apparent flux, where some things seem to be constantly undergoing change, no doubt each of us must make our own individual decisions about what

Dewey believed, or thought about subjects such as God, evil, death, philosophy and truth. Throughout the pages of this book, the present writer has endeavored to share his interpretation of Dewey's views on the various subjects. However, it seems obvious that as long as we keep living here on earth, none of us shall ever really know for certain the beliefs or thoughts that Dewey held. Moreover, even if he were yet living among us himself, and communicating with us daily, it seems that we still would not necessarily know what he was actually thinking. For example, in the following statement Dewey alludes to the private domain of human beings, and says,

> A new idea is an unsettling of received beliefs; otherwise, it would not be a new idea. This is only to say that the production of new ideas is peculiarly a private performance.[32]

It is this private domain of being human, where new ideas, beliefs, thoughts, sensations, and consciousness occur, that apparently prevents one person from knowing what another person may be really thinking. No doubt, then, this is the sense in which we would have limited access to Dewey's actual thoughts. Nevertheless, he does note a principle that one may employ when considering what another person might be thinking; for he informs us that "Every scientific inquirer, even when he deviates most widely from current ideas, depends upon methods and conclusions that are a common possession and not private ownership, even though all of the methods and conclusions may at some time have been initially the product of private invention."[33]

So it seems clear that there are some difficulties involved in knowing what a person is actually thinking. Therefore, perhaps one of the best ways for us to know what Dewey was really thinking, is to consider his work in light of his own assertions about Instrumentalism. That is, as we observed in the conclusion of Chapter 2, he claims that his instrumentalism, as a "behaviorist theory of thinking and knowing," interprets the thoughts of a "knower" in terms of "obvious overtness." In other words, it is the habitual behavior of a knower that tends to reflect the way one thinks. For instance, Feuer tells us that "the historic men of wisdom felt that a religious ingredient was essential to their philosophy; though none of them were theologians, all found an intellectual ballast in traditional religious beliefs."[34] Those historic men of wisdom, no doubt, had disclosed their thoughts or beliefs through obvious overtness; and quite like them, says Feuer,

Dewey's longing for the community one finds in a church with "a common faith" never abated. Once, at Columbia University, Dewey happened to be "entertaining a visiting humanist from England." To the surprise of his assembled "horrified" students, "who were more doctrinaire than the master," Dewey "joined with this gentleman in proposing to establish some sort of humanist church in the United States."[35]

This obviously overt action of a historic man of wisdom was reported by Robert E. Fitch, a student of Dewey's at Columbia University and later Dean of the Pacific School of Religion at Berkeley, California.[36] Now in light of Fitch's and Feuer's report, perhaps the reader can see that Dewey continued to show his deep concern for the church during his later years, just as he had done during his early and middle years. Thus, to be sure, this seems to imply that he retained his belief in God; and consequently, his good works enabled him to go to his grave in peace.

As further confirmation of this interpretation, let us bear in mind that only five years before retiring from Columbia, Dewey published *Experience and Nature* (1925); and in it he informs us that

Beliefs about God, Nature, society and man are precisely the things that men most cling to and most ardently fight for. It is easier to wean a miser from his hoard, than a man from his deeper opinions. . . . In traditional discussion the fact is overlooked that the subject matter of belief is a good, since belief means assimilation and assertion. . . . [However] The "true" is indeed set up along with the good and the beautiful as a transcendent good, but the role of empirical good, of value, in the sweep of ordinary beliefs is passed by. The counterpart of this error, which isolates the subject matter of intellect from the scope of values and valuations, is a coresponding isolation of the subject matter of esthetic contemplation and immediate enjoyment from judgment. . . . Hence the primary function of philosophy at present is to make it clear that there is no such difference as this division assumes between science, morals, and esthetic appreciation. . . . Philosophic discourse partakes both of scientific and literary discourse. It has no stock of information or body of knowledge peculiarly its own . . . . Its business is to accept and utilize for a purpose the best available knowledge of its own time and place. And this purpose is criticism of beliefs, institutions, customs, policies with respect to their bearings upon good. . . . [yet] philosophy has no private score or knowledge or of methods for attaining truth, [and] it has no private access to good. . . . It has no Mosaic nor Pauline authority of revelation entrusted to it.  But it has the authority of intelligence, of criticism of these common and natural goods.

The difficulty is that philosophy, even when professing catholicity, has often been suborned.  [That is], Instead of being a free messenger of communication it has been a diplomatic agent of some special and partial interest; insincere, because in the name of peace it has fostered divisions that lead to strife, and in the name of loyalty has promoted unholy alliances and secret understandings.  One might say that profuseness of attestations to supreme devotion to truth on the part of philosophy is matter to arouse suspicion.  For it has usually been a preliminary to the claim of being a peculiar organ of access to highest and ultimate truth.  Such it is not; and it will not lose its esoteric and insincere air until the profession is disclaimed.  Truth is a collection of truth; and these constituent truths are in keeping of the best available methods of inquiry and testing . . . when collected under a single name, science.  As to truth, then, philosophy has no pre-eminent status . . . .  To note, however, contingency in connection with a concrete situation of life is that fear of the Lord which is at least the beginning of wisdom.[37]

In the preceding statement, as we can see, Dewey exhibits his thoughts about the subjects of God, philosophy, and truth through obviously overt assertions.  However, as this study has tried to show, John Dewey furnishes ample evidence that tends to indicate his beliefs.

For instance, the very first year after he became Philosopher Emeritus, Columbia, Dewey published *Philosophy and Civilization* (1931), and it provides some useful insight concerning the subjects of philosophy, truth, God, and heaven.  For he tacitly explains how we may use some of the heterogeneous students who wish to climb the continuous ladder of higher education.  If we really want to bring to light increasing measures of truth, then according to Dewey we should employ them in "the hunt for truth, beauty, virtue, wealth, social well-being, and even of heaven and of God."[38]

Approximately three years later *A Common Faith* (1934) was published, and he addressed the difficult problems that gather around the question of reference and divinity.  In this work we can see that Dewey anticipated those who would misinterpret his use of the term "God," for he tells us, "There are those who hold that the associations of the term with the supernatural are so numerous and close that any use of the word 'God' is sure to give rise to misconception and be taken as concession to traditional ideas."[39]   However, despite the various interpretations of what Dewey meant by the term "God," at least it should be clear to the reader that in this particular writing he definitely tries to point out "all the elements for a religious faith that shall not be confined to sect, class, or race."[40]

As another example of Dewey's obviously overt behavior, one can see that in 1940, beyond any reasonable doubt, he still was trying to get philosophers to consider the question of God's existence in light of his open-minded perspective.  For during that time Dewey published a review of Douglas Macintosh's *Social Religion*, and he tells us,

> The book itself discusses but one religion, namely Christianity. Professor Macintosh would not, I am confident, deny that the social aspects and implications of other great historic religions are worth examining, even though they fall outside the scope of this book. . . . Mr. Macintosh's book is divided into two parts . . . . [The] first part, "Principles of Social Religion," is an examination of the meaning of the idea of the Kingdom of God as that is presented in the New Testament when it is taken to be the central and controlling principle of the Christian faith. . . .
>
> As far as the present writer can judge, Mr. Macintosh does full justice to what has been urged regarding the influence of eschatological beliefs upon Jesus.  He also accepts many of the conclusions of what used to be called "higher criticism" regarding interpolations in the record and attributions to Jesus of interpretations made in light of later events.  But he holds that, even when the mode of expression of Jesus is influenced by the idea of a sudden eschatological change, what he asserted were ethical principles intended to be universally applicable.  This position is supported by examination of the social contents of the Old Testament literature which Jesus was presumably familiar, and by a detailed examination of the records of his teachings, especially the parables.[41]

Now don't Dewey's statements in his review of Macintosh's *Social Religion* seem to substantiate the validity of implications  (1) and (2) above?  The present writer thinks so.

Surely one does not need to be a great mathematician or statistician to calculate the numerous years that he must have spent thinking about the subject of God.  As this study has endeavored to show, Dewey employed the term "God" throughout the course of his highly productive seventy-year publishing career.  Moreover, the present writer could go on and on producing illustrations of Dewey's thoughts about God as a proper subject matter of philosophy. Likewise, more and more citations and explanations of Dewey's notion of truth could be produced. However, due to a delimited amount of space, it is hoped that those presented thus far has shed sufficient light on the evolution of Dewey's conception of philosophy and his notion of truth.

It is hoped, moreover, that the reader recognizes how Dewey apparently prepared himself to enter "a city which [has] foundations, whose builder and maker is God."[42] In other words, Dewey evidently believed that some forms of knowledge cannot be obtained from spoken or written texts. For as he takes care to remind us, "Without knowing how to use books our ability to get and understand actual facts would be reduced to almost zero. But the usual course is to treat what is in books as an end in themselves instead of means of creating ability to see and judge things which are outside of books."[43] Hence, it will help to keep this in mind, perhaps, whenever we are reading Dewey's works.

Anyway, in light of what he seems to have thought about the proper use of books, and what he seems to have thought about philosophy, truth, and God, it appears that the wisdom of Dewey's logic is based upon his view of communication in a world of two dimensions; one is visible to the physical eye, and the other is invisible. In the former, which we all have probably experienced, it seems that the occurrence of death is the most persistent factor of human existence; but in the latter dimension, which probably none of us have examined, it appears that death must be nonexistent. If we grant the possibility that this two dimensional world does indeed exist, then logically speaking, it sustains our observations regarding the twofold aspect of Dewey's theory of communication.

In addition, it seems that the twofold aspect of his theory of communication is the main reason why he tells us that in his *Logic*, "the absence of any attempt at symbolic formulation will doubtless cause serious objection in the minds of my readers."[44] But he goes on to explain that there is an absence of symbolization, first of all, because of "the need for development of a general theory of language in which form and matter are not separated," and secondly because he did not want to "perpetuate existing mistakes while strengthening them by seeming to give them scientific standing."[45] Thus, in view of his thoughts about symbolic logic, it is apparent that Dewey's theory of communication was designed to avoid the kind of paradoxical problems such as the Third Man argument posed by Plato's theory of Forms;

that is to say, the muliplication of entities needing to be explained or accounted for.

Unfortunately, though, when Dewey employs the word "experience" to explain how his logic is based upon his theory of communication, it seems to create confusion for some of his readers. In his explanation of the relation between discourse and experience, what he tries to make clear is that

> A universe of experience is the precondition of a universe of discourse. [Because] Without its controlling presence, there is no way to determine the relevancy, weight or coherence of any designated distinction or relation. . . . [And furthermore] It is a commonplace that a universe of discourse cannot be a term or element within itself. One universe of discourse may, however, be a term of discourse within *another* universe. The same principle applies in the case of universes of experience.[46]

Why didn't he provide an example to show what he meant by a "universe of discourse" and a "universe of experience"? Dewey says, "It *would* be a contradiction if I attempted to demonstrate by means of discourse, the existence of universes of experience."[47] Why? The reader can get a good grasp of what Dewey means by "contradiction," perhaps, if we consider the following example. For instance, let us suppose that eventually the day does come when "every knee shall bow to [God], and every tongue shall confess to God. So then every one of us shall give account to God of himself [or herself]."[48] This scenario, so it seems, is fairly illustrative of a situation in which only the individual can experience the uniqueness of the circumstances. With respect to such a case, no doubt Dewey would be correct in saying that, "It is not a contradiction by means of discourse to invite the reader to have for himself [or herself] that kind of an immediately experienced situation in which the presence of a situation as a universe of experience is seen to be the encompassing and regulating condition of all discourse."[49]

Dewey continued his efforts to clarify the logical relations between discourse and experience when he published "Experience, Knowledge and Value: A Rejoinder" (1939). In this article he responds to Russell's failure to recognize what he meant by an individual experiencing an "indeterminate situation," and he says,

> I have pointed out that one person cannot communicate an experience as immediate to another person. He can only invite that person to

institute the conditions by which the person himself will have that kind of situation the conditions for which are stated in discourse. Even if this difficult condition is fulfilled, there is no assurance that any one will so act as to have the experience.[50]

From Dewey's perspective, then, the most that a narrator could do to help Russell realize what it means to experience such a situation, especially a problematic one, is to describe "the experimental set-up, the material involved, the apparatus employed, the series of acts performed, the observations which result and state the conclusions reached."[51]    Once the narrator has done this, it would be left to the inquirer to accept the invitation and attempt to experience the given situation.    As Dewey reminds us, however, "Any one who refuses to go outside [one's own] universe of discourse—as Mr. Russell apparently does—has of course shut himself off from understanding what a 'situation,' as directly experienced subject matter, is."[52]    Nevertheless, Dewey kept trying to clarify his position; but it is not likely that he could help Russell, if he refused to make any serious effort to understand.

The present writer wonders whether Russell read "Whitehead's Philosophy" (1937), which Dewey published just one year before his *Logic.*    If he did read it, then seemingly he would have recognized that what Dewey liked most about Whitehead's work was that

> Upon the positive side there is the rather complex intermediary apparatus of God, harmony, mathematical relations, natural laws, that is required to effect the interweaving of eternal objects and immediate occasions.    I do not think that the difficulties found in reading Mr. Whitehead are due to his fundamental conception of experience.    On the contrary, given a reasonable degree of emancipation of philosophic imagination from philosophic tradition and its language, that idea seems to me extraordinarily luminous as well as productive.[53]

As we can see, Dewey explicitly endorses Whitehead's "generalized idea of experience," and clearly states that, "The conception of God in the total system seems to indicate that this is the proper interpretation, since some principle is certainly necessary, upon this premise, to act selectively in determining what eternal objects ingress in any given immediate occasion."[54]    So, even if it may be useless to wonder about Russell's reading of "Whitehead's Philosophy," at least it seems clear that Dewey retained his belief in God.

Anyway, four years earlier, in "The Adventures of Persuasion" (1934), Dewey had acknowledged how highly impressed he was with Whitehead's philosophical treatment of "the question of how eternal objects can be influentially embodied in the processes of change that constitute the actuality of the universe."[55] In this particular writing Dewey reviews Whitehead's *Adventures of Ideas* (1933), and he maintains that Whitehead's devotion to Plato "goes to show that Plato's attempt to unite a mathematical and religious interpretation of the universe is not the merely 'mystical' thing it is often taken to be."[56] Regarding Whitehead's interpretation of the course of historical events, moreover, Dewey explains that

> The religious reformation, to be of fortunate issue, must primarily base itself upon "moral and metaphysical intuitions" scattered throughout the germinal epoch lying between the Hebrew prophets and Plato and the stabilization of Western theology by Augustine. The elements that Mr. Whitehead believes the new reformation must recover and develop are, first of all, the fact brought out by Plato, that "the divine element in the world is to be conceived as a persuasive agency and not as a coercive agency"; second, the exemplification of this principle by Christ in act.[57]

For present purposes, the most pertinent point to notice about Whitehead's philosophy is that Dewey found it amenable with his theory of communication and his notion of truth. He informs us that certain chapters of *Adventures of Ideas* had been selected for specific reference "because of Whitehead's identification of the cosmological with (ultimately) the theological, but more because it brings the idea of 'persuasion' to the front."[58] As Dewey also points out, "The mutual relations of coercion and persuasion in Western history are the chief theme of the sociological section, which traces the means by which the idea of persuasion, formulated by Plato in connection with the general character of 'soul' and freedom, finally found its way, in conflict against ideas of slavery and coercion of circumstances, into power in Western civilization."[59] Hence it seems that Dewey may have considered Whitehead's process theology to be in line with his own idea of truth as "processes of change so directed that they achieve an intended consummation."[60]

As we prepare to bring this final chapter to a close, it is hoped that our brief look at Whitehead's philosophy has aided the reader in comprehending the developmental stages of Dewey's mature conceptions of philosophy and truth. For Dewey reminds us that "Alfred North Whitehead has called attention to the progressive shortening of the time-span of social change."[61] Presently, however, for those of us who reside in the visible world of "time and place," where the velocity of history appears to be accelerating at an almost alarming pace, what does the future hold for philosophy and human beings?

Before departing to the eternal dimension of the invisible world, Dewey made a statement that seems to be an appropriate reply to the latter question. He said, "Would there were prophets who are genuine seers who will warn against reactions to the past and who will show us how to take full advantage of the resources now at our disposal!"[62] In describing the human predicament during his own era, Dewey pointed out that, "Put in the language of common sense, the movement that goes by the name of *Individualism* is very largely responsible for the chaos now found in human associations—the chaos which is at the root of the present debasement of human beings."[63] Moreover, says Dewey,

> Separation and opposition of *individual* and *social* has its roots far back in history. It was initiated when man was linked to "the next world" instead of to his fellows in this world. . . . We can not grasp the significance of the crisis without a long look backward into the abyss of time. We cannot judge how to meet it without a long look ahead. My complementary point, in fine, is that we can understand the crisis only as we take it out of its narrow geographical and temporal setting and view it in long historical perspective.[64]

If we really wish to resolve this crisis in human history, as Dewey has reminded us, we must face the fact that "The economic aspect of human association decides the conditions under which human beings actually live."[65] For as we can see from his observations, it seems safe to say that he was a genuine seer himself, and a valiant warner as well.

With respect to the problem of economics, for example, he addresses the problem in "Philosophy's Future in Our Scientific Age: Never Was Its Role More Crucial" (1949). In this article he reiterates that "most moral problems are now what they are because of the conditions and problems of economic life."[66] What has happened in philosophy, according to Dewey's perception of the predicament, is that there has been "a creation of dualisms that are the intellectual manifestations of the divisions in life between what is regarded as supreme in value," and even today this insulation seems to prevail between "the subject matter of economic theory and the subject matter of moral theory."[67]   Thus, in order to counter the problem, Dewey contends that

> It is for the philosophers today to encourage and further methods of inquiry into human and moral subjects . . . to bring into existence a kind of knowlege which, by being thoroughly humane, is entitled to the name moral. . . . It is not of urgent importance that it be done by philosophers, or by any other special group of intellectuals. It is, however, in harmony with the claim of philosophers to deal with what is comprehensive and fundamental that they take a hand, perhaps a leading one, in promoting methods that will result in the understanding that is now absent. This type of activity at least seems to be the only way to halt the decline of philosophy in influence and in public esteem and bring about something like restoration.[68]

As our study has endeavored to show, of course, non-American critics such as Russell misconstrued Dewey's message regarding economics and moral matters.   We've seen how he spent time and energy trying to defend the pragmatic doctrine of Peirce and James against Russell's attacks.   However, Dewey's "Discussion of 'Freedom, in Relation to Culture, Social Planning, and Leadership'" (1932), provides an explicit statement of his own position; and in concurrence with George S. Counts, Dewey says, "One dominant tradition, with which I am no more in sympathy than is Dr. Counts, is for example that of getting ahead in a competitive struggle for pecuniary gain."[69] More than a decade earlier, however, Dewey had asserted that "So repulsive is a conception of truth which makes it a mere tool of private ambition and aggrandizement, that the wonder is that critics have attributed such a notion to sane men."[70]  In any case, for those Americans who recognize the urgent need to improve the economic system of capitalism, and are willing to do so, no doubt some of us may have to take the time to defend our beliefs, as Dewey did.

He has told us that "Communication can alone create a great community.  Our Babel is not one of tongues but of the signs and symbols without which shared experience is impossible."[71]  With respect to the employment of "signs and symbols," then, let us  heed Dewey's message that "Signs and symbols, language, are means of communication by which a fraternally shared experience is urshered in and sustained.   But the winged words of conversation in immediate intercourse have a vital import lacking in the fixed and frozen words of written speech."[72]  That is to say, for those of us who are serious in our efforts to discuss and employ the wisdom of Dewey's teachings, it seems expedient for us to understand that "Presentation is fundamentally important, and presentation is a question of art. . . . [Because] The function of art has always been to break through the crust of conventionalized and routine consciousness."[73]

Rather unfortunately, perhaps, Dewey does not provide an explicit solution for resolving the complex problems concerning philosophy and truth, but he surely seems to point us in the right direction when he says,

> It is no part of my task to outline in detail a program for renascent liberalism. But the question of "what is to be done" cannot be ignored. Ideas must be organized, and this organization implies an organization of individuals who hold these ideas and whose faith is ready to translate itself into action. . . . I for one do not believe that Americans living in the tradition of Jefferson and Lincoln will weaken and give up without a whole-hearted effort to make democracy a living reality. This, I repeat, involves organization.[74]

In light of Dewey's noteworthy directive, as we communicate among ourselves and the other heterogeneous members of society, let us also bear in mind that

> In national life as well as in our scholastic undertakings we best honor those whom we call Founding Fathers by trying to do for our own conditions what they accomplished in their time. Political and economic activities, as well as educational activities, have to adapt themselves to changed conditions. Democracy has to be continually fought for and won over again by every generation. . . . We cannot live upon the past in our national life any more than we can in bodily life.[75]

In communicating about our current society, and our prospects for a happy future, what we should be concerned about is that, as Dewey has tried to make clear to us, "There is urgent need for a philosophy of personal and institutional life that is consequent with present knowledge."[76] In other words, it is highly important for us to understand that, "The special technical problems of ageing are all connected with processes of growth, but in addition our philosophy of all life and of all social relations demands reconstruction of traditional beliefs upon the basis of Growth as the fundamental category."[77] Of course, the only way that we can achieve succesful communication and organization to resolve such issues, is to find enough people who have overcome the problem of "fear."

For as Dewey also reminds us, "Insecurity and fear make people adhere to some fixed body of social truth supposed to be already scientifically established."[78] But this was not the case with philosophers such as Peirce and James; for according to Dewey, "They rule[d] out all dogmatism, all cocksureness, all appeal to authority and ultimate first truths; they [kept] alive the spirit of doubt as the spring of the work of continually renewed inquiry—which is a work and not an argumentative skepticism."[79] Very much like Peirce and James, then, we find that for John Dewey, truth is apparently an ongoing and never ending process. That is to say, if he retained his belief in God, as asserted in implications (1) and (2) above.[80] Either way we consider the implications, however, it is evident that John Dewey has made his decisions, and we apparently must do the same, even if it means suspending judgment concerning the existence of God. Apart from our individual decisions, though, the question still remains: What shall we do about the future of philosophy? To be sure, as Dewey has reminded us, regardless of the course of action that we take, it definitely must include some kind of collective organizational effort. In this respect, he has tried to make it clear to us that "[Democracy] can be won only by extending the application of democratic methods, methods of consultation, persuasion, negotiation, cooperative intelligence in the task of making our own politics, industry, education—our culture generally—a servant and an evolving manifestation of democratic ideas."[81] So let's remember, then, as Hook has pointed up,

> We can list in broad outline the groups whose interests are represented in Dewey's philosophy. He speaks first of all for those who do productive labor of hand or brain, who desires not only continuous work but significant work commensurate with their capacities. . . . He speaks for those who wish to see the crucial problems and conflicts of our day settled by a voluntary consent obtained by persuasion, and not by terror and bloodshed.[82]

Also, however, let us bear in mind that it is not necessary that we all agree with Dewey in determining our course of action. For instance, some Deweyan supporters may take a stand similar to Ratner, who says,

> Despite my negative verdict on Dewey's peace efforts, the nonviolence movement led by Ghandi in India and by Martin Luther

King in the United States demonstrated that the resort to force could be effectively renounced on domestic issues in countries where the ruling groups could be influenced by appeals to human rights and by democratic governmental processes.[83]

In other words, as Dewey reminds us himself,

Democracy is a way of life controlled by a working faith in the possibilities of human nature. Belief in the Common Man is a familiar article in the democratic creed. That belief is without basis and significance save as it means faith in the potentialities of human nature as that nature is exhibited in every human being irrespective of race, color, sex, birth and family, of material cultural wealth. . . . Intolerance, abuse, calling of names because of differences of opinion about religion or politics or business, as well as differences of race, color, wealth or degree of culture are treason to the democratic way of life.[84]

In full agreement with Dewey's message, the present writer wishes to conclude by reminding his readers that, like Dewey says, "It is less important that we all believe alike than that we all inquire freely and put at the disposal of one another such glimpses as we may obtain of the truth for which we are in search."[85] Perhaps one of the best ways for us to "put at the disposal of one another" a sufficient glimpse of "the truth" for which we are in search, is to get clear on the form of holism that Dewey held; and he seems to express it rather well in *Experience and Nature* (1925), where he tells us that

Discourse itself is both instrumental and consummatory. Communication is an exchange which procures something wanted . . . . [Indeed] Language is always a form of action for an end, while at the same time it finds in itself all the goods of its possible consequences. For there is no mode of action as fulfilling and as rewarding as is concerted consensus of action. It brings with it the sense of sharing and merging in a whole.[86]

With respect to Dewey's holism, or his holistic perspective, unfortunately for us, too few philosophers have understood how he thought that "words" come to be. Regarding the process of generation, apparently they fail to recognize that from his perspective,

The sound, gesture, or written mark which is involved in language is a particular existence. But as such it is not a *word*, and it does not become a word by declaring mental existence; it becomes a word by gaining meaning; and it gains meaning when its use establishes a genuine community of action.[87]

As we continue our quest for truth, let us bear in mind the wisdom of Dewey's holism. Let's remember that we are the ones who can make communication easy or difficult. As Dewey points out, "Language is specifically a mode of interaction of at least two beings, a speaker [writer] and a hearer [reader]; it presupposes an organized group to which these creatures belong, and from whom they have acquired their habits of speech [writing]."[88] So let's keep Dewey's view in mind as we look for the truth in which we are in search.

# Notes

1.  Dewey, "The Value of Historical Christianity" (1889), in *Later Works,* Vol. 17, p. 529.
2.  Perhaps it should be noted here that there are some cases where, as Dewey puts it, "we must be content with an order of probability." See "What Are Universals?" (1936), in *Later Works*, Vol. 11, p. 112. Also, the probable suggestions that are presented by the present writer attempts to follow what Dewey refers to as "Peirce's philosophy he called Probabilism, which he opposed to Infallibilism in its myriad forms. . . . his assertion [is] that every scientific proposition is only probable." See Dewey's "Charles Sanders Peirce" (1937), in *Later Works*, Vol. 11, p. 483.
3.  Plato, *Apology* (40c), reprinted in Melchert's *The Great Conversation,* p. 93.
4.  Plato, *Apology* (41b), *Ibid.*, p. 94.
5.  Plato, *Apology* (41c), *Ibid.*, p. 94.
6.  Dewey, "Introduction" to *Problems of Men* (1946), in *Later Works,* Vol. 15, p. 169.
7.  Dewey, "Introduction" to *Problems of Men* (1946), in *Later Works,* Vol. 15, p. 157.
8.  Dewey, *Experience and Nature* (La Salle, Illinois: The Open Court Publishing Company, 1925). p. 138.
9.  Dewey, "Philosophy" (1934), in *Later Works,* Vol. 8, p. 21.
10. Dewey, "Has Philosophy a Future?" (1949), in *Later Works,* Vol. 16, p. 358.
11. Dewey, "Has Philosophy a Future?" (1949), in *Later Works,* Vol. 16, p. 365.
12. *Ibid.*, p. 359.
13. *Ibid.*
14. Dewey, "On Immortality" (1928), in *Later Works*, Vol. 17, p. 126.
15. Dewey, "Dewey Describes Child's New World" (1932), in *Later Works,* Vol. 6, p. 139.
16. *Ibid.*, p. 140.
17. Dewey, "Dewey Describes Child's New World" (1932), in *Later Works,* Vol. 6, p. 140.
18. Dewey, "Intimmations of Mortality" (1935), in *Later Works,* Vol. 11, p. 425.
19. Dewey, "Common Sense and Science" in *Knowing and the Known* (1949), reprinted in *Later Works,* Vol. 16, p. 243. Possibly, so it seems, Dewey's assertion that "every human being is a *Party* " may be in accord with Emerson's view. That is, as observed by Frederick Mayer, "The wise man, Emerson felt, is his own court and creates his own party, and he seeks direct contact with God." See Mayer's *A History of Educational Thought,* p. 352.

20.  T. Z. Lavine, "Introduction" in *Later Works*, Vol. 16, p. xii.
21.  *St. John* 5: 28-29 (King James Version).
22.  *St. Matthew* 25: 41 (King JamesVersion).
23.  *Ibid.*, 8: 12 (King James Version).
24.  McDermott, "Introduction" in *Later Works,* Vol. 11, p. xxxii.
25.  Dewey, "A Resume of Four Lectures on Common Sense, Science and Philosophy" (1932), in *Later Works,* Vol. 6, p. 431.
26.  Dewey, "Context and Thought" (1931), in *Later Works,* Vol. 6, p. 5.
27.  *Ibid.*, p. 4.
28.  *Ibid.*, p. 5.
29.  Dewey, "Context and Thought" (1931), in *Later Works,* Vol. 6, p. 19.
30.  Dewey, "Intimations of Mortality" (1935), in *Later Works*, Vol. 11, p. 426.
31.  *Ibid.*
32.  Dewey, *The Public and Its Problems* (1927), in *Later Works*, Vol. 2, p. 272.  With regard to the domain of private ideas that humans possess, we are reminded by Dewey that, "When the most assured dogmatist starts out to act in conformity with his dogma, he may have some private and subjective certainty as to the rightness and beneficence of his course. He may deem it absolutely warranted by the assured truths which he assumes that he possesses.  But actually he is *trying* something."  See "The Underlying Philosophy of Education" (1933), in *Later Works*, Vol. 8, p. 94.
33.  Dewey, "Authority and Social Change" (1936), in *Later Works*, Vol. 11, p. 142.  For the individual who is a "scientific inquirer," as Dewey also points out, "Record and communication are indispensable to knowledge. Knowledge cooped up in a private consciousness is a myth, and knowledge of social phenomena is peculiarly dependent upon dissemination, for only by distribution can such knowledge be either obtained or tested."  See *The Public and Its Problems* (1927), in *Later Works,* Vol. 2, p. 345. With respect to private ideas, perhaps it should be mentioned here that above seven years earlier, Dewey already had maintained that, "Left to himself, the individual can do little or nothing; he is likely to become involved in his own self-spun web of misconceptions.  The great need is the organization of co-operative research, whereby men attack nature collectively and the work of inquiry is carried on continuously from generation to generation."  See *Reconstruction in Philosophy* (1920), pp. 36-37.
34.  Lewis S. Feuer, "Introduction," in *Later Works,* Vol. 15, p. xxxi.
35.  *Ibid.*, p. xxxiii.
36.  *Ibid.*
37.  Dewey, *Experience and Nature* (La Salle, Illinois: The Open Court Publishing Company, 1925). pp. 328-34.
38.  Dewey, "Interpretation of the Savage Mind," in *Philosophy and Civilization* (New York: Capricorn Books, 1931). p. 187.  Dewey says,

"It is true that all valuable as well as new ideas begin with minorities, perhaps even a minority of one. The important consideration is that opportunity be given that idea to spread and to become the possession of the multitude." See *The Public and Its Problems* (1927), in *Later Works*, Vol. 2, p. 365.

39. Dewey, *A Common Faith* (New Haven: Yale University Press, 1934). p. 51.

40. *Ibid.*, p. 87.

41. Dewey, Review. "*Social Religion* by Douglas Clyde Macintosh" (1940), in *Later Works*, Vol. 14, pp. 286-88.

42. *Hebrews* 11: 10 (King James Version). The following statement seems to divulge Dewey's ideas about things that may be found outside the "immediate grasp" of spoken and written communication. Dewey says, "That Plato and Aristotle should have borrowed from the communal objects of the fine arts, from ceremonies, worship and the consummatory objects of Greek culture, is something to be thankful for. That, after having enforced the loan, they spurned the things from which they derived their models and criteria is not so admirable. This lack of piety concealed from them the poetic and religious character of their own constructions, and established in the classic Western philosophic tradition the notions that immediate grasp is knowledge; that things are placed in graded reality . . . and that the order of reality in Being is coincident with a predetermined rank of Ends." See *Experience and Nature* (1925), p. 91.

43. Dewey, "Between Two Worlds" (1944), in *Later Works*, Vol. 17, p. 464. In light of Dewey's reminder about how to treat books, perhaps we should also note his assertion that "it was man and and not science that educated man into becoming a scientific man; and it is man, not science, that commends and eulogizes science." Moreover, says Dewey, "What is called the conflict of science and religion is not a conflict of two abstractions, two Platonic entities, but of social groups and forces. In spite of what literary critics say, literature is written by men and women and not by imagination and abstract faculties, and men and women are subject to the influences of their time." See "Some Connexions of Science and Philosophy" (1911), in *Later Works*, Vol. 17, pp. 403, 412.

44. Dewey, *Logic: The Theory of Inquiry* (1938), in *Later Works*, Vol. 12, p. 4.

45. *Ibid.* Seemingly, a clue to Dewey's thinking about symbols may be seen in his assertion that, "Many years ago I heard a distinguished English mathematician, Cayley, say there was dispute about whether the method of mathematics was inductive or deductive, but that, as he saw it, it was neither, being more like *poetry.*" In other words, according to Dewey, "Mathematics, in short, is fruitfully applicable in our dealings with the world, but no more than any other language is it part of that world save as man himself is part of it." See "Man and Mathematics" (1947), in *Later Works*, Vol. 15, pp. 376-77. Approximately six years earlier, though,

Dewey was arguing that, "A special point is made of insisting that the main connection of valid philosophy is with mathematics and that mathematics is the science that has nothing to do with anything which actually exists either in man or nature. This self-denying ordinance of philosophers is in part by way of doing penance for exaggerated claims previous philosophers have put forth. But it is also in effect if not in intention a way of evading contact with social issues. It is no matter of surprise then that this school of philosophy has made an alliance with linguistic students who hold that if we only eliminated all emotive quality and bearing from the words we use, thereby depriving them of any connection whatever with what we do and have to do, the great step needed for advance in social science would be taken. . . . Nothing I have said indicates disrespect for the importance that is now taken by the study of language in contemporary philosophy. On the contrary, communication, which is, I take it, the definitive trait of language, is the central social fact. The dual relation of language, its connection on one side with ideas and emotions, and on the other side with social process, only affords another reason why one basic problem of philosophy at the present concerns the relation of emotion and intelligence in the make-up of human beings." See "Lessons from the War—in Philosophy" (1941), in *Later Works,* Vol. 14, pp. 324-25.

46. Dewey, *Logic: The Theory of Inquiry* (1938), in *Later Works*, Vol. 12, p. 74. As an example of the difficulty that Dewey encountered employing the word "experience," approximately six years later we find him corresponding with Arthur F. Bentley; and Dewey says to him, "I agree with what you say about dropping 'experience,' as not needed. I should like the mode of treatment a little more sympathetic—probably because of my own past struggles." Dewey made this statement to Bentley on May 12, 1944. See *John Dewey and Arthur F. Bentley: A Philosophical Correspondence, 1932-1951.* Sidney Ratner and Jules Altman, eds. (New Brunswick, N. J.: Rutgers University Press, 1964). p. 246. About five years later, however, we find that Dewey still was convinced about the importance of employing the term "experience" in his discourse; for he says, "I always wondered on what ground those who reject the generalized view of 'experience,' such as is presented for example in *Experience and Nature,* justify their own acceptance of the findings of, say, astronomers and/or physicists working in the field of infra-atomic events. . . . Were they to examine what the word 'experience' stands for and names, . . . I think they might refrain from adverse criticism of a generalized view of experience upon which their own criticisms must rest for validity. . . ." See "Experience and Existence: A Comment" (1949), in *Later Works,* Vol. 16, p. 386.

47. Dewey, *Logic: The Theory of Inquiry* (1938), in *Later Works,* Vol. 12, p. 75.

48. *Romans* 14: 11 (King James Version).

49. Dewey, *Logic: The Theory of Inquiry* (1938), in *Later Works,* Vol. 12, p. 75. With regard to the problem of clarifying his meaning of "experience," Dewey also tells us that, "There is another difficulty in grasping the meaning of what has been said. It concerns the use of the word 'quality'" (*Ibid.*). It seems, then, that he had trouble getting his readers to see that all experiences must have some kind of quality. Four years later, for instance, he tries to further clarify this matter in "Inquiry and Indeterminateness of Situations" (1942). Dewey responds to D. S. Mackay's "What Does Mr. Dewey Mean by an 'Indeterminate situation'?" and he clearly contends that "no word can describe or convey a *quality*." "The words used," as Dewey informs us, "can at best only serve to produce in the hearer or reader an experience in which the quality mentioned is directly had or experienced." Reprinted in *Later Works*, Vol. 15, p. 34.

50. Dewey, "Experience, Knowledge and Value: A Rejoinder" (1939), in *Later Works*, Vol. 14, pp. 30-31.

51. *Ibid.*, p. 31.

52. *Ibid.* Although Russell might have refused to take seriously Dewey's "substitution of 'inquiry' for 'truth' as the fundamental concept of logic and theory of knowledge," it is apparent that the former recognized how firmly the latter had fixed his belief in God. For Russell informs us himself that, "In every writer on philosophy there is a concealed metaphysic, usually unconscious; even if his subject is not metaphysics, he is almost certain to have an uncritically believed system which underlies his explicit arguments. Reading Dr. Dewey makes me aware of my own unconscious metaphysic as well as his." See Russell's "Dewey's New Logic," in *The Basic Writings of Bertrand Russell* , R. E. Egner and L. E. Dennon, eds. (New York: Simon and Schuster, 1961). p. 191.

53. Dewey, "Whitehead's Philosophy" (1937), in *Later Works*, Vol. 11, p. 153. Perhaps it should be noted here that approximately four years later, in "The Philosophy of Whitehead" (1941), Dewey discussed the initial philosophical principles postulated by Plato and Aristotle, and he informs us that their principles "seemed to descend directly via pure intellect, out of the ether of reason, situated next to God or perhaps in his own intrinsic abode." Reprinted in *Later Works,* Vol. 14, p. 123.

54. Dewey, "Whitehead's Philosophy" (1937), in *Later Works*, Vol. 11, p. 152.

55. Dewey, "The Adventure of Persuasion" (1934), in *Later Works,* Vol. 8, p. 356.

56. *Ibid.*, p. 357.

57. Dewey, "The Adventure of Persuasion" (1934), in *Later Works*, Vol. 8, p. 357. It is also interesting to note that several years earlier Dewey pointed out that "The attempt to decide by law that the legends of a primitive Hebrew people regarding the genesis of man are more authoritative than the results of scientific inquiry might be cited as a

typical example of the sort of thing which is bound to happen when the accepted doctrine is that a public organized for political purposes, rather than experts guided by specialized inquiry, is the final umpire and arbiter of issues." See *The Public and Its Problems* (1926), in *Later Works,* Vol. 2, pp. 312-13.

58. Dewey, "The Adventure of Persuasion" (1934), in *Later Works,* Vol. 8, p. 358.

59. *Ibid.*

60. Dewey, *Experience and Nature* (La Salle, Illinois: The Open Court Publishing Company, 1925). p. 135. Perhaps it should be mentioned here that in "The Changing Intellectual Climate" (1926), Dewey presented a review of Whitehead's *Science and The Modern World* (1925), which also indicates the affinity between their views on discourse and experience as a logically related process.

61. Dewey, "Science and Society" (1931), in *Later Works,* Vol. 6, p. 53.

62. Dewey, "The Crisis in Human History: The Danger of the Retreat to Individualism" (1946), in *Later Works,* Vol. 15, p. 223. With respect to the need for true "prophets," Dewey says, "Intellectual prophecy is dangerous; but if I read the cultural signs of the times aright, the next synthetic movement in philosophy will emerge when the significance of the social sciences and arts has become an object of reflective attention in the same way that mathematical and physical sciences have been made the objects of thought in the past, and when their full import is grasped." See "From Absolutism to Experimentalism" (1930), in *Later Works,* Vol. 5, p. 159. Also, according to Dewey, "One thing is sure: [William James] was a prophet of the future; all the vital currents of science and philosophy have set in the direction in which he pointed." Moreover, says Dewey, "If you wish to know what it was in American life that William James stood for, no better answer can be found than that given by Mr. Kallen in his Introduction. Mr. James gave intellectual expression to the life of the pioneer who made the country. There is similarity between the personal, the private, experiences of James whereby his own thought was nurtured and 'the free responses of the American people to the American scene.' The latter have to do 'with the unprecedented, the hazardous, the unpredictable in the adventure of the white man on the American continent. . . . They are most at play in the effort of the pioneer; the will to believe at one's own risk in the outcome of an enterprise the success of which is not guaranteed in advance is what they sum up to." See "William James in Nineteen Twenty-Six" (1926), in *Later Works,* Vol. 2, pp. 158-59.

63. Dewey, "The Crisis in Human History: The Danger of the Retreat to Individualism" (1946), in *Later Works*, Vol. 15, p. 212.

64. Dewey, "The Crisis in Human History: The Danger of the Retreat to Individualism" (1946), in *Later Works,* Vol. 15, p. 212. According to Dewey, "The emphasis James places upon the individual quality of human

beings and all things is, of course, central in his pluralism. But the adjective 'individual' is often converted into a noun, and then human beings and all objects and events are treated as if they were individual and nothing but individual. The result is that identification of human beings with something supposed to be completely isolated which is the curse of the so-called individualistic movement in economics, politics, and psychology. I find the actual position of James to be well represented in a remark he quotes . . . 'There is very little difference between one man and another; but what little there is, is *very important*.' It is this element which is precious because it is that which nobody and nothing else can contribute, and which is the source of all creativity. Generic properties on the other hand are replaceable, and express routines of nature." See "William James and the World Today" (1942), in *Later Works*, Vol. 15, pp. 4-5.

65. Dewey, "The Crisis in Human History: The Danger of the Retreat to Individualism" (1946), in *Later Works,* Vol. 15, p. 218.

66. Dewey, "Philosophy's Future in Our Scientific Age: Never Was Its Role More Crucial" (1949), in *Later Works*, Vol. 16, p. 371.

67. *Ibid.*

68. Dewey, "Philosophy's Future in Our Scientific Age: Never Was Its Role More Crucial" (1949), in *Later Works*, Vol. 16, pp. 375-76.

69. Dewey, "Discussion of 'Freedom, in Relation to Culture, Social Planning, and Leadership" (1932), in *Later Works*, Vol. 6, p. 142.

70. Dewey, *Reconstruction in Philosophy* (1920), p. 157.

71. Dewey, *The Public and Its Problems* (1927), in *Later Works,* Vol. 2, p. 324.

72. Dewey, *The Public and Its Problems* (1927), in *Later Works*, Vol. 2, p. 371.

73. *Ibid.*, p. 349. With respect to Dewey's concept of "art," perhaps it should be reiterated here that according to him, "In the case of material things, possession by one excludes possession, use, and enjoyment by others. In the case of the intangibles of art the exact opposite is the case. The more the arts flourish, the more they belong to all persons alike, without respect to wealth, birth, race, or creed. . . . This is what is meant when we say that art is universal—more universal than is that other intangible, science, since the arts speak a language which is closer to the emotions and imaginations of every man." Indeed, says Dewey, it is "the values of the arts which nourish the human spirit with the accomplishment of our past history which strengthens that legitimate pride, which enables one to say, 'I am an American citizen!'." See "Art as Our Heritage" (1940), in *Later Works*, Vol. 14, pp. 256-57.

74. Dewey, *Liberalism and Social Action* (1935), in *Later Works,* Vol. 11, p. 64. Perhaps we should stress again that Dewey evidently believed that the proper employment of "propaganda" is the key to a collective organizational effort. For as he reminds us, "Intelligence in politics

when it is identified with discussion means reliance upon symbols. The invention of language is probably the greatest single invention achieved by humanity. . . . The nineteenth-century establishment of parliamentary institutions, written constitutions and suffrage as a means of political rule, is a tribute to the power of symbols. . . . [But] 'Propaganda' is the inevitable consequence of the combination of these influences and it extends to every area of life." See *Liberalism and Social Action* (1935), in *Later Works*, Vol. 11, p. 51. Regarding the way we should employ propaganda, unfortunately we find Dewey saying, "The discussion of propaganda and propagandism alone, however, demand a volume, and could be written only by one much more experienced than the present writer. Propaganda can accordingly only be mentioned, with the remark that the present situation is one unprecedented in history." See *The Public and Its Problems* (1927), in *Later Works*, Vol. 2, p. 348.

75. Dewey, "Education: 1800-1939" (1939), in *Later Works*, Vol. 14, pp. 271-72.

76. Dewey, "Introduction" to *Problems of Ageing* (1939), in *Later Works*, Vol. 14, p. 349.

77. *Ibid.* No doubt Dewey wished for a society in which individuals (infants) could grow to maturity and die— if it must happen—with grace, instead of growing up in a world full of fear and suffering.

78. Dewey, "Charles Sanders Peirce" (1937), in *Later Works*, Vol. 11, p. 484. With regard to the problem of "fear," for example, Dewey says, "The writings of Thomas Hobbes, the real founder of British theory are important in this connection. . . . . . . he appealed especially to fear and the need of security. English political thought after Hobbes consistently interpreted human nature in terms of the primacy of non-rational factors . . . . The economists who set out to give intellectual expression to the rising industrialism started from the affective side of human nature in accordance with prevailing English doctrine." See "Human Nature" (1932), in *Later Works*, Vol. 6, p. 36.

79. Dewey, "Charles Sanders Peirce" (1937), in *Later Works*, Vol. 11, p. 484.

80. We have cited several explicit statements of his belief in God already, and he also seems to be implying it when says, "We either should surrender our professed belief in the supremacy of ideal and spiritual values and accomodate our beliefs to the predominant material orientation, or we should through organized endeavor institute the socialized economy of material security and plenty that will release human energy for pursuit of higher values. . . . [Because] Regimentation of material and mechanical forces is the only way by which the mass of individuals can be released from regimentation and consequent suppression of their cultural possibilities." See *Liberalism and Social Action* (1935), in *Later Works*, Vol. 11, pp. 62-63.

81. Dewey, "Democratic Ends Need Democratic Methods for Their Realization" (1939), in *Later Works*, Vol. 14, p. 367.
82. Sidney Hook, *John Dewey: An Intellectual Portrait* (Connecticut: Greenwood Press Publishers, 1939, 1971). p. 238.
83. Sidney Ratner, "Introduction" (1989) to *Later Works*, Vol. 17, p. xxi. Although Ratner seems to think that Dewey's "peace efforts" were insufficient, it is interesting to note the following observations. In 1940, for instance, Ratner said, "John Dewey is today the embodiment of America's most sensitive conscience, constructive intelligence, and intense democratic faith. Eighy years of his life have grown out of, and have been woven into, the fabric of American civilization. He came out of the heart of the American tradition. . . and his place is as secure there as that of Jefferson, Emerson, Whitman or Lincoln. Like them he is a symbol to the people, a molder of tradition, an architect of the future." See Ratner's "Foreword" to *The Philosopher of the Common Man* (New York: Greenwood Press Publishers, 1940). p. 7.
84. Dewey, "Creative Democracy—The Task Before us" (1939), in *Later Works*, Vol. 14, pp. 226-27. Let us remember, now, just one decade before departing from this visible world of error, terror, and confusion, Dewey explicitly asserted that, "Genuine toleration does not mean merely putting up with what we dislike, nor does it mean indifference and a conviction that difference of faith is of no importance because none of them matters. It includes active sympathy with the struggles and trials of those of other faiths than ours and a desire to cooperate with them in the give-and-take process of search for more light." See "Religion and Morality in a Free Society" (1942), in *Later Works,* Vol. 15, p. 183.
85. Dewey, "Experience, Knowledge and Value: A Rejoinder" (1939), in *Later Works*, Vol. 14, pp. 89-90.
86. Dewey, *Experience and Nature* (La Salle: Open Court, 1925). p. 152.
87. *Ibid.*, p. 153.
88. Dewey, *Experience and Nature* (La Salle: Open Court, 1925). p. 153.

# Bibliography

## I. Works by John Dewey

All citations refer to the original source or reprinted references in the Southern Illinois University edition of *The Collected Works of John Dewey, 1882-1953,* 37 Vols., under the general editorship of Jo Ann Boydston: *The Early Works of John Dewey, 1882-1898.* 5 vols. (henceforth abbreviated as *Early Works*). *The Middle Works of John Dewey, 1899-1924.* 15 vols. (henceforth abbreviated as *Middle Works*). *The Later Works of John Dewey, 1925-1953.* 17 vols. (henceforth abbreviated as *Later Works*).

"Address to the National Association for the Advancement of Colored People" (1932), reprinted in *Later Works,* Vol. 6, p. 224.

"The Adventures of Persuasion" (1933). Review of Alfred North Whitehead's *Adventures of Ideas.* Reprinted in *Later Works*, Vol. 8, p. 355.

"Aesthetic Experience as a Primary Phase and as an Artistic Development" (1950), reprinted in *Later Works*, Vol. 16, p. 395.

"Affective Thought" (1926), reprinted in *Later Works*, Vol. 2, p. 104.

"The Ambiguity of 'intrinsic Good'" (1942), reprinted in *Later Works*, Vol. 15, p. 42.

"Anti-Naturalism in Extremis" (1943), reprinted in *Later Works*, Vol. 15, p. 46.

"Are Naturalists Materialists?" (1945), reprinted in *Later Works*, Vol. 15, p. 109.

"Art as Our Heritage" (1940), reprinted in *Later Works*, Vol. 14, p. 255.

"Art in Education—Education in Art" (1926), reprinted in *Later Works*, Vol. 2, p. 111.

"The Art of Thought" (1926). Review of *The Art of Thought* (1926), by Graham Wallas. Reprinted in *Later Works,* Vol. 2, p. 231.

"Authority and Social Change" (1936), reprinted in *Later Works*, Vol. 11, p. 130.

"The Basic Values and Loyalties of Democracy" 1941), reprinted in *Later Works,* Vol. 14, p. 275.

"Bergson on Instinct" (1935). Review of *The Two Sources of Morality and Religion* (1935), by Henri Bergson. Reprinted in *Later Works*, Vol. 11, p. 428.

"Between Two Worlds" (1944), reprinted in *Later Works*, Vol. 17, p. 451.

"Bishop Brown: A Fundamentalist Modernist" (1926), reprinted in *Later Works*, Vol. 2, p. 163.

"By Nature and by Art" (1944), reprinted in *Later Works*, Vol. 15, p. 84.

"The Case for Bertrand Russell" (1940), reprinted in *Later Works,* Vol. 14, p. 231.

"The Case of Odell Waller: The Supreme Court to Be Asked Again to Hear Negro's Petition" (1942), reprinted in *Later Works*, Vol. 15, p. 356.

"The Changing Intellectual Climate" (1926). Review of Alfred North Whitehead's *Science and the Modern World. Reprinted in LaterWorks,* Vol. 2, p. 221.

"Characteristics and Characters: Kinds and Classes" (1936), reprinted in *Later Works*, Vol. 11, p. 95.

"Charles Sanders Peirce" (1937), reprinted in *Later Works,* Vol. 11, p. 479.

"Church Leaders Ask Church Act on Unemployment" (1932), reprinted in *Later Works*, Vol. 6, p. 381.

"The Church and Society" (1885), reprinted in *Later Works*, Vol. 17, p. 19.

"The Collapse of a Romance" (1932), reprinted in *Later Works,* Vol. 6, p. 69.

"Comment on 'Religion at Harvard'" (1947), reprinted in *Later Works,* Vol. 17, p. 135.

*A Common Faith* (New Haven: Yale University Press, 1934). Reprinted in *Later Works,* Vol. 9, pp.1-60.

"Context and Thought" (1931), reprinted in *Later Works*, Vol. 6, p. 3.

"'Contrary to Human Nature'" (1940), reprinted in *Later Works*, Vol. 14, p. 258.

"Contribution to Democracy in a World of Tensions" (1951), reprinted in *Later Works,* Vol. 16, p. 399.

"Contribution to 'Religion and the Intellectuals'" (1950), reprinted in *Later Works*, Vol. 16, p. 390.

"Corporate Personality" (1926), reprinted in *Later Works*, Vol. 2, p. 22.

"Creative Democracy—The Task Before Us" (1939), reprinted in *Later Works*, Vol. 14, p. 224.

"The Crisis in Human History: The Danger of the Retreat to Individualism" (1946), reprinted in *Later Works*, Vol. 15, p. 210.

"Dedication Address of the Barnes Foundation" (1925), reprinted in *Later Works,* Vol. 2, p. 382.

*Democracy and Education* (New York: MacMillan Company, 1916). Reprinted in *Later Works,* Vol. 9.

"Democracy Joins the Unemployed" (1932), reprinted in *Later Works,* Vol. 6, p. 239.

"Democratic Ends Need Democratic Methods for Their Realization" (1939), reprinted in *Later Works,* Vol. 14, p. 367.

"The Development of American Pragmatism" (1922), reprinted in *Later Works*, Vol. 2, p. 3.

"Dewey Describes Child's New World" (1932), reprinted in *Later Works,* Vol. 6, p. 137.

"The Dewey School: Appendix 2" (1936), reprinted in *Later Works,* Vol. 11, p. 202.

"Discussion of 'Freedom, in Relation to Culture, Social Planning, and Leadership'" (1932), reprinted in *Later Works*, Vol. 6, p. 142.

"The Economic Situation: A Challenge to Education" (1932), reprinted in *Later Works*, Vol. 6, p. 123.

"Education: 1800-1939" (1939), reprinted in *Later Works*, Vol. 14, p. 266.

"Education and New Social Ideals" (1936), reprinted in *Later Works*, Vol. 11, p. 167.

"Education and Social Change" (1937), reprinted in *Later Works,* Vol. 11, p. 408.

*Educational Lectures Before Brigham Young Academy* (1901), reprinted in *Later Works,* Vol. 17, pp. 211-347.

"An Emprical Survey of Empiricisms" (1935), reprinted in *Later Works,* Vol. 11, p. 69.

*Essays in Experimental Logic* (Chicago: University Press, 1916), reprinted in *Later Works*, Vol. 10, p. 319.

"Ethical Subject-Matter and Language" (1945), reprinted in *Later Works*, Vol. 15, p. 127.

"Events and the Future" (1926), reprinted in *Later Works,* Vol. 2, p. 62.

*Experience and Education* (1938), reprinted in *Later Works*, Vol. 13, pp. 1-62.

"Experience and Existence: A Comment" (1949), reprinted in *Later Works*, Vol. 16, p. 383.

*Experience and Nature* (La Salle, Illinois: Open Court Publishing Company, 1925), reprinted in *Later Works*, Vol. 1.

"Experience, Knowledge and Value: A Rejoinder" (1939), reprinted in *Later Works,* Vol. 14, p. 3.

"The Federal Government and Unemployment" (1931), reprinted in *Later Works,* Vol. 6, p. 377.

"The Field of 'Value'" (1949), reprinted in *Later Works*, Vol. 16, p. 343.

"Foreword" (1926) to *The Story of Philosophy,* by W. J. Durant, reprinted in *Later Works*, Vol. 2, p. 387.

"The Founder of American Pragmatism" (1935). Review of *Collected Papers of Charles Sanders Peirce,* Charles Hartshorne and Paul Weiss, eds., reprinted in *LaterWorks*, Vol. 11, p. 421.

*Freedom and Culture* (New York: G. P. Putnam's Sons, 1939), reprinted in *Later Works*, Vol. 13, p. 63.

"From Absolutism to Experimentalism" (1930), reprinted in *Later Works*, Vol. 5, p. 147.

"Full Warehouses and Empty Stomachs" (1931), reprinted in *Later Works*, Vol. 6, p. 341.

"Future of Liberalism" (1935), reprinted in *Later Works,* Vol. 11, p. 258.

"The Future of Liberalism" (1935), reprinted in *Later Works,* Vol. 289.

"The Future of Philosophy" (1947), reprinted in *Later Works*, Vol. 17, p. 466.

"General Propositions, Kinds, and Classes" (1936), reprinted in *Later Works*, Vol. 11, p. 118.

"George Herbert Mead as I Knew Him" (1931), reprinted in *Later Works*, Vol. 6, p. 22.

"A God or The God?" Review. *Is There a God? A Conversation.* New York: Willett, Clark and Co., 1932. Douglas C. Macintosh, Max Carl Otto and Henry Nelson Wieman. Reprinted in *Later Works*, Vol. 9. Ed. Jo Ann Boydston. pp. 213-22.

"Has Philosophy a Future?" (1949) reprinted in *Later Works*, Vol. 16, p. 358.

"Health and Sex in Higher Education" (1885), reprinted in *Early Works*, Vol. 1, p. 64.

"The Health of Women and Higher Education" (1885), reprinted in *Later Works,* Vol. 17, p. 7.

"'The Higher Learning in America'" (1937), reprinted in *Later Works*, Vol. 11, p. 402.

"How Do Concepts Arise from Precepts?" (1891), reprinted in *Early Works*, Vol. 3, p. 142.

"How Is Mind to Be Known"? (1942), reprinted in *Later Works*, Vol. 15, p. 27.

*How We Think: A Restatement of the Relation of Reflective Thinking to the Educative Process* (1910), reprinted in *Later Works*, Vol. 8, p. 105.

"How, What, and What for in Social Inquiry" (1951), reprinted in *Later Works*, Vol. 16, p. 333.

"Human Nature" (1932), reprinted in *Later Works*, Vol. 6, p. 29.

*Human Nature and Conduct* (New York: Henry Holt and Company, 1920). Reprinted in *Middle Works*, Vol. 14.

"I Believe" (1939), reprinted in *Later Works,* Vol. 14, p. 91.

"Importance, Significance, and Meaning" (1950), reprinted in *LaterWorks,* Vol. 16, p. 318.

*Individualism, Old and New* (New York: Minton, Balch and Company, 1930), reprinted in *Later Works,* Vol. 5, p. 41.

"Individuality and Experience" (1926), reprinted in *Later Works,* Vol. 2, p. 55.

*The Influence of Darwin on Philosophy: And Other Essays in Contemporary Thought* (New York: Henry Holt and Company, 1910). "The Influence of Darwinism on Philosophy," reprinted in *Middle Works*, Vol. 4, p. 3.

"Inquiry and Indeterminateness of Situations" (1942), reprinted in *Later Works*, Vol. 15, p. 34.

"Interpretation of the Savage Mind" (1902), reprinted in *Middle Works*, Vol. 2, p. 39.

"Intimations of Immortality" (1935), reprinted in *Later Works*, Vol. 11, p. 425.

"Introduction" (1939), to *James's Talks to Teachers on Psychology*; written with William Heard Kilpatrick. Reprinted in *Later Works*, Vol. 14, p. 337.

"Introduction" (1935) to *Looking Forward* (1936), reprinted in *Later Works*, Vol. 16, p. 48.

"Introduction" to *Problem of Ageing* (1939), reprinted in *Later Works*, Vol. pp. 341-50.

"Introduction" (1946) to *Problems of Men:The Problems of Men and The Present State of Philosophy* reprinted in *Later Works*, Vol. 15, p. 154.

"Introduction" to *Selected Poems of Claude McKay* (1953), reprinted in *Later Works*, Vol. 17, p. 53.

"Introduction" to *The Bertrand Russell Case* (1941); edited with Horace M. Kallen. Reprinted in *Later Works*, Vol. 14, p. 357.

"Inventory of Philosophy Taught in American Colleges" (1886), reprinted in *Early Works*, Vol. 1, p. 116.

"Is Logic a Dualistic Science?" (1890), reprinted in *Early Works,* Vol. 3, p. 75.

"James Hayden Tufts " (1943), reprinted in *Later Works*, Vol. 15, p. 324.

"The Jameses" (1936). Review of *The Thought and Character of William James,* by Ralph Barton Perry. Reprinted in *Later Works*, Vol. 11, p. 441.

"The Jobless—A Job for All of Us" (1931), reprinted in *Later Works*, Vol. 6, p. 153.

"John Dewey Responds" (speech delivered at the Hotel Commodore, New York City, 20 October 1949). First published in *John Dewey at Ninety*, H. W. Laidler, ed. (New York: League for Industrial Democracy, 1950). Reprinted in *Later Works,* Vol. 17, p. 84.

"Kant and Philosophic Method" (1884), reprinted in *Early Works,* Vol. 1, p. 34.

"A Key to the New World" (1926). Review of *Education and the Good Life* (1926), by Bertrand Russell. Reprinted in *Later Works*, Vol. 2, p. 226.

*Knowing and the Known* (1949), co-authored with Arthur F. Bentley, reprinted in *Later Works*, Vol. 16, p. 3.

"Knowledge and Existence" (1909 ca.), reprinted in *Later Works*, Vol. 17, p. 361.

"The Late Professor Morris" (1889), reprinted in *Early Works*, Vol. 3, p. 3.

*Leibnitz's New Essays Concerning the Human Understanding: A Critical Exposition* (1888), reprinted in *Early Works*, Vol. 1, pp. 253-435.

"The Lesson of Contemporary French Literature" (1889), reprinted in *Early Works,* Vol. 3, p. 36.

"Lessons From the War—in Philosophy" (1941), reprinted in *Later Works,* Vol. 14, p. 312.

"Liberalism and Civil Liberties" (1936), reprinted in *Later Works,* Vol. 11, p. 372.

"Liberalism and Equality" (1936), reprinted in *Later Works,* Vol. 11, p. 368.

*Liberalism and Social Action* (New York: G. P. Putnam's Sons, 1935), reprinted in *Later Works,* Vol. 11.

"Liberalism in a Vacuum: A Critique of Walter Lippmann's Social Philosophy" (1937). Review of *An Inquiry into the Principles of the Good Society* (1937), by Walter Lippmann. Reprinted in *Later Works,* Vol. 11, p. 489.

"Liberty and Social Control" (1935), reprinted in *Later Works,* Vol. 11, p. 360.

"Literature or Mathematics" (1925), reprinted in *Later Works,* Vol. 2, p. 386.

"Logic" (1933), reprinted in *Later Works,* Vol. 8, p. 3.

"The Logic of Verification" (1890), reprinted in *Early Works,* Vol. 3, p. 83.

*Logic: The Theory of Inquiry* (New York: Henry Holt and Company, 1938), reprinted in *Later Works,* Vol. 12.

"Man and Mathematics" (1947), reprinted in *Later Works,* Vol. 15, p. 376.

"Marx Inverted" (1932). Review of *The Emergence of Man* (1931), by Gerald Heard. Reprinted in *Later Works,* Vol. 6, p. 278.

"The Metaphysical Assumptions of Materialism" (1882), reprinted in *Early Works,* Vol. 1, p. 3.

"Methods in Philosophy and the Sciences" (1937), reprinted in *Later Works,* Vol. 17, p. 442.

"Modern Philosophy" (1952), reprinted in *Later Works,* Vol. 16, p. 407.

"Moral Theory and Practice" (1891), reprinted in *Early Works,* Vol. 3, p. 93.

"My Philosophy of Law" (1941), reprinted in *Later Works,* Vol. 14, p. 115.

"Nature in Experience" (1940), reprinted in *Later Works,* Vol. 14, p. 141.

"A Naturalistic Theory of Sense-Perception" (1925), reprinted in *Later Works,* Vol. 2, p. 44.

"The Need for a Recovery of Philosophy" (1917), first printed in *Creative Intelligenge: Essays in the Pragmatic Attitude* (New York: Octagon books, 1970). pp. 3-69. Reprinted in *Middle Works,* Vol. 10, p. 3.

"The Obligation to Knowlege of God" (1884), reprinted in *Early Works,* Vol. 1, p. 61.

"The Objectivism-Subjectivism of Modern Philosophy" (1941), reprinted in *Later Works,* Vol. 14, p. 189.

"On Immortality" (1928), reprinted in *Later Works,* Vol. 17, p. 126.

"On Philosophical Synthesis" (1951), reprinted in *Later Works,* Vol. 17, p. 35.

"One Current Religious Problem" (1936), reprinted in *Later Works*, Vol. 11, p. 115.

*Outlines of a Critical Theory of Ethics* (1891), reprinted in *Early Works,* Vol. 3, pp. 239-388.

"The Pantheism of Spinoza" (1882), reprinted in *Early Works*, Vol. 1, p. 9.

"Peirce's Theory of Linguistic Signs, Thought, and Meaning" (1946), reprinted in *Later Works*, Vol. 15, p. 141.

"Peirce's Theory of Quality" (1935), reprinted in *Later Works*, Vol. 11, p. 86.

"Philosophy" (1934), reprinted in *Later Works*, Vol. 8, p. 19.

*Philosophy and Civilization* (New York: Minton, Balch and Company, 1931).

"Philosophy's Future in Our Scientific Age: Never Was Its Role More Crucial" (1949), reprinted in *Later Works*, 16, p. 369.

"A Philosophy of Scientific Method" (1931). Review of *Reason and Nature: An Essay on the Meaning of Scientific Method,* by M. R. Cohen. Reprinted in *Later Works,* Vol. 6, p. 299.

"The Philosophy of Whitehead" (1941), reprinted in *Later Works,* Vol. 14, p. 123.

"The Philosophy of William James" (1937). Review of Ralph Barton Perry's *The Thought and Character of William James.* Reprinted in *Later Works*, Vol. 11, p. 464.

"The Place of Religious Emotion" (1886), reprinted in *Early Works*, Vol. 1. p. 90.

"Poetry and Philosophy" (1890), reprinted in *Early Works,* Vol. 3, p. 110.

"Politics and Culture" (1932), reprinted in *Later Works*, Vol. 6, p. 40.

"Practical Democracy" (1925). Review of *The Phantom Public* (1925), by Walter Lippmann. Reprinted in *Later Works*, Vol. 2, p. 213.

"Preface" (1952) to Japanese Translation of *Democracy and Education,* reprinted in *Later Works*, Vol. 17, p. 57.

"Prefatory Remarks" (1932), in *The Philosophy of The Present,* by G. H. Meade, reprinted in *Later Works*, Vol. 6, p. 307.

"The Present Position of Logical Theory" (1891), reprinted in *Early Works*, Vol. 3, p. 125.

"Presenting Thomas Jefferson" (1940), reprinted in *Later Works*, Vol. 14, p. 201.

"President Dewey Calls on Hoover to Recognize Government Responsibility for Unemployment" (1931), reprinted in *Later Works*, Vol. 6, p. 372.

"President Dewey Opposes Community Chest Drives for Unemployment" (1931), reprinted in *Later Works*, Vol. 6, p. 374.

"President Hutchin's Proposals to Remake Higher Education" (1937), reprinted in *Later Works,* Vol. 11, p. 398.

"The *Principles*" (1943), reprinted in *Later Works*, Vol. 15, p. 18.

"Problems of Contemporary Philosophy: The Problem of Experience" (1933), reprinted in *Later Works*, Vol. 17, p. 429.

*Problems of Men* (New York: Philosopical Library, 1946).

"The Problems of the Liberal Arts College" (1944), reprinted in *Later Works*, Vol. 15, p. 276.

"Propositions, Warranted Assertibilty, and Truth" (1941), reprinted in *Later Works,* Vol. 14, p. 168.

"Prosperity Dependent on Building from the Bottom Up" (1932), reprinted in *Later Works*, Vol. 6, p. 383.

"Psychology as Philosophic Method" (1886), reprinted in *Early Works*, Vol. 1, p. 144.

"The Psychological Standpoint" (1886), reprinted in *Early Works*, Vol. 1, p. 122.

*The Public and Its Problems* (New York: Henry Holt and Company, 1927), reprinted in *Later Works,* Vol. 2, p. 235.

*The Quest for Certainty* (New York: Minton, Balch and Company, 1929), reprinted in *Later Works*, Vol. 4.

"Rationality in Education" (1936), reprinted in *Later Works,* Vol. 11, p. 391.

*Reconstruction in Philosophy* (New York: Henry holt and Company, 1920), reprinted in *Middle Works*, Vol. 12, p. 77.

"The Reflex Arc Concept in Psychology" (1896), reprinted in *Early Works*, Vol. 5, p. 96.

"Religion and Morality in a Free Society" (1949), reprinted in *Later Works*, Vol. 15, p. 170.

"Religion, Science, and Philosophy" (1936). Review of *Religion and Science* (1935), by Bertrand Russell. Reprinted in Later Works, Vol. 11, p. 454.

"A Resume of Four Lectures on Common Sense, Science and Philosophy" (1932), reprinted in *Later Works*, Vol. 6, p. 424.

Review (1940). Douglas C. Macintosh's *Social Religion* (1939). Reprinted in *Later Works*, Vol. 14, p. 286.

"The Revival of the Soul" (1885), reprinted in *Later Works*, Vol. 17, p. 10.

*The School and Society* (Chicago: University of Chicago Press, 1900). Reprinted in *Middle Works*, Vol. 1, pp. 1-111.

"The Schools and the White House Conference" (1932), reprinted in *Later Works*, Vol. 6, p. 131.

"Science and Society" (1931), reprinted in *Later Works,* Vol. 6, p. 53.

"Science and the Idea of God" (1886). Review of *The Idea of God as Affected by Modern Knowledge,* by John Fiske. Reprinted in *Later Works,* Vol. 17, p. 93.

"The Social-Economic Situation in Education" (1933); written with John L. Childs. Reprined in *Later Works,* Vol. 8, p. 43.

"Social Science and Social Control" (1931), reprinted in *Later Works*, Vol. 6, p. 64.

"The Social Significance of Academic Freedom" (1936), reprinted in *Later Works*, Vol. 11, p. 376.

"The 'Socratic Dialogues' of Plato" (1925), reprinted in *Later Works,* Vol. 2, p. 124.

"Some Connexions of Science and Philosophy" (1911), reprinted in *Later Works*, Vol. 17, p. 402.

"Some Thoughts Concerning Religion" (1910), reprinted in *Later Works*, Vol. 17, p. 374.

"Statement on Jefferson" (1943), reprinted in *Later Works*, Vol. 15, p. 366.

"Subject-Matter in Art" (1936). Review of *Representation and Form: A Study of Aesthetic Values in Representational Art* (1936), by Walter Abell. Reprinted in *Later Works*, Vol. 11, p, 487.

"The Subject-Matter of Metaphysical Inquiry" in *The Journal of Philosophy, Psychology, and Scientific Methods*, Vol. XII, no. 13, June 24, 1915.

"Substance, Power and Quality in Locke" (1926), reprinted in *Later Works*, Vol. 2, p. 141.

"The Teacher and the Public" (1935), reprinted in *Later Works*, Vol. 11, p. 158.

"The Techniques of Reconstruction" (1940). Review of *Man and Society in an Age of Reconstruction* (1940), by Karl Mannheim. Reprinted in *Later Works*, Vol. 14, p. 293.

"Toward a National System of Education" (1935), reprinted in *Later Works*, Vol. 11, p. 356.

"Time and Individuality" (1940), reprinted in *Later Works*, Vol. 14, p. 98.

"Tribute to James Hayden Tufts" (1942), reprinted in *Later Works*, Vol. 15, p. 321.

"Tribute to Schiller" (1935), reprinted in *Later Works*, Vol. 11, p. 155.

"'Truth Is on the March'" (1937), reprinted in *Later Works*, Vol. 11, p. 310.

"The Underlying Philosophy of Education" (1933); written with John L. Childs. Reprinted in *Later Works*, Vol. 8, p. 77.

"United, We Shall Stand" (1935), reprinted in *Later Works*, Vol. 11, p. 348.

"The Unity of Human Being" (1937), reprinted in *Later Works*, Vol. 13, p. 323.

"Value, Objective Reference and Criticism" (1925), reprinted in *Later Works*, Vol. 2, p. 78.

"The Value of Historical Christianity" (1889), reprinted in *Later Works*, Vol. 17, p. 529.

"Values, Valuations, and Social Facts" (1945), reprinted in *Later Works*, Vol. 16, p. 310.

"The Vanishing Subject in the Psychology of James" (1940), reprinted in *Later Works*, Vol. 14, p. 155.

*Theory of Valuation* (1939), reprinted in *Later Works*, Vol. 13, p. 189.

"War's Social Results" (1917), reprinted in *Later Works*, Vol. 17, p. 21.

"What Are Universals?" (1936), reprinted in *Later Works*, Vol. 11, p. 105.

"What Is Democracy?" (ca. 1946?), reprinted in *Later Works*, Vol. 17, p. 471.

"What Is It to Be a Linguistic Sign or Name?" (1945), reprinted in *Later Works*, Vol. 16, p. 297.

"What Is the Demonstration of Man's Spiritual Nature?" (1886), reprinted in *Later Works*, Vol. 17, p. 15.

"What Is the Matter with Teaching?" (1925), reprinted in *Later Works*, Voll. 2, p. 116.

"Whitehead's Philosophy" (1937), reprinted in *Later Works*, Vol. 11, p. 146.

"William James and the World Today" (1942), reprinted in *Later Works*, Vol. 15, pp. 3-8.

"William James as Empiricist" (1942), reprinted in *Later Works*, Vol. 15, pp. 9-17.

"The Work of George Mead" (1936). Review of G. H. Mead's *Mind, Self and Society* (1934) *and Movements of Thought in the Nineteenth Century* (1936). Reprinted in *Later Works*, Vol. 11, p. 450.

"World High Court for Knowledge" (1936), reprinted in *Later Works*, Vol. 11, p. 127.

"Youth in a Confused World" (1935), reprinted in *Later Works*, Vol. 11, p. 353.

# II. Other Works

Adams, George, et al., *Studies in the Nature of Truth*. Berkeley: University of California Press, 1929.

Ammerman, Robert R., ed. *Classics of Analytic Philosophy*. Cambridge: Hackett Publishing Company, Inc., 1990.

Arendt, Hannah. *The Human Condition*. Chicago: University of Chicago Press, 1958.

Arkes, Hadley. *The Philosopher in the City*. Princeton: Princeton University Press, 1981.

Ayer, A. J. *The Origins of Pragmatism*. San Francisco, California: Freeman, Cooper & Company, 1968.

Beineke, John A. "The Investigation of John Dewey by the FBI." *Educational Theory*. Winter 1987, Vol. 37, No. 1, pp. 43-52.

Bernal, Martin. *Black Athena: The Afroasiatic Roots of Classical Civilization*. New Jersey: Rutgers University Press, 1987. Vol. 1.

Bernstein, Richard J. *Beyond Objectivism and Relativism: Science, Hermeneutics, and Praxis*. Philadephia: University of Pennsylvania Press, 1988.

———. *John Dewey*. New York: Washington Square Press, 1966.

———. Ed. *Habermas and Modernity*. Cambridge: The MIT Press, 1985.

Bertocci, Peter A. *Mid-Twentieth Century American Philosophy: Personal Statements*. New York: Humanities Press, 1974.

Bertocci, Peter A. *The Person God Is*. New York: Humanities Press, 1970.

Blanshard, Brand. "Dewey," in *The Philosophy of Brand Blanshard*. The Library of Living Philosophers. Vol. XV; Paul A. Schilpp, ed. La Salle, Illinois: Open Court, 1980. pp. 44-50.

———. *Reason and Analysis*. New Haven: Yale University Press, 1975.

———. *Reason and Belief*. New Haven: Yale University Press, 1975.

———. "Reply to Mr. Bertocci: *Does Blanshard Escape Epistemic Dualism?*" in *The Philosophy of Bland Blanshard*. The Library of Living Philosophers. Vol. XV; Paul A. Schilpp, ed. La Salle, Illinois: Open Court, 1980. pp. 618-628.

———. "Reply to Mr. Hartshorne: *Understanding as Seeing to Be Necessary,*" in *The Philosophy of Bland Blanshard*. The Library of Living Philosophers. Vol. XV; Paul A. Schilpp, ed. La Salle, Illinois: Open Court, 1980. pp. 636-45.

———. "Reply to Mr. Howie: Blanshard on 'Intrinsic Good'" in *The Philosophy of Bland Blanshard*. The Library of Living Philosophers. Vol. XV; Paul A. Schilpp, ed. La Salle, Illinois: Open Court, 1980. pp. 314-19.

———. "Reply to Mr. Rorty: *Idealism, Holism, and 'The Paradox of Knowledge'*" in *The Philosophy of Bland Blanshard*. The Library of Living Philosophers. Vol. XV; Paul A. Schilpp, ed. La Salle, Illinois: Open Court, 1980. pp. 756-73.

———. *The Nature of Thought*. 2 Vols. London: George Allen, 1939. Vols. 1 & 2.

Blum, John M., E. S. Morgan, W. L. Rose, A. M. Schlesinger, Jr., K. M. Stampp and C. V. Woodward, eds. *The National Experience: A History of the United States*. New York: Harcourt Brace Jovanovich, Inc., 1963, 1973.

Bowden, Henry W. *Church History in the Age of Science: Historiographical Patterns in the United States 1876-1918*. Chapel Hill: The University of North Carolina Press, 1971.

Bowden, Henry W. *Church History in An Age of Uncertainty: Historiographical Patterns in the United States, 1906-1990*. Carbondale and Edwardsville: Southern Illinois University Press, 1991.

Boydston, Jo Ann, ed. *Guide to the Works of John Dewey*. Carbondale and Edwardsville: Southern Illinois University Press, 1970.

Burns, James M., Thomas E. Cronin and J. W. Peltason, eds. *Government by the People*. New Jersey: Prentice-Hall Inc., 1952, 1978.

Caputo, David A. *Urban America: The Policy Alternatives*. San Francisco: W. H. Freeman and Company, 1976.

Chatalian, George. *Epistemology and Skepticism: An Inquiry into the Nature of Epistemology*. Carbondale: Southern Illinois University Press, 1991.

Christian, James L. *Philosophy: An Introduction to the Art of Wondering*. San Francisco: Holt, Rinehart and Winston, Inc., 1973, 1990.

Clarke, David S., Jr. *Principles of Semiotic*. New York: Routledge & Kegan Paul, Inc., 1987.

Clarke, John H., ed. *American Negro Short Stories*. New York: Hill and Wang, 1954.

———. "The Boy Who Painted Christ Black" (1940). *American Negro Short Stories*. New York: Hill and Wang, 1954. pp. 109-15.

Corbin, Raymond M. *1999 Facts About Blacks: A Source of African-American Accomplishment*. Beckham House Publishers, Inc., 1986.

Coser, Lewis A. *Masters of Sociological Thought: Ideas in Historical and Social Context*. New York: Harcourt Brace Jovanovich, Inc., 1971. Ed. Robert K. Merton.

Coughlan, Neil. *Young John Dewey*. Chicago: University of Chicago Press, 1975.

Custance, Arthur C. *Noah's Three Sons: Human History in Three Dimensions*. Grand Rapids, Michigan: Zondervan Publishing House, 1975. The Doorway Papers, Vol. 1.

Dallmayer, Fred. *Critical Encounters: Between Philosophy and Politics*. Notre Dame: Notre Dame University Press, 1987.

———. *Language and Politics*. Notre Dame: Notre Dame University Press, 1984. and Thomas McCarthy, eds. *Understanding and Social Inquiry*. Notre Dame: Notre Dame University Press, 1977.

David, Stephen M. and Paul E. Peterson, eds. *Urban Politics and Public Policy: The City in Crisis*. New York: Praeger Publishers, 1976.

De George, Richard, ed. *Classical and Contemporary Metaphysics*. New York: Holt, Rinehart and Winston, 1962.

Descartes, Rene. *Discourse on the Method*. Trans. John Cottingham, Dugald Murdock and Robert Stoothoff. *The Philosophical Writings Of Descartes*. 2 Vols. Cambridge: Cambridge University Press, 1985. Vol. 1.

———. *Principles of Philosophy*. Trans. John Cottingham, Dugald Murdock and Robert Stoothoff. *The Philosophical Writings Of Descartes*. 2 Vols. Cambridge: Cambridge University Press, 1985. Vol. 1. Original text 1644.

Desmond, William, ed. *Hegel and His Critics: Philosophy in the Aftermath of Hegel*. Albany: State University of New York Press, 1989.

Diop, Cheikh Anta. *Civilization or Barbarism: An Authentic Anthropology*. New York: Lawrence Hill Books, 1991. Trans. Yaa-Lengi Meema Ngemi. Ed. Harold J. Salemson and Marjolin de Jager. Originally published by Presence Africaine, Paris, 1981.

Downs, James F. *Cultures in Crisis*. Beverly Hills, California: Glencoe Press, 1971.

Drennen, D. A., ed. *A Modern Introduction to Metaphysics: Readings From Classical and Contemporary Sources*. New York: The Free Press, 1962.

Eames, Elizabeth R. *Bertrand Russell's Dialogue With His Contemporaries*. Carbondale: Southern Illinois University Press, 1989.

———. "Quality and Relation as Metaphysical Assumptions in The Philosophy of John Dewey." *The Journal of Philosophy*, Vol. LI, no. 26, December 23, 1954. pp. 166-69.

Eames, S. Morris. "Introduction" to *John Dewey: The Early Works, 1889-1892*. Ed. Jo Ann Boydston. Vol. 3.

Egner, Robert and Lester Denonn, eds. *The Basic Writings of Bertrand Russell.* New York: Simon & Schuster, 1967.

Emerson, Ralph W. "The America Scholar." *Factual Prose: Introduction to Explanatory and Persuasive Writing.* Chicago: Scott, Foresman and Company, 1959. Eds. Walter Blair and John Gerber. Original text 1837. pp. 281-94.

Feigl, Herbert and Grover Maxwell, eds. *Current Issues in the Philosophy of Science.* New York: Holt, Rinehart and Winston, Inc., 1961.

Feuer, Lewis S. "Introduction" to *John Dewey: The Later Works, 1942-1948.* Ed. Jo Ann Boydston. Vol. 15.

Franklin, John H. *From Slavery to Freedom: A History of Negro Americans.* New York: Alfred A. Knopf, Inc., 1947, 1974.

Gardiner, James J. and J. Deotis Roberts, eds. *Quest for a Black Theology.* Philadephia: Pilgrim Press, 1971.

Garry, Ann and Marilyn Pearsall, eds. *Women, Knowledge, and Reality: Explorations in Feminist Philosophy.* Boston: Unwin Hyman, Inc., 1989.

Gormon, Benjamin L., Richard F. Larson and Gerald R. Leslie, eds. *Order and Change: Introductory Sociology.* New York: Oxford University Press, 1973.

Gouinlock, James. "Introduction" to *John Dewey: The Later Works, 1925-1953.* Ed. Jo Ann Boydston. Vol. 2.

Hahn, Lewis E. "Aesthetics and Education." *The Chinese University of Hong Kong Education Journal.* 12 December, 1984, Vol. 12 No 2, pp. 71-76.

———. "John Dewey's World Hypothesis." *The Chinese University of Hong Kong Education Journal* 13 June, 1985, pp. 82-87.

Hahn, Lewis E. "John Dewey's World View." *Religious Humanism* 14 Winter, 1980, pp. 32-37.

———. "Dewey's Philosophy and Philosophic Method." *Guide to the Works of John Dewey.* Ed. Jo Ann Boydston, pp. 15-60.

———. "Dewey's View of Experience and Culture." *Two Centuries of Philosophy in America.* Totowa, New Jersey: Rowman and Littlefield, 1980. Ed. Peter Caws. pp. 167-173.

———. "Introduction: From Intuitionalism to Absolutism." *John Dewey: The Early Works, 1882-1888.* Ed. Jo Ann Boydston. Vol. 1. pp. vii-xxi.

Hamilton, Edith and Huntington Cairns, eds. *Plato: The Collected Dialogues.* Princeton: Princeton University Press, 1961.

Harbermas, Jurgen. *The Theory of Communicative Action: Reason and the Rationalization of Society.* Boston: Beacon Press, 1984. Trans. Thomas McCarthy. Vol. 1.

Hartshorne, Charles and Paul Weiss, eds. *The Collected Papers of Charles Sanders Peirce.* Cambridge: Harvard University Press, 1931-35.

Heidegger, Martin. *Being and Time*. New York: Harper & Row, Publishers, 1962. Trans. John Macquarrie and Edward Robinson. Original text 1927.

Heilbroner, Robert L. *The Worldly Philosophers: The Lives, Times, and Ideas of the Great Economic Thinkers*. New York: Simon and Schuster, 1953.

Hempel, Carl G. *Fundamentals of Concept Formation in Empirical Science*. 2 Vols. Chicago: University of Chicago Press, 1952.

Hickman, Larry A. *John Dewey's Pragmatic Technology*. Indianapolis: Indiana University Press, 1990.

"Why Peirce Didn't Like Dewey's Logic." *Southwest Philosophy Review* 3, 1986, pp. 178-89.

Hodgson, Peter C., ed. and trans. *Ferdinand Christian Baur on The Writing of Church History*. New York: Oxford University Press, Inc., 1968.

Hoekema, David A. "Letter From the Editor." *The American Philosophical Association*. Proceedings (1990). Vol. 63, no. 5, p. 3.

Hook, Sidney, ed. *American Philosophers at Work: The Philosophic Scene in the United States*. New York: Criterion Books, Inc., 1956.

———. "Introduction: The Relevance of John Dewey's Thought." *John Dewey: The Later Works, 1925-1953*. Ed. Jo Ann Boydston. Vol. 17, pp. pp. xvii-xxxiv.

———. *John Dewey: An Intellectual Portrait*. Westport, Connecticut: Greenwood Press Publishers, 1939/1971.

James, George G. M. *Stolen Legacy: The Greeks Were Not the Authors of Greek Philosophy, but the People of North Africa, Commonly Called the Egyptians*. San Francisco: Julian Richardson Associates, Publishers, 1988. Originally published by Philosophical Library, New York, 1954.

James, William. *The Meaning of Truth: A Sequel to Pragmatism* (1907) and *Pragmatism: A New Name for Some Old Ways of Thinking* (1907. Ed. Frederick Burkhardt. Cambridge: Harvard University Press, 1978.

———. *The Principles of Psychology*. New York: Holt Company, 1890.

Jefferson, Thomas. *The Life and Morals of Jesus of Nazareth*. Cleveland, Ohio: The World Publishing Company, 1940. Ed. Douglas E. Lurton. Originally printed in 1904.

Jones, W. T. *A History of Western Philosophy*. New York: Harcourt, Brace and Company, Inc., 1952.

Kallen, Horace M. and Sidney Hook, eds. *American Philosophy Today and Tomorrow*. Freeport, New York: Books for Library Press, 1935.

———. "Freedom and Education." *The Philosopher of the Common Man: Essays in Honor of John Dewey to Celebrate His Eightieth Birthday*. New York: Greenwood Press, Publishers, 1940, 1968.

Kant, Immanuel. *Critique of Judgment* (1790). Trans. J. H. Bernard. New York: Hafner Press, 1951.

———. *Critique of Pure Reason* (1781). Trans. Norman Kemp Smith. New York: St. Martin's Press, 1929, 1965.

Kelly, Alfred H., Winfred A. Harbison and Herman Beltz. *The American Constitution:*
*Its Origin and Development.* New York: W. W. Norton & Company, Inc., 1948, 1983.

Kent, Beverly. *Charles S. Peirce: Logic and the Classification of the Sciences.* Kingston and Montreal: McGill-Queen's University Press, 1987.

Kestenbaum, Victor. *The Phenomenological Sense.* New Jersey: Humanities Press, 1977.

Kolenda, Konstantin. *Philosophy's Journey: A Historical Introduction.* Reading, Massachusetts: Addison-Wesley Publishing Company, 1974.

Kuklick, Bruce. *Churchmen and Philosophers: From Jonathan Edwards to John Dewey.* New Haven: Yale University Press, 1985.

Lavine, T. Z. "Introduction" to *John Dewey: The Later Works, 1949-1952.* Ed. Jo Ann Boydston. Vol. 16.

Levin, Michael. "To the Editor." *The American Philosophical Association Proceedings* (1990). Vol. 63, no. 5, p. 63.

Locke, John. *An Essay Concerning Human Understanding.* Ed. Peter Nidditch. Oxford: Clarendon Press, 1975. Original text 1690.

Madden, Edward H. "Joseph L. Blau: The American Scholar." *Transactions of the Charles S. Peirce Society* 23 Fall, 1987, pp. 477-506.

Maxcy, Spencer J. "Ethnic Pluralism, Cultural Pluralism, and John Dewey's Program of Cultural Reform: A Response to Eisele." *Educational Theory,* Summer 1984, Vol. 34, No. 3, pp. 301-305.

Mayer, Frederick. *A History of Educational Thought.* Columbus, Ohio: Charles E. Merrill Publishing Company, 1960, 1973.

Matson, Wallace I. *A New History of Philosophy: Modern.* 2 Vols. Gen Ed. Robert J. Fogelin. New York: Harcourt Brace Jovanovich, Publishers, 1987. Vol. 2.

McDermott, John J. "Introduction" to *John Dewey: The Later Works, 1935-1937.* Ed. Jo Ann Boydston. Vol. 11.

———. Ed. *The Philosophy of John Dewey.* 2 Vols. Chicago: The University of Chicago Press, 1973, 1981.

Mead, George H. "A Pragmatic Theory of Truth." *University of California Publications in Philosophy.* Eds. George Adams, J. Lowenberg and Stephen C. Pepper. Berkeley, California: The University of California Press, Vol. 11.

———. "Scientific Method and Individual Thinker." *Creative Intelligence: Essays in the Pragmatic Attitude.* New York: Octagon Books, Inc., 1917.

Melchert, Norman. *The Great Conversation: A Historical Introduction to Philosophy.* Mountain View, California: Mayfield Publishing Company, 1991.

Meyer, Samuel, ed. *Dewey and Russell: An Exchange.* New York: Philosophical Library, 1985.

Morgenbesser, Sidney. *Dewey and His Critics: Essays From The Journal of Philosophy.* New York: The Journal of Philosophy, Inc., 1977.

Morris, George. *Philosophy and Christianity*. New York: The Regina Press, 1975.

Nagel, Ernest. "Introduction" to *John Dewey: The Later Works, 1925-1953*. Ed. Jo Ann Boydston. Vol. 12.

Noss, John B. *Man's Religions*. New York: Macmillan Publishing Co., Inc., 1949, 1974.

Pojman, Louis P. *Philosophy of Religion: An Anthology*. Belmont, California: Wadsworth Publishing Company, 1987.

Phillips, Llad and Harold L. Votey, Jr., eds. *Economic Analysis of Pressing Social Problems*. Chicago: Rand McNally College Publishing Company, 1974.

Rachels, James. *The Elements of Moral Philosophy*. New York: McGraw-Hill, Inc., 1986.

Ratner, Sidney. "Foreword" to *The Philosopher of the Common Man: Essays in Honor of John Dewey to Celebrate His Eightieth Birthday*. New York: Greenwood Press, Publishers, 1940, 1968.

Ratner, Sidney. "Introduction" to *John Dewey: The Later Works, 1931-1932*. Ed. Jo Ann Boydston. Vol. 6.

Rorty, Richard. "Introduction" to *John Dewey: The Later Works, 1925-1933*. Ed. Jo Ann Boydston. Vol. 8.

―――. *Philosophy and the Mirror of Nature*. Princeton: Princeton University Press, 1979.

Russell, Bertrand. *The Analysis of Mind*. New York: The Macmillan Company, 1921.

―――. "Dewey's New *Logic*." *The Basic Writings of Bertrand Russell*. New York: Simon & Schuster, 1967. Eds. Robert Egner and Lester Denonn. pp. 191-206.

―――. *An Inquiry into Meaning and Truth*. London: George Allen and Unwin LTD, 1940.

―――. "An Outline of Intellectual Rubbish." *The Basic Writings of Bertrand Russell*. New York: Simon & Schuster, 1967. Eds. Robert Egner and Lester Denonn. pp. 84-85.

―――. "John Dewey." *The Basic Writings of Bertrand Russell*. New York: Simon & Schuster, 1967. Eds. Robert Egner and Lester Denonn. pp. 207-214.

―――. *Our Knowledge of the External World: As a Field for Scientific Method in Philosophy*. Chicago: Open Court Publishing Company, 1914.

Schrag, Calvin O. *Communicative Praxis and the Space of Subjectivity*. Bloomington: Indiana University Press, 1986.

Sertima, Ivan Van, ed. *African Presence in Early Europe*. New Brunswick, New Jersey: Transaction Publishers, 1985, 1990.

Sidorsky, David. *John Dewey: The Essential Writings*. New York: Harper & Row, Publishers, 1977.

Sire, James W. *The Universe Next Door*. Downers Grove, Illinois: InterVarsity Press, 1976, 1988.

Sleeper, R. W. "Introduction" to *John Dewey: The Later Works, 1939-1941.* Ed. Jo Ann Boydston. Vol. 14.

Snowden, Frank M. Jr. *Blacks in Antiquity. Ethiopians in the Greco Roman Experience.* Cambridge: Harvard University Press, 1970.

Toffler, Alvin. *Future Shock.* New York: Bantam Books, 1970.

———. *Powershift.* New York: Bantam Books, 1990.

Tong, Rosemarie. *Feminist Thought: A Comprehensive Introduction.* San Francisco: Westview Press, Inc., 1989.

Unger, Debi and Irwin Unger. *Postwar America: The United States since 1945.* New York: St. Martin's Press, 1990.

Urofsky, Melvin I. *Louis D. Brandeis and the Progressive Tradition.* Boston: Little, Brown and Company, 1981. Ed. Oscar Handlin.

Vaughan, George B. *The Community College Presidency.* New York: Macmillan Publishing Company, 1986.

Vaughn, Stephen. *Holding Fast the Inner Lines: Democracy, Nationalism, and the Committee on Public Information.* Chapel Hill: The University of North Carolina Press, 1980.

Weinberger, Paul E. *Perspectives on Social Welfare: An Introductory Anthology.* New York: Macmillan Publishing Co., Inc., 1964, 1974.

Weiss, Paul. *The Making of Men.* Carbondale and Edwardsville: Southern Illinois University Press, 1967.

———. *Philosophy in Process, 1964.* 3 Vols. Carbondale and Edwardsville: Southern Illinois University Press, 1968. Vol. 3.

Wheelwright, Philip. Ed. *The PreSocratics.* New York: The Odyssey Press, 1966.

White, Morton. *The Origin of Dewey's Instrumentalism.* New York: Octagon Books, 1943.

Williamson, William B. *Decisions in Philosophy of Religion.* Columbus, Ohio: Charles E. Merrill Publishing Company, 1976.

Wittgenstein, Ludwig. *Philosophical Investigations.* Trans. G.E.M. Anscombe. New York: Macmillan Publishing Company, Inc., 1953.

Woodson Carter G. *The Mis-Education of the Negro.* Trenton, 1New Jersey: Africa World Press, Inc., 1990. Originally published Washington, D. C.: The Associated Publishers, 1933.

# Index

Page numbers followed by *n* indicate endnotes.